Part 1	EXERCISES 1-20	Preparatory Exercises to Acquire Speed, Precision, Agility and Strength in the Fingers of Both Hands as well as Flexibility of the Wrists.
Part 2	EXERCISES 21-43	Further Exercises for the Development of a Virtuoso Technique.
Part 3	EXERCISES 44-60	Virtuoso Exercises for Mastering the Greatest Technical Difficulties.

an introduction by C. L. Hanon

The study of the piano is now so wide-spread and good pianists are so numerous, that mediocrity on this instrument is no longer acceptable. Consequently, one must study the piano for eight or ten years before performing a piece of any difficulty, even at a gathering of amateurs. Few are in a position to devote so many years to this study. It often happens, that for lack of sufficient practice, the playing is uneven and incorrect. The left hand gives out in passages of slight difficulty; the 4th and 5th fingers are almost useless for lack of special exercises; and when passages in octaves, in tremolo or trills occur, they are usually executed with such great exertion and strain, the performance is incorrect and expressionless.

For several years we have worked to overcome this problem. It is our goal to combine in one book, special exercises which make possible a complete study of piano technique in far less time.

To attain this end, it was necessary to find a solution to the following problem: if all five fingers of both hands were equally well-trained, they would be ready to play anything written, and the only question remaining would be that of fingering, which could be easily solved.

The solution to this problem is our work, "The Virtuoso Pianist, in 60 Exercises." In this book are found the exercises necessary to gain speed, precision, agility and strength in all of the fingers as well as flexibility of the wrists – all indispensable qualities for fine execution. Furthermore, these exercises are designed to make the left hand as skillful as the right and in addition, are interesting to play.

The exercises are written so that having read them a few times, they can be played quite rapidly and become excellent practice for the fingers with no time lost in their study. They are arranged so in each successive exercise, the fingers are rested from the fatigue caused by the previous one. The result of this is that all technical difficulties are easily executed and the fingers attain an astonishing facility.

This book is intended for all piano pupils. It may be taken up after the student has studied for about a year. As for more advanced students, they will learn these exercises quickly and never again experience any stiffness or technical problems.

Pianists and teachers who cannot find the time for sufficient practice to keep up their playing need only play these exercises a few hours to regain their technique. The entire book can be played through in one hour and if, after it has been thoroughly mastered, it can be repeated daily for a while, all difficulties will disappear and that beautiful, clear, clean execution will have been acquired which is the secret of distinguished artists.

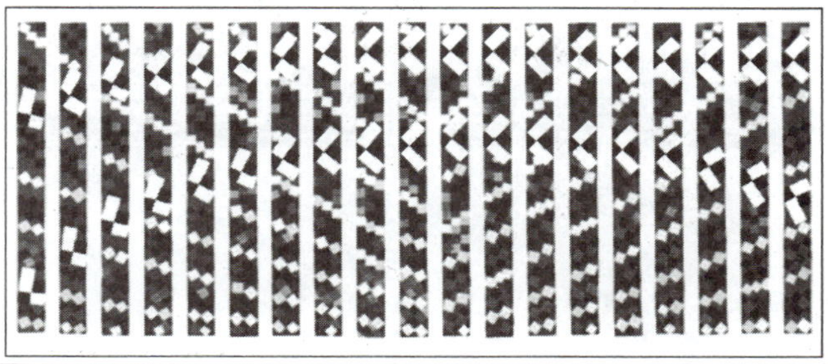

Second Edition

Cover art: The Bees
by Henri Matisse
Musée Matisse, Nice, France
© *1992. Succession Henri Marisse/ARS New York*

THE VIRTUOSO PIANIST, PART 1

Preparatory Exercises to Acquire Speed, Precision, Agility and Strength in the Fingers of Both Hands as well as Flexibility of the Wrists.

The two "Metronome Marks" (M.M.) at the head of the first exercise means to begin playing at "60" and gradually increase the speed to "108". Play all exercises in Part 1 in this manner.

Exercise 1 gives practice in stretching the 4th and 5th fingers of the left hand while ascending, the 4th and 5th fingers of the right hand while descending. Lift the fingers high and play each note distinctly.

M M. ♩ = 60 to 108 C. L. HANON

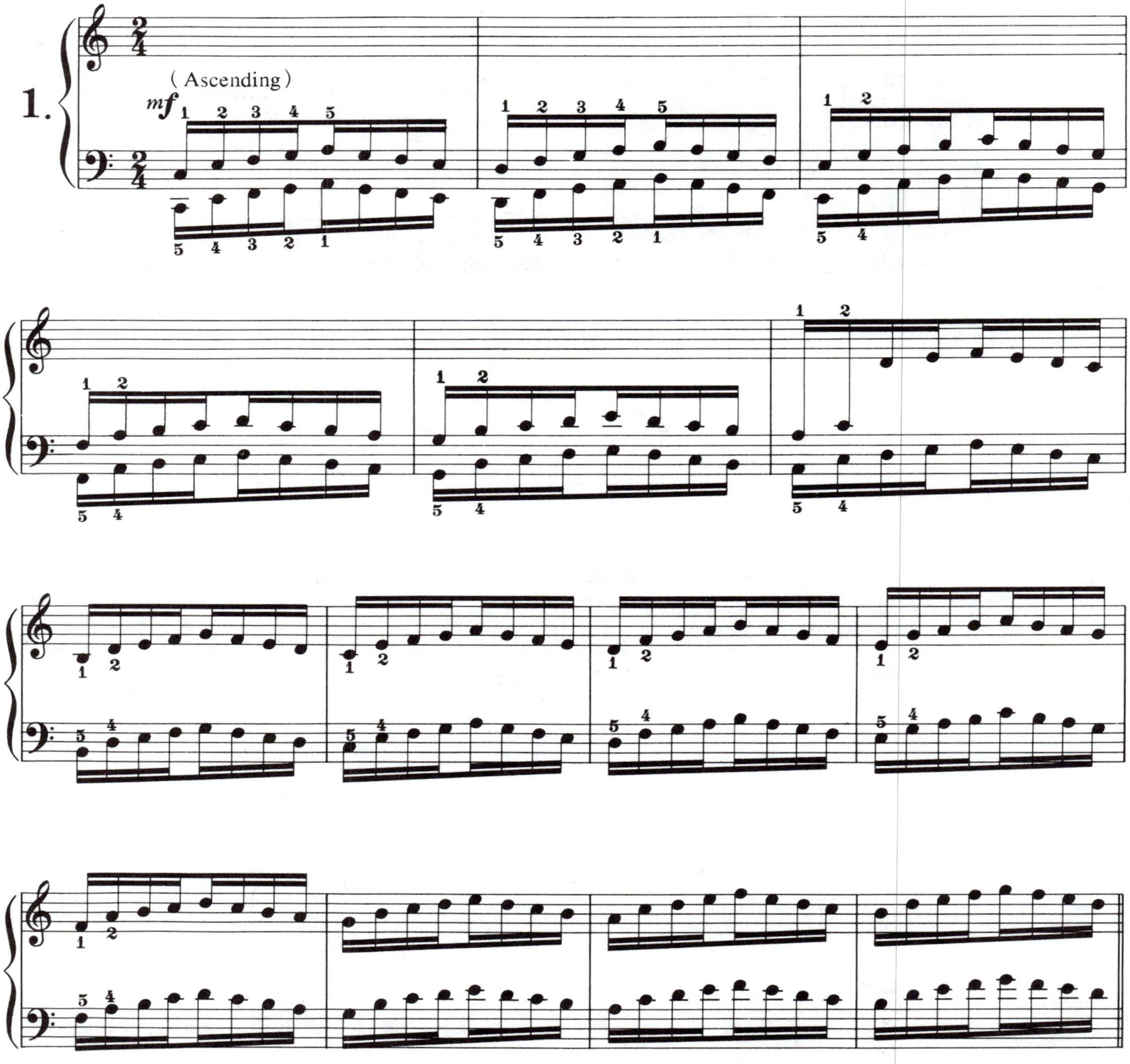

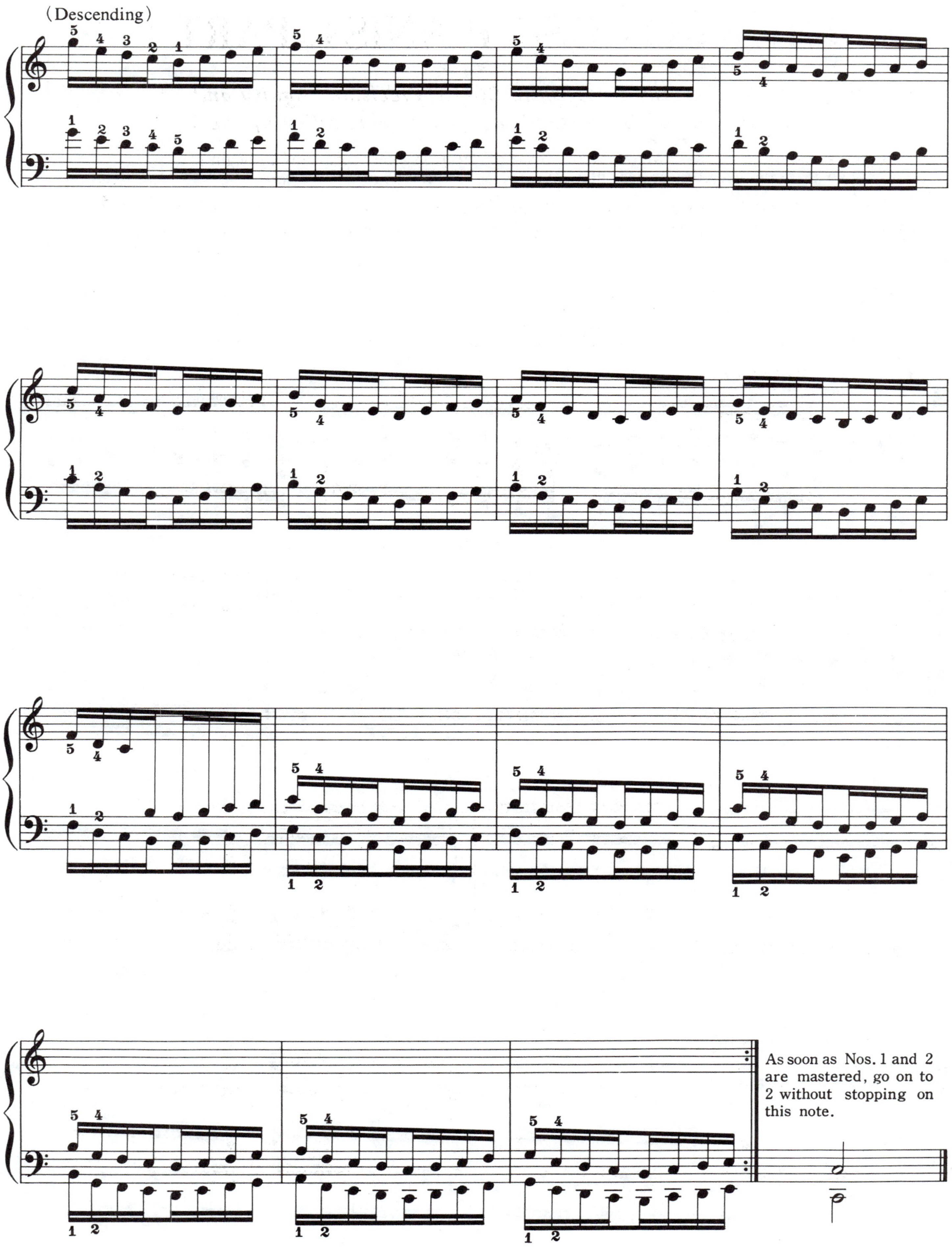
(Descending)
As soon as Nos. 1 and 2 are mastered, go on to 2 without stopping on this note.

At the beginning of each exercise, the numbers within the parentheses indicate the fingers which receive special training.

Notice that throughout the book, both hands receive similar practice because the problems the left hand has in ascending are executed by the right hand in descending. The hands will, therefore, acquire equal dexterity.

(3–4) When this exercise is mastered, play 1 and 2 four times together without stopping. Your technique will be improved substantially by practicing all the exercises in this manner.

The 4th and 5th fingers are naturally weak. It is the purpose of this exercise and those up to No. 31 to make them as strong and agile as the 2nd and 3rd.

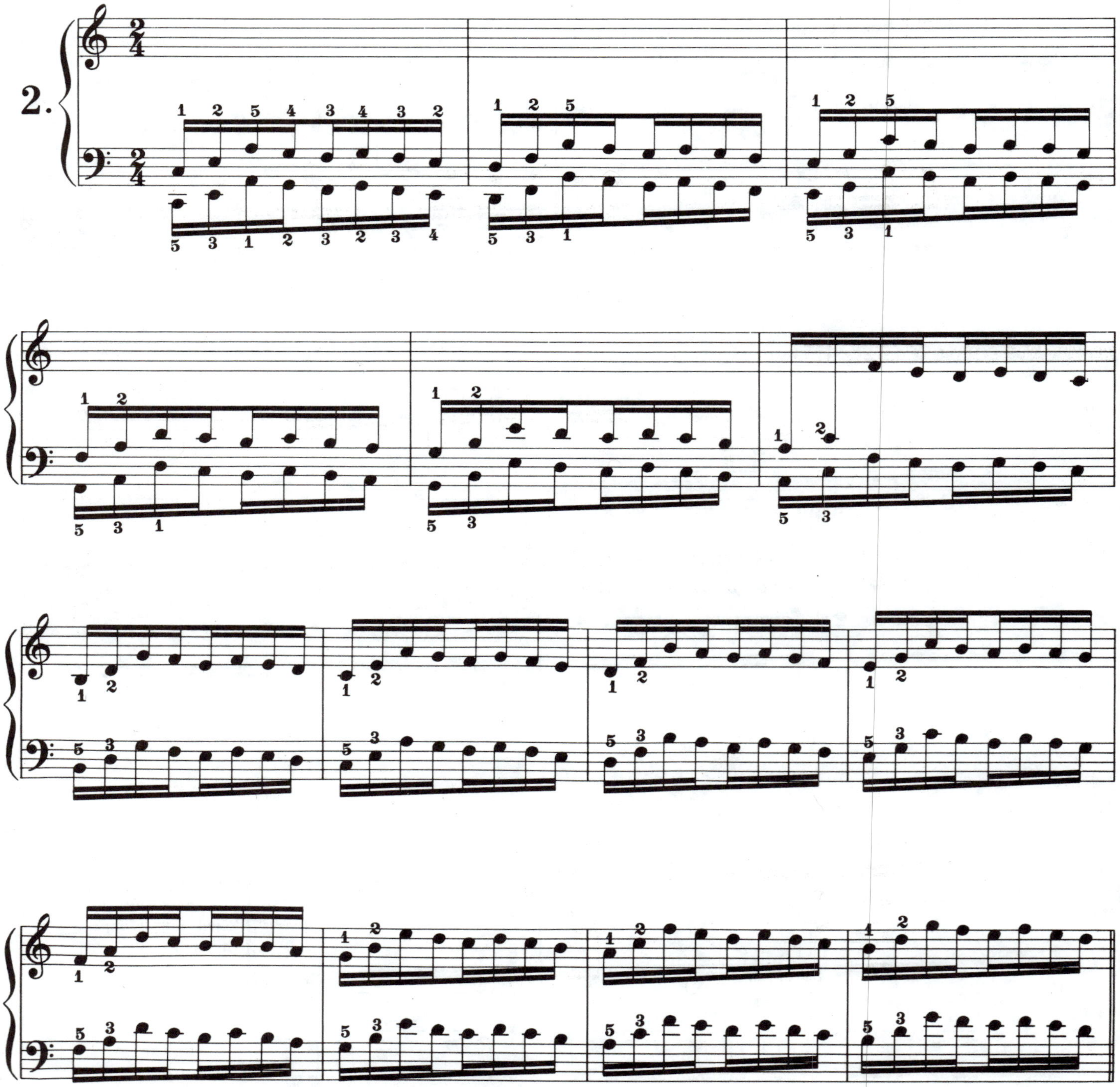

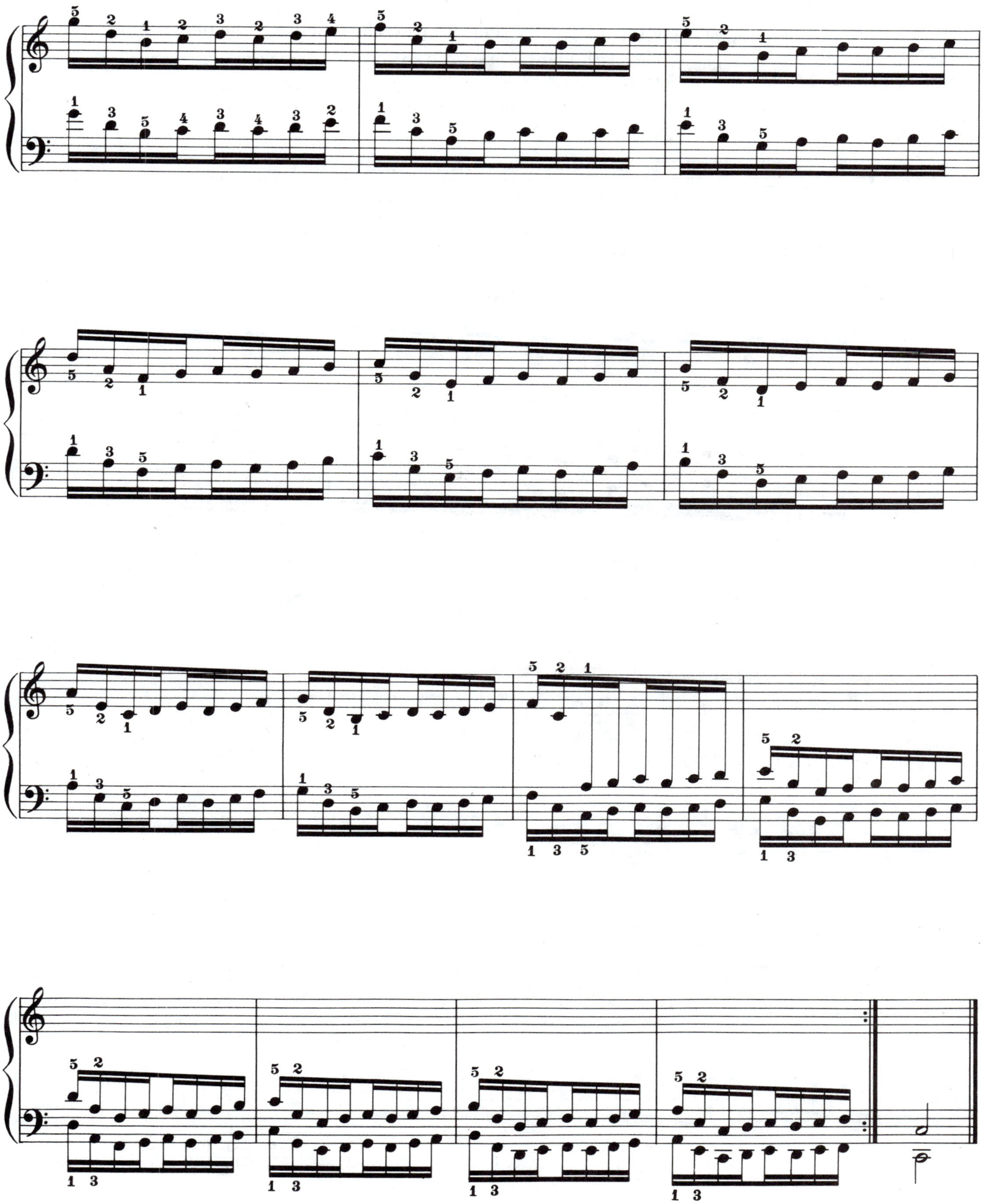

(2-3-4) Before beginning No. 3, play Exercises 1 and 2 once or twice without stopping. When Ex. 3, 4 and 5 are thoroughly mastered, play all three at least four times without interruption, not stopping until the last note on page 11. All exercises in Part 1 should be practiced in this manner. Stop only on the last note on **pgs. 5, 11, 17, 23, 26, 29 and 32.**

3.

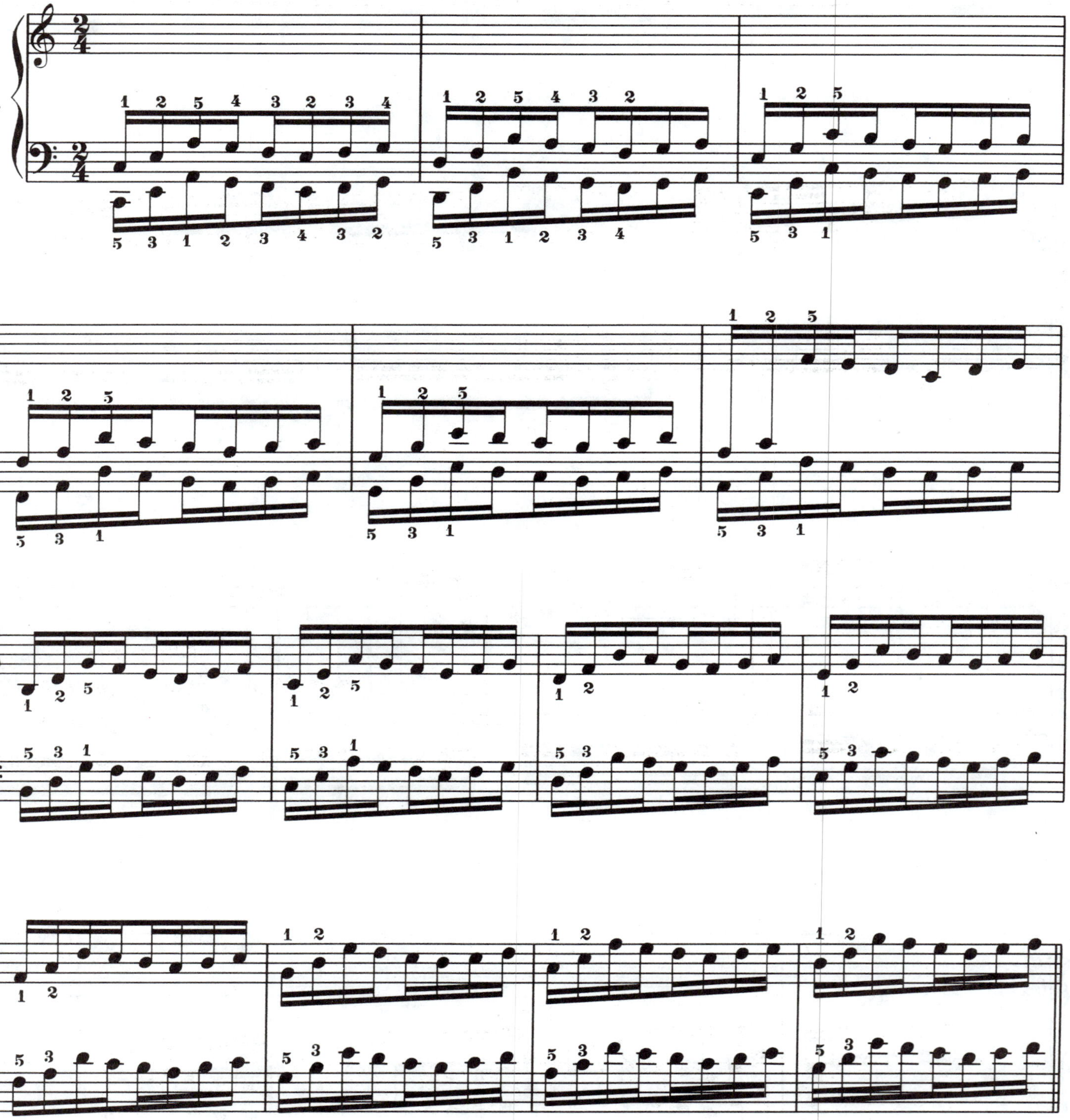

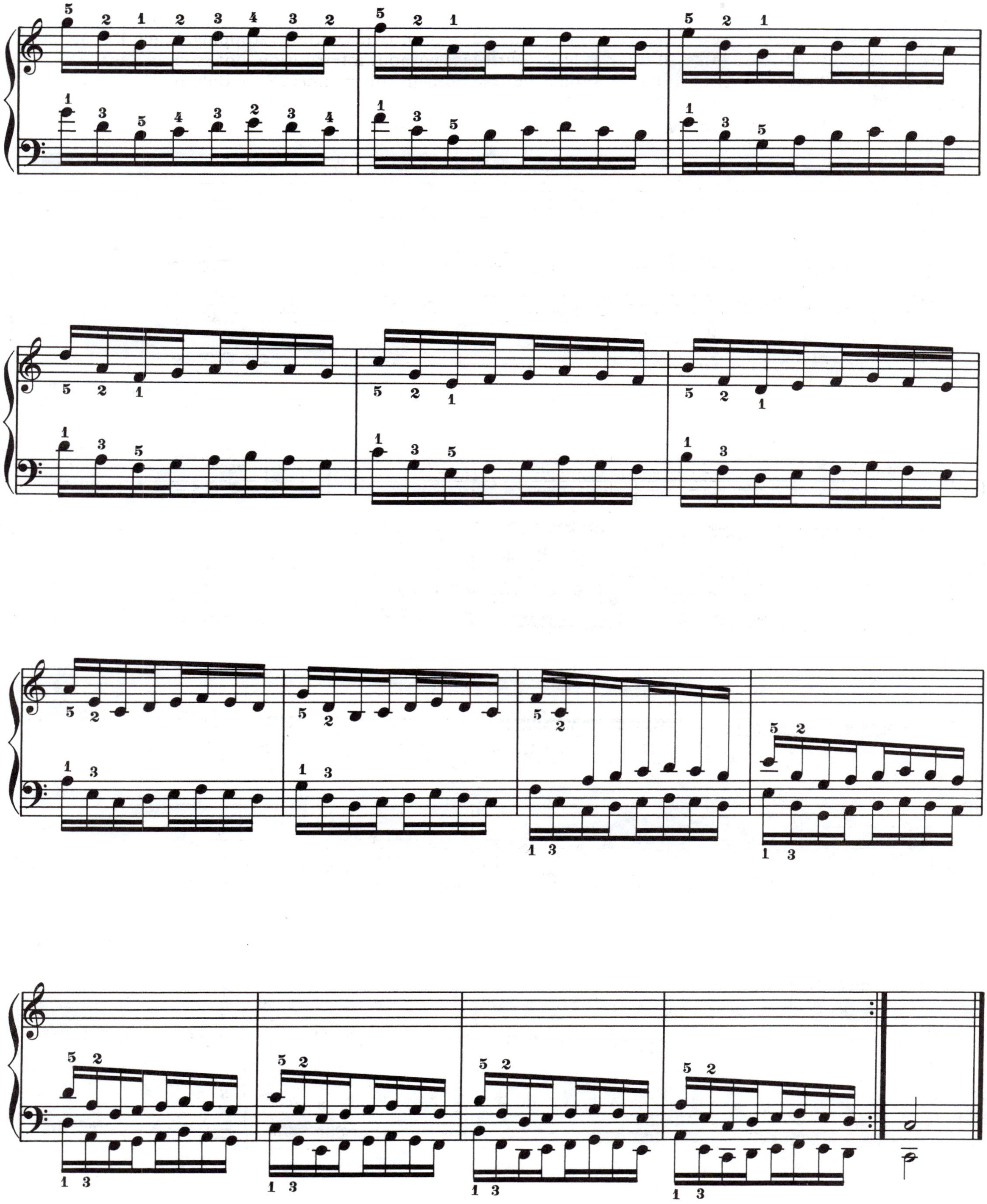

(3-4-5) Exercise for the 3rd, 4th and 5th fingers.

4.

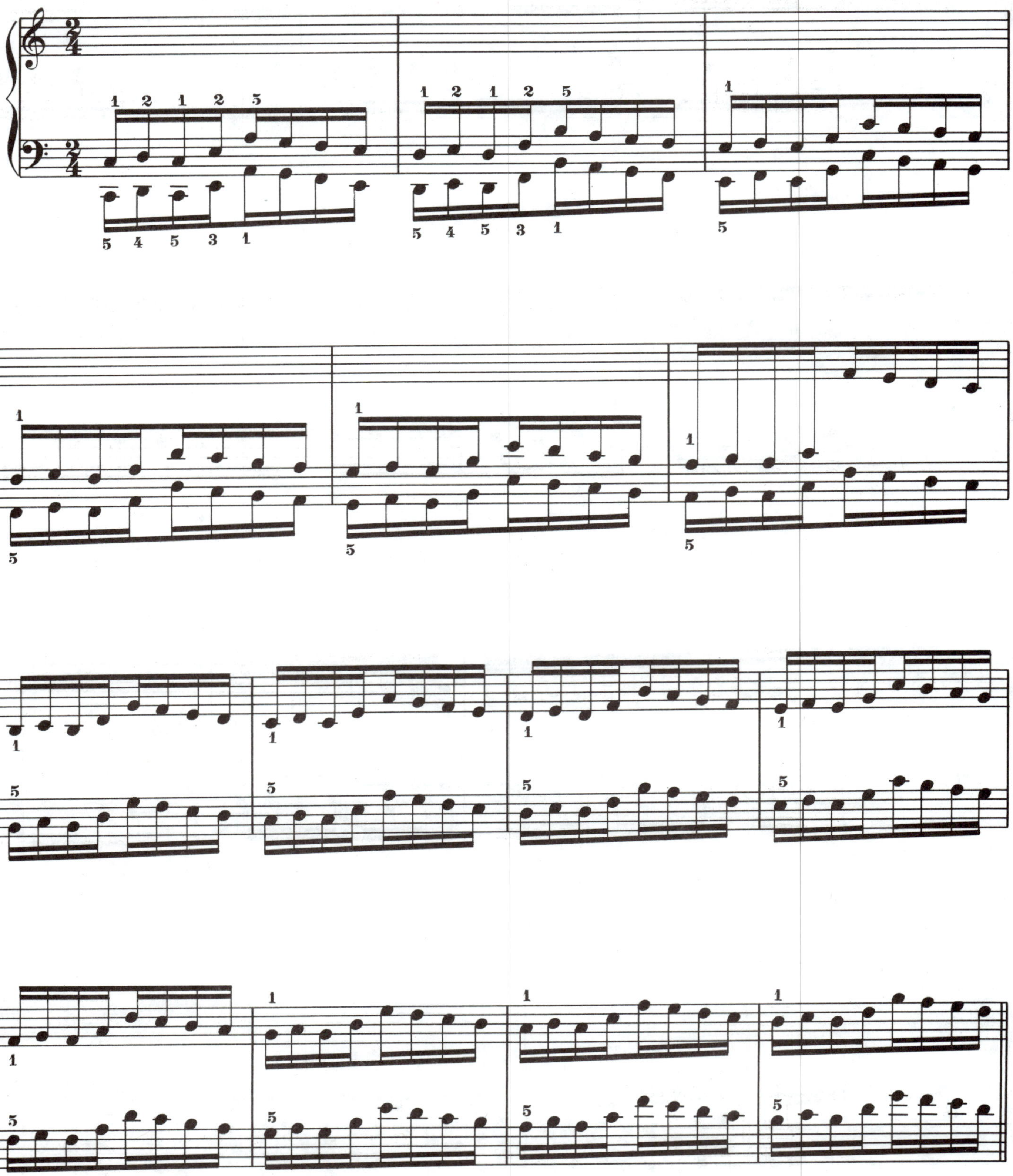

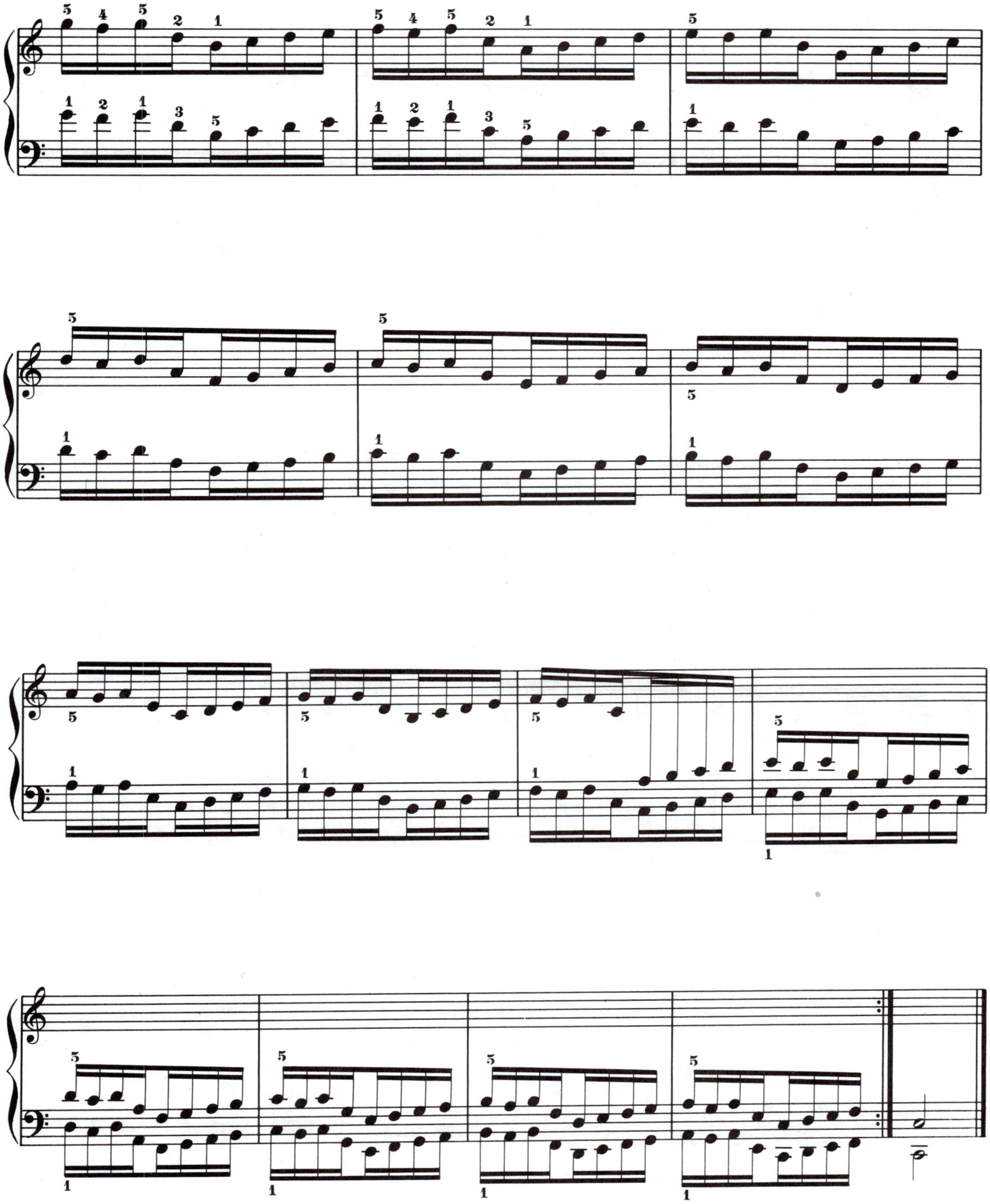

(1-2-3-4-5) Lift the fingers high and with precision in all exercises. This exercise prepares the pianist to play the trill with the 4th and 5th fingers of the right hand.

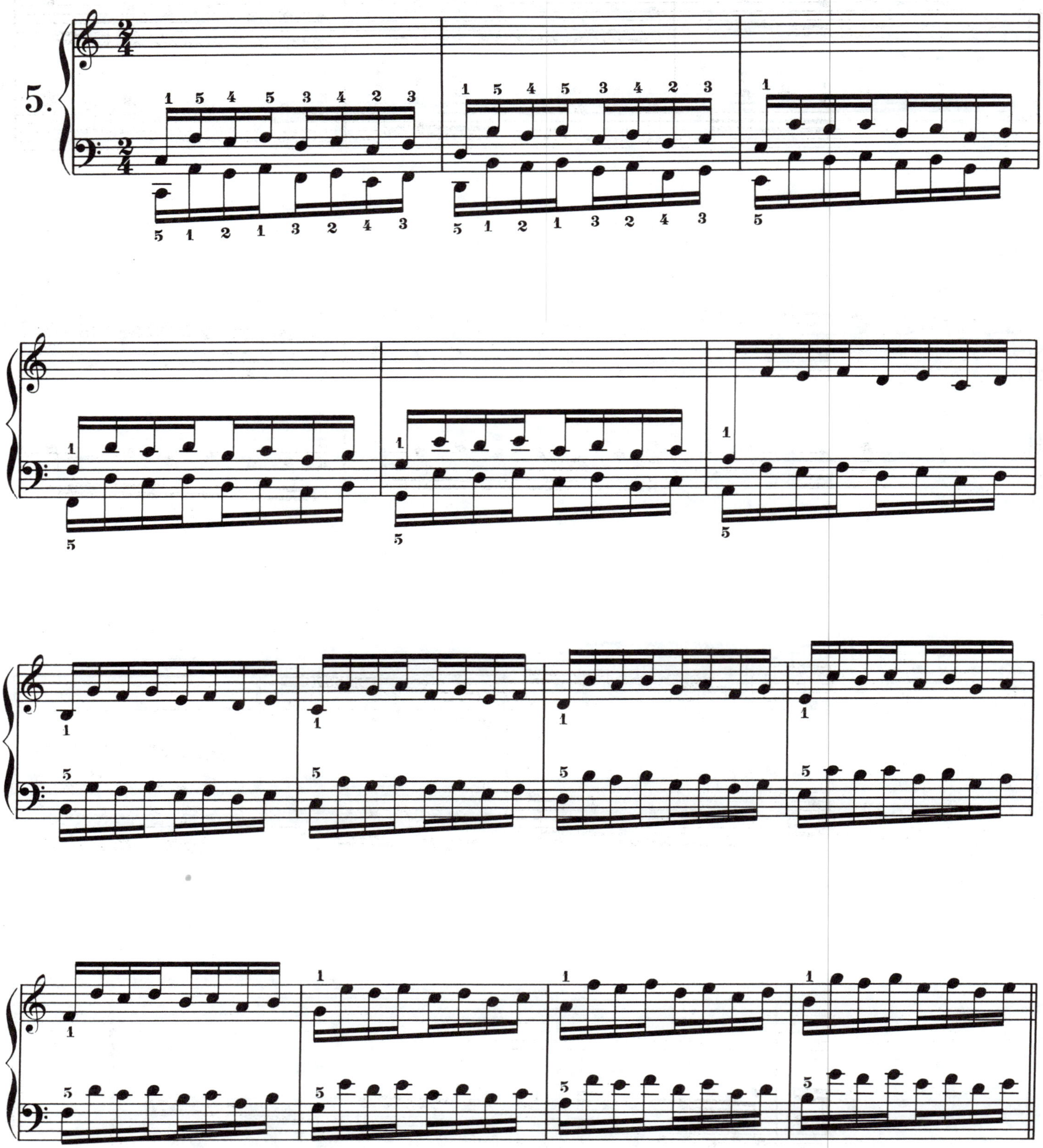

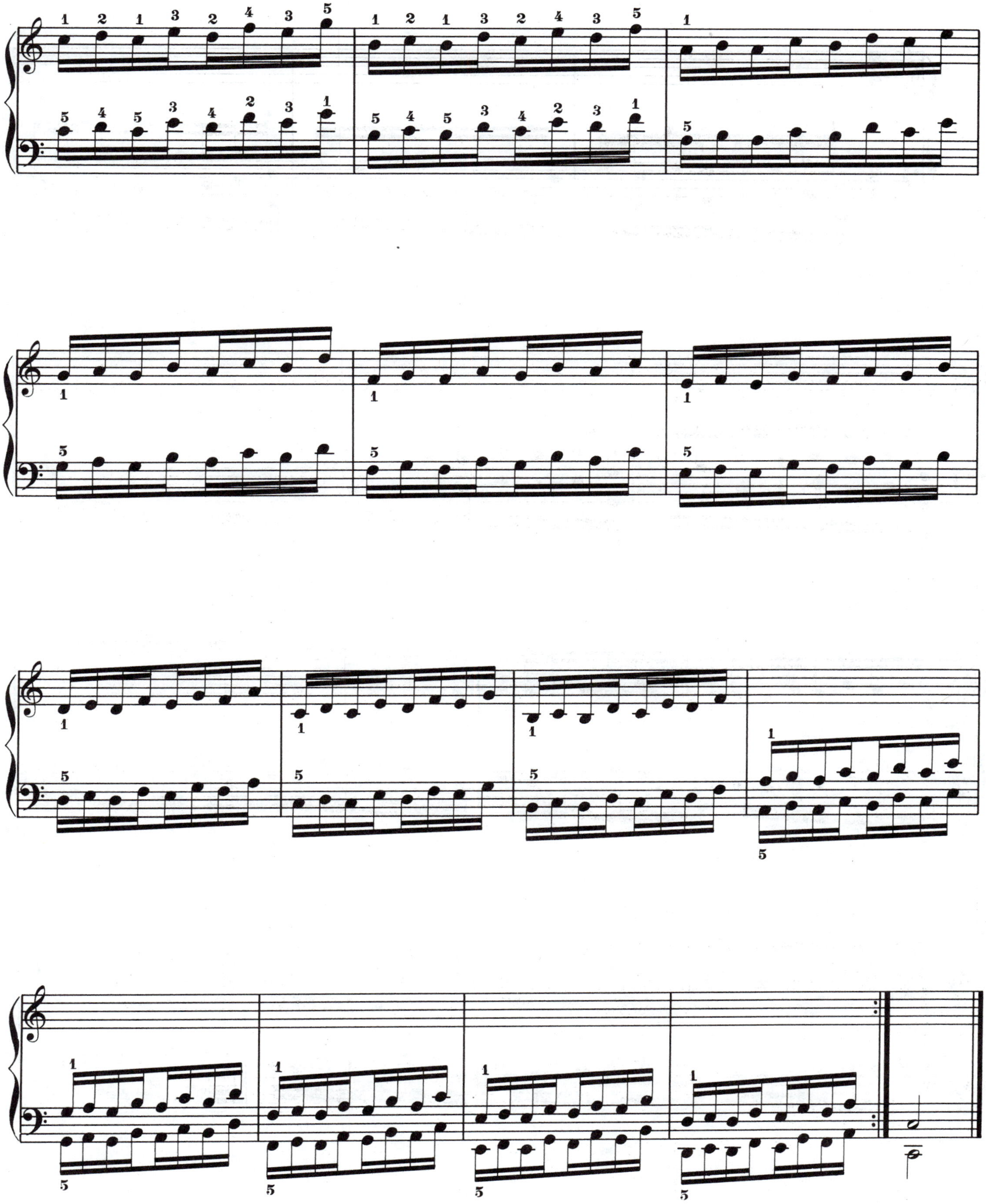

(5) For best results, play the exercises already learned at least once daily.

6.

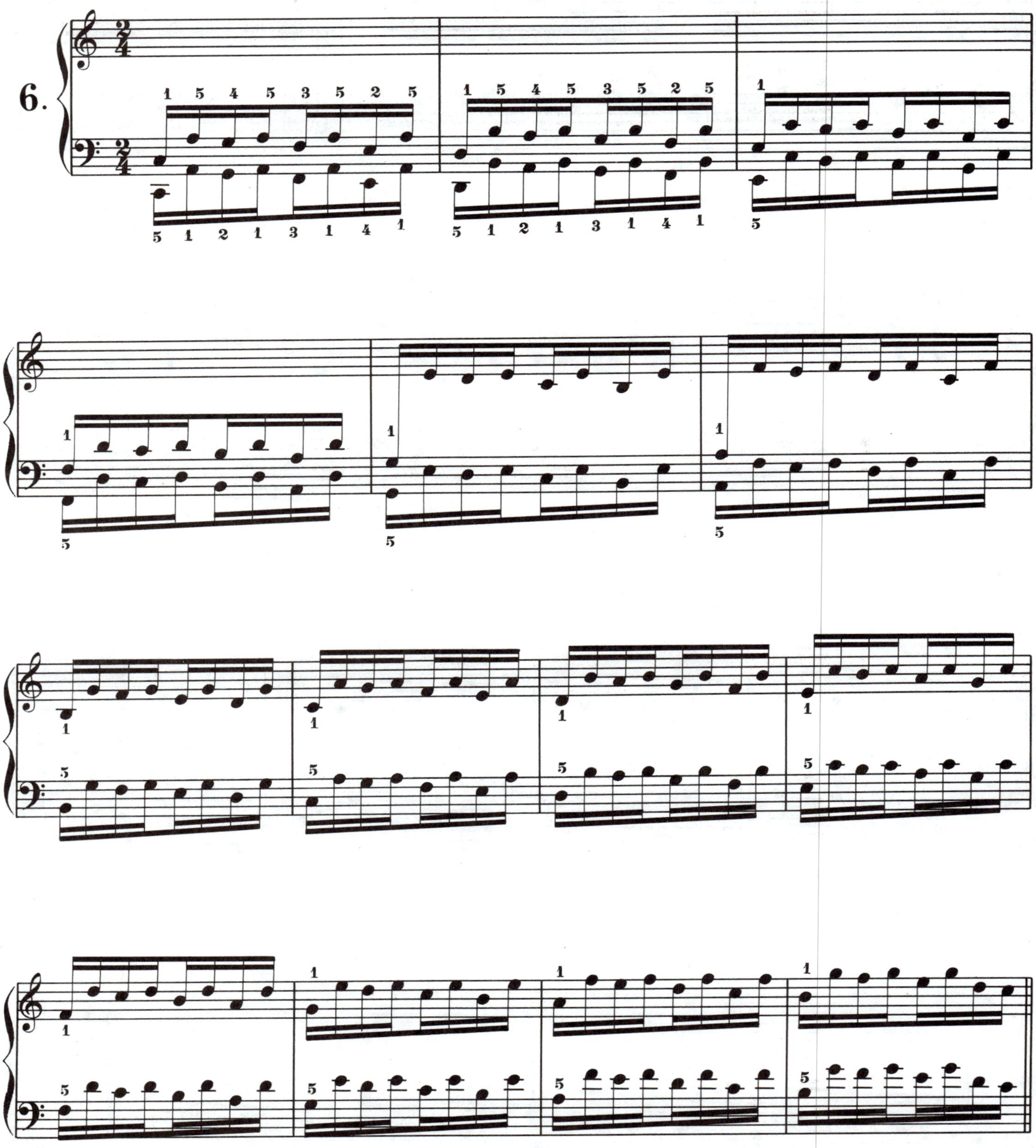

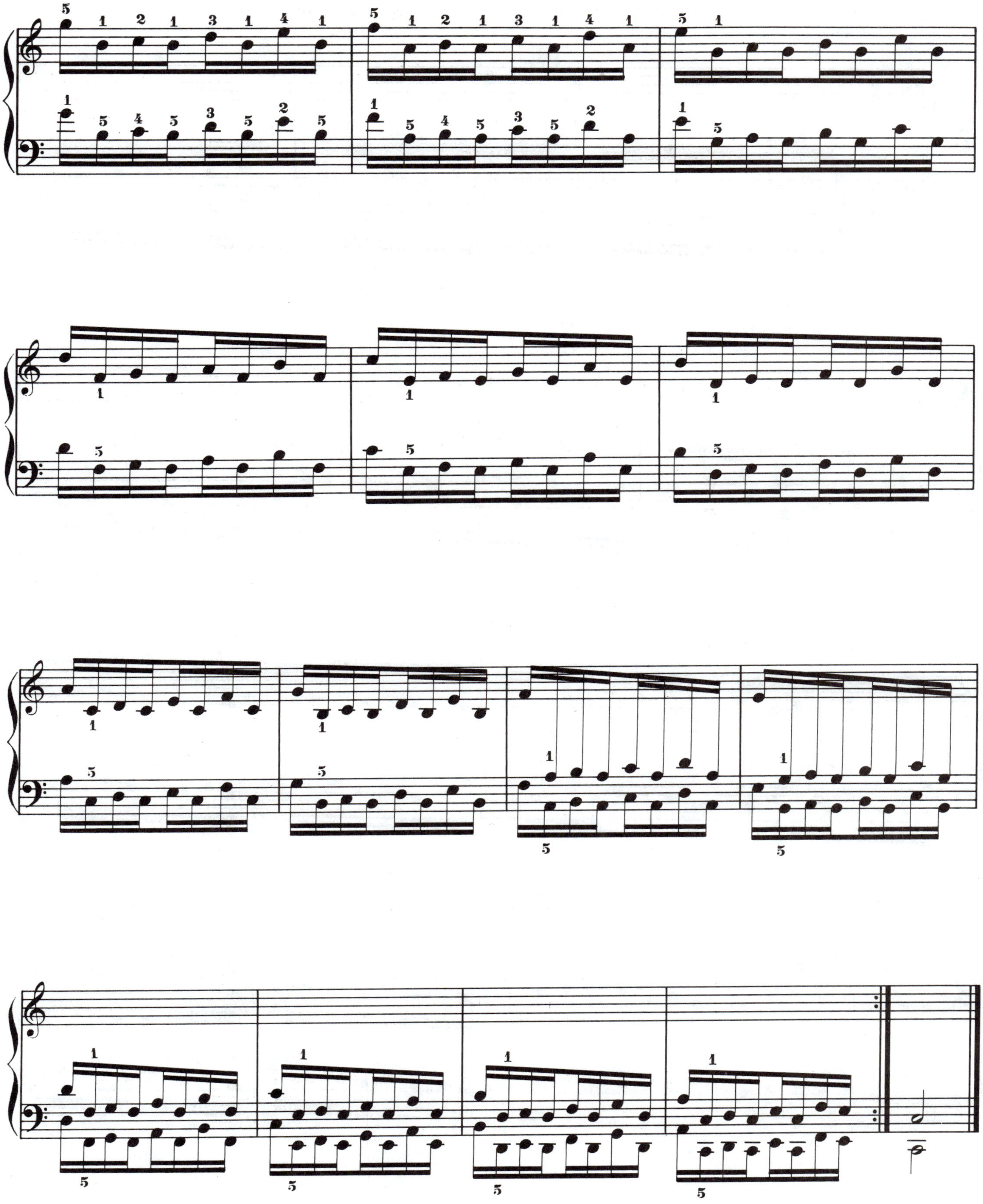

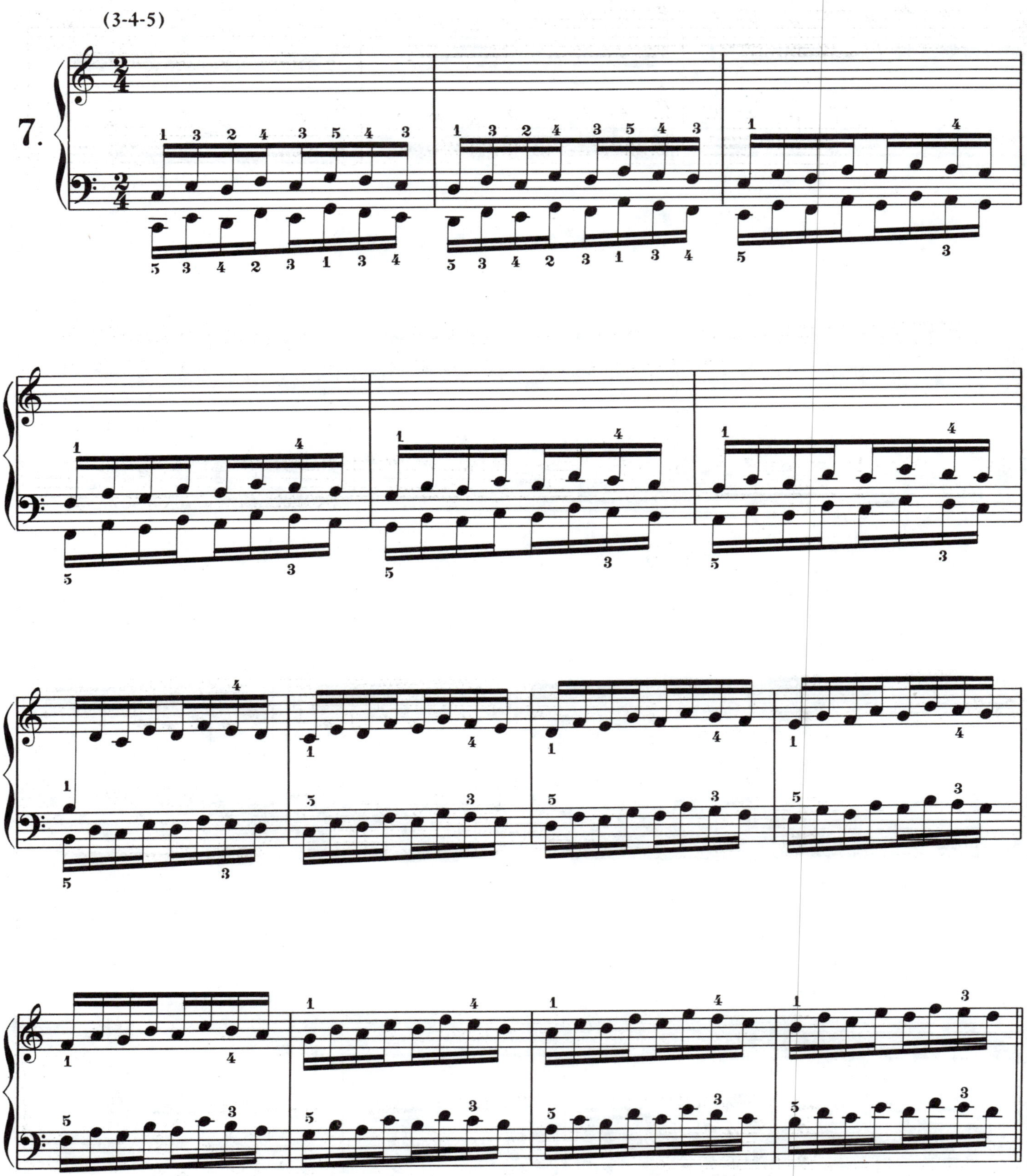
(3-4-5)
7.

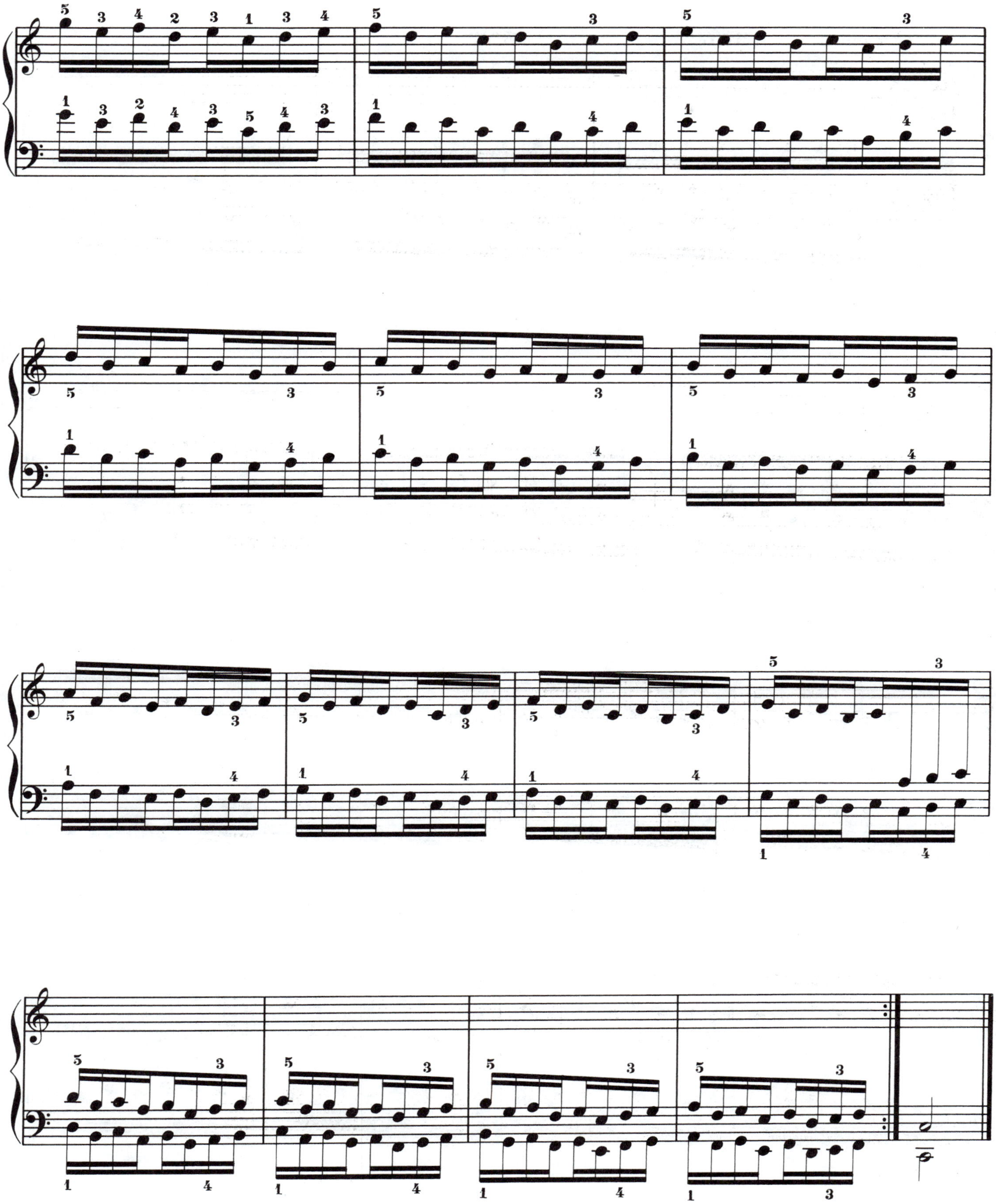

(1-2-3-4-5)

8.

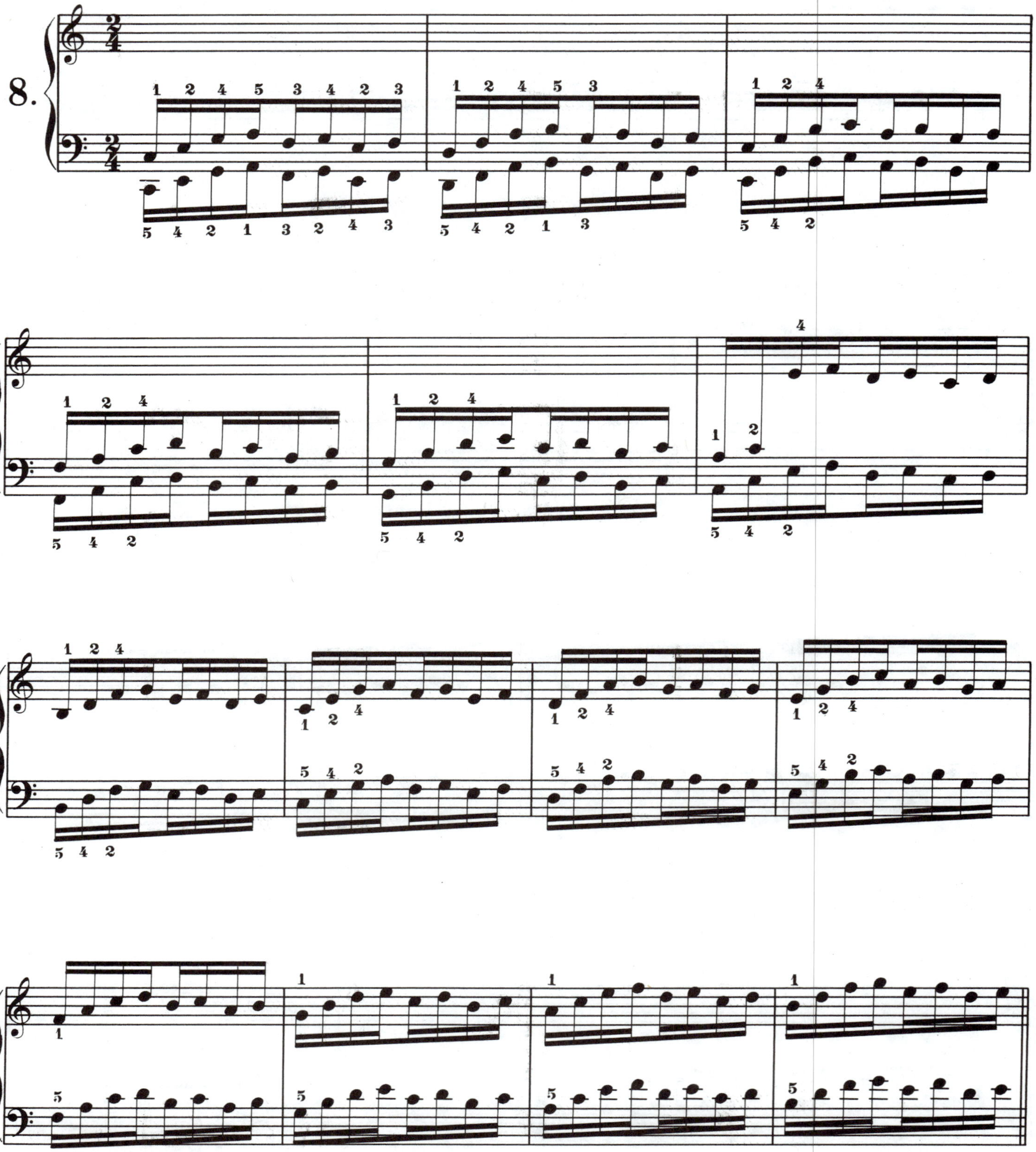

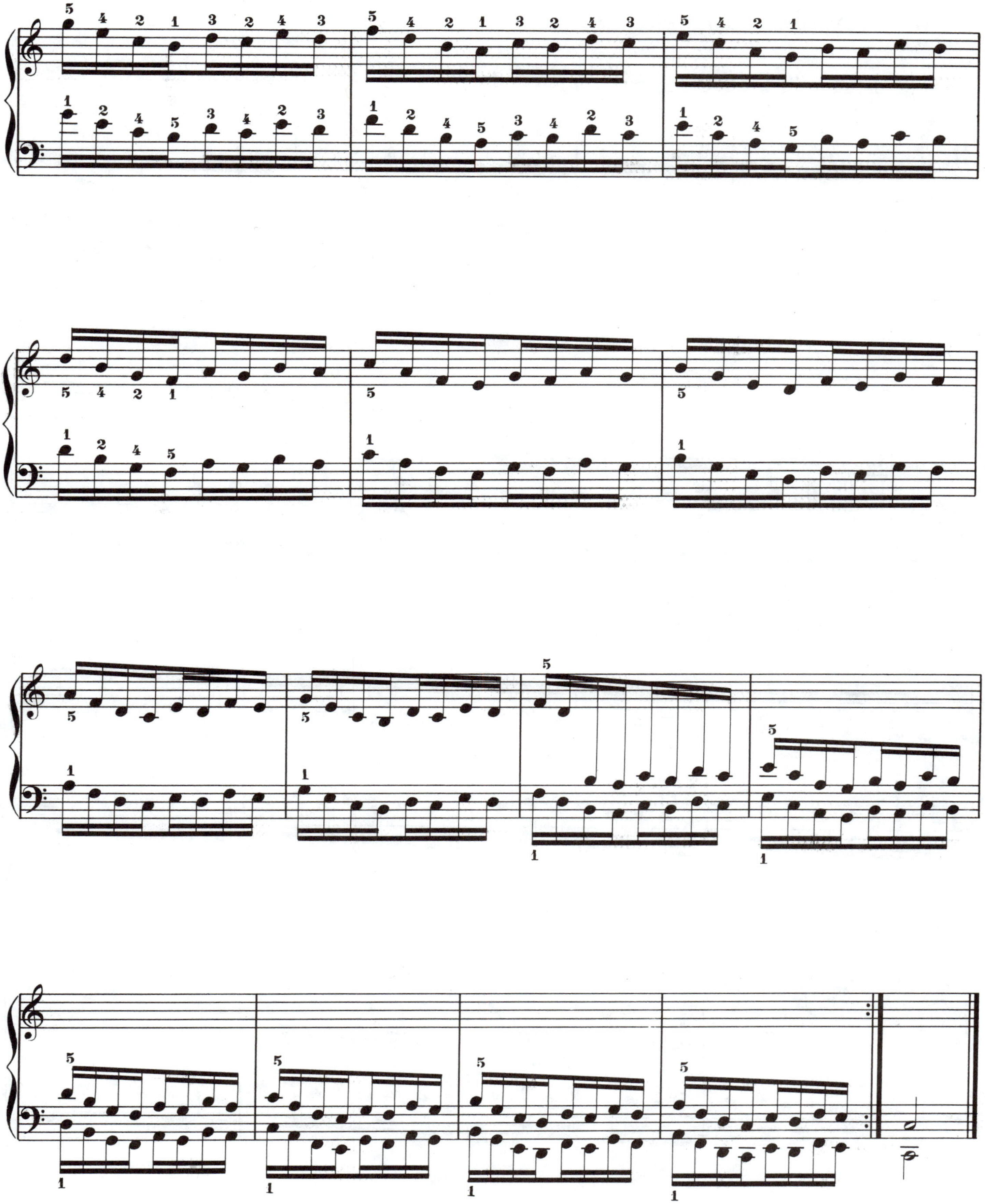

(1-2-3-4-5) Extension of the 4th and 5th fingers.

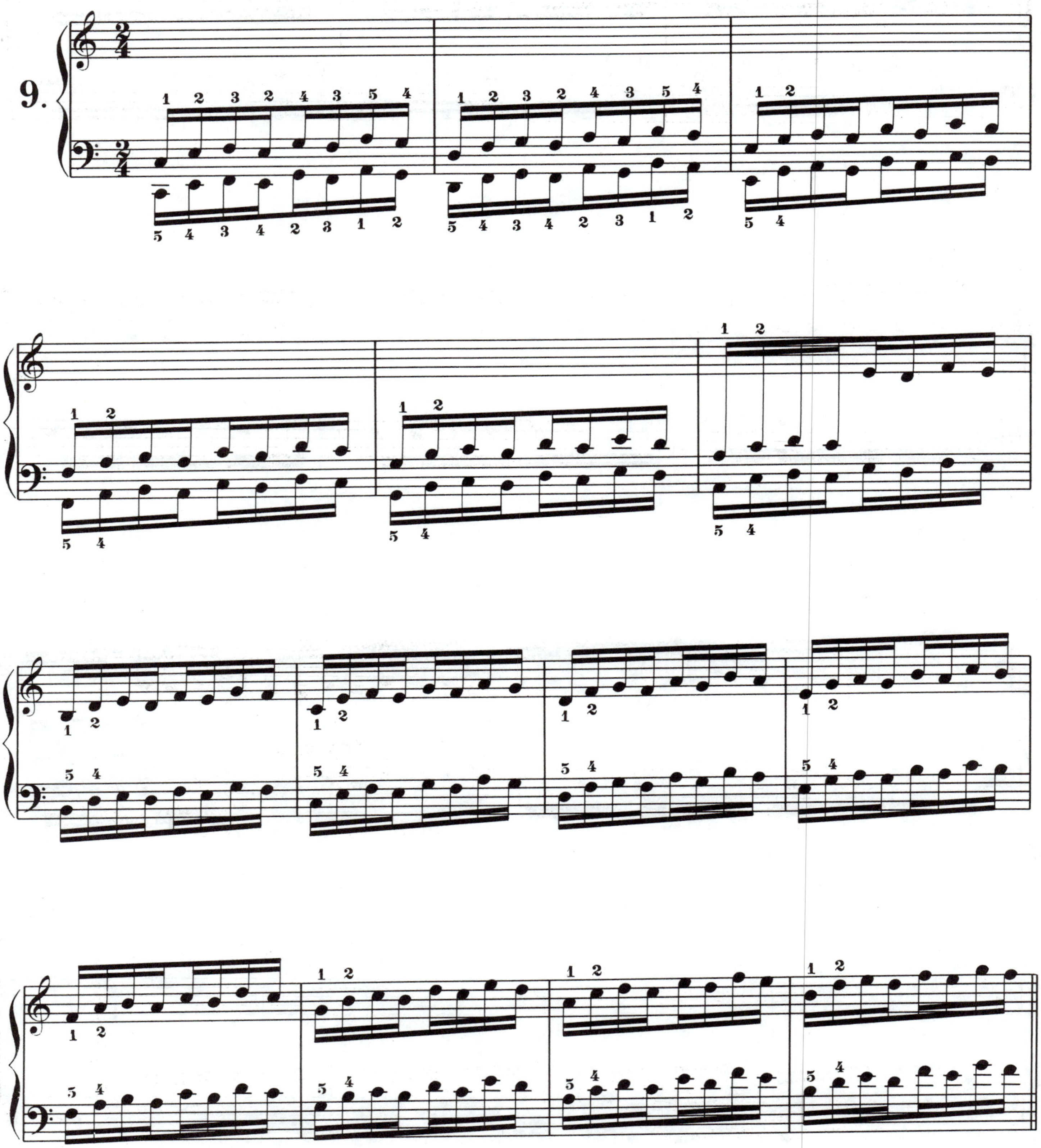

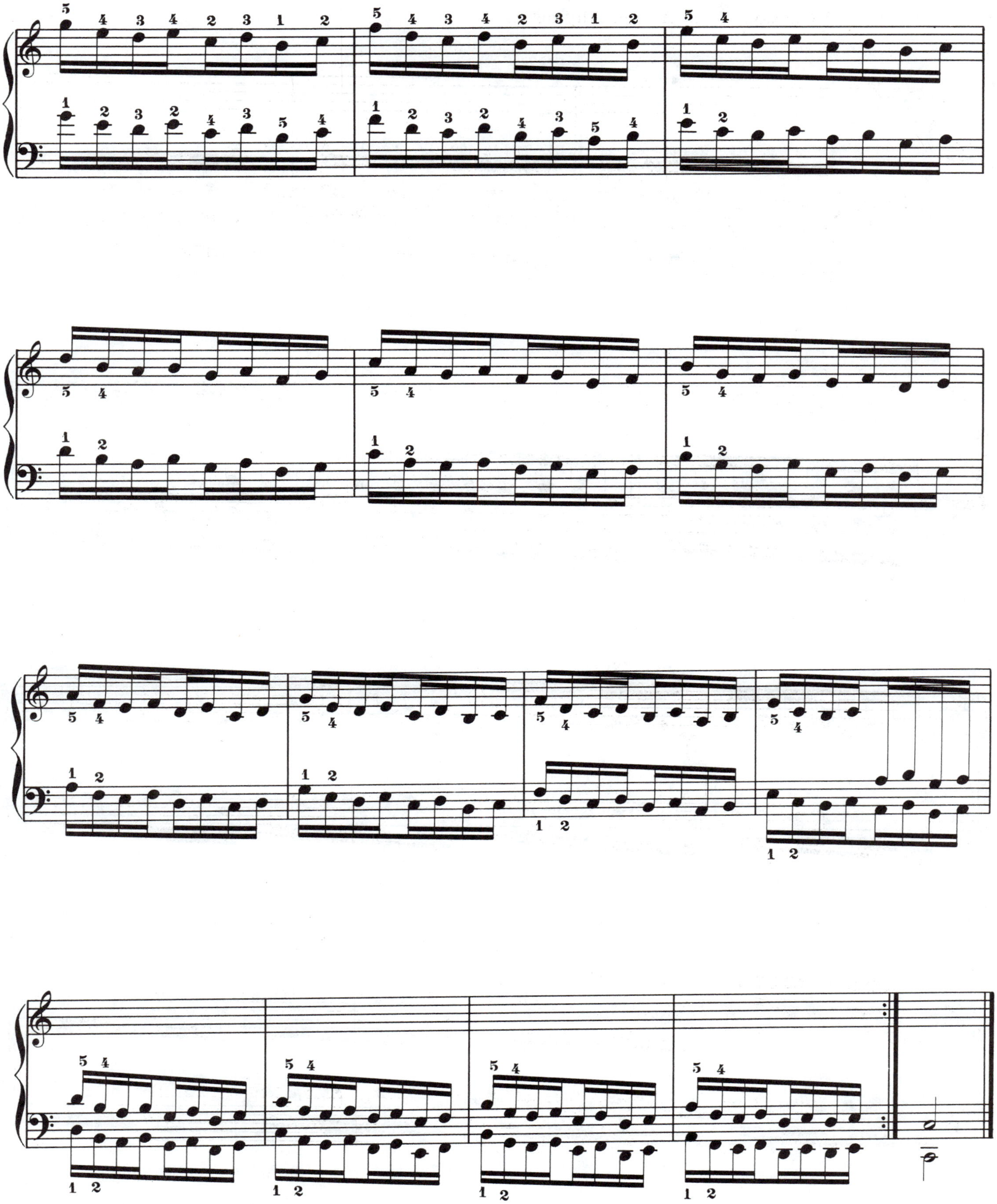

(3-4) Preparation for the trill for the 3rd and 4th fingers of the left hand in ascending and the right hand in descending.

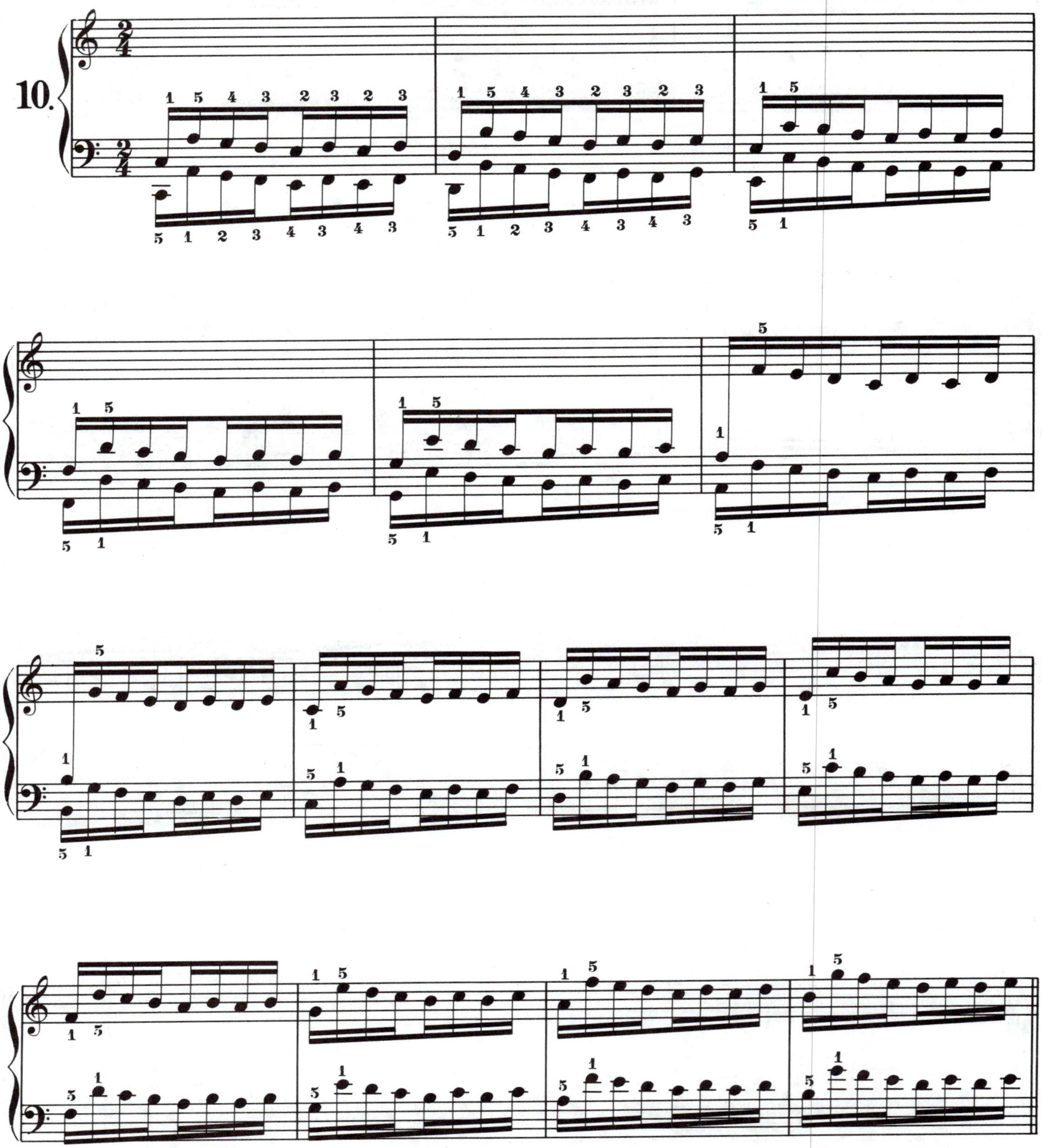

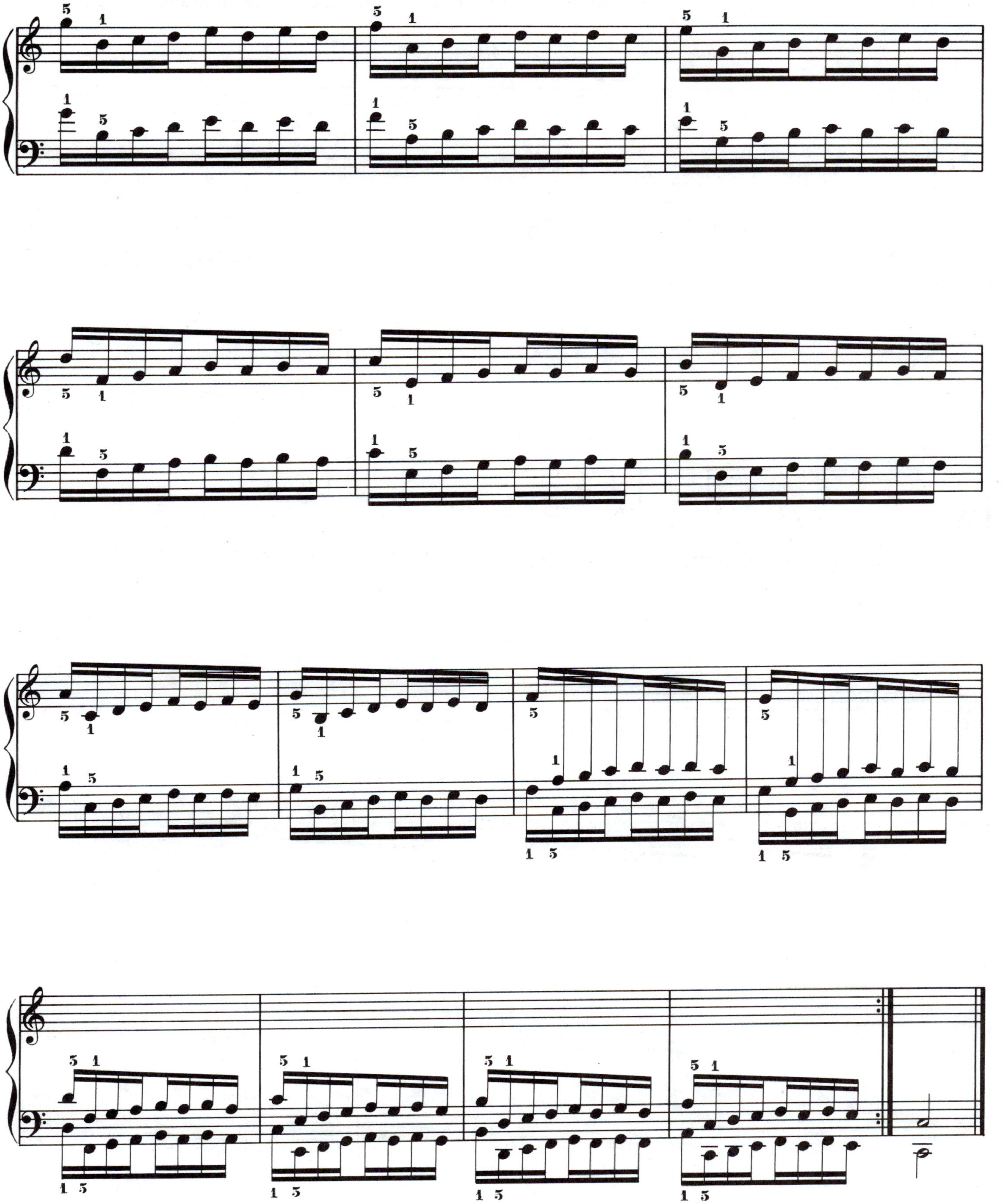

(3-4-5) Another preparation for the trill, for the 4th and 5th fingers.

11.

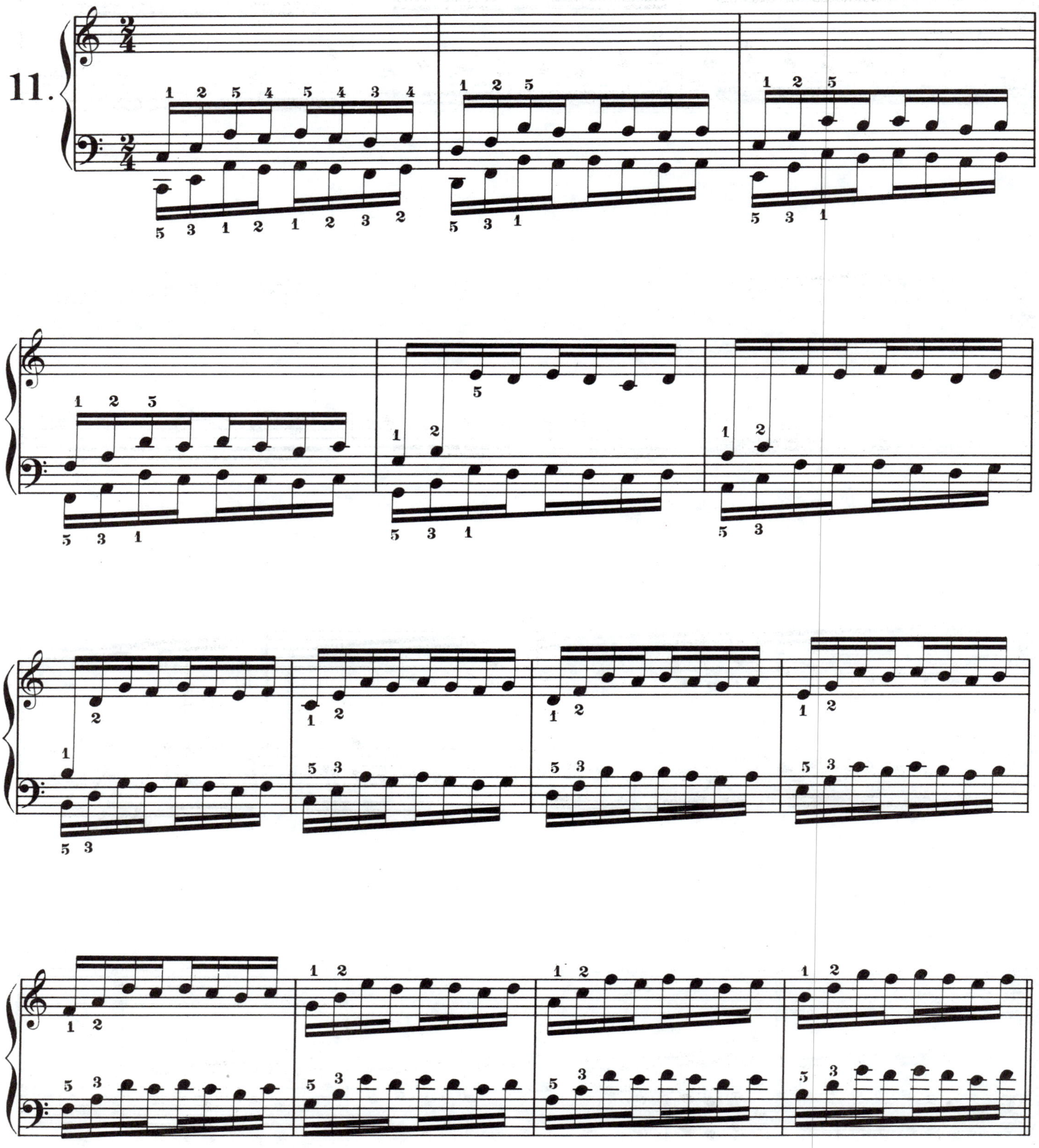

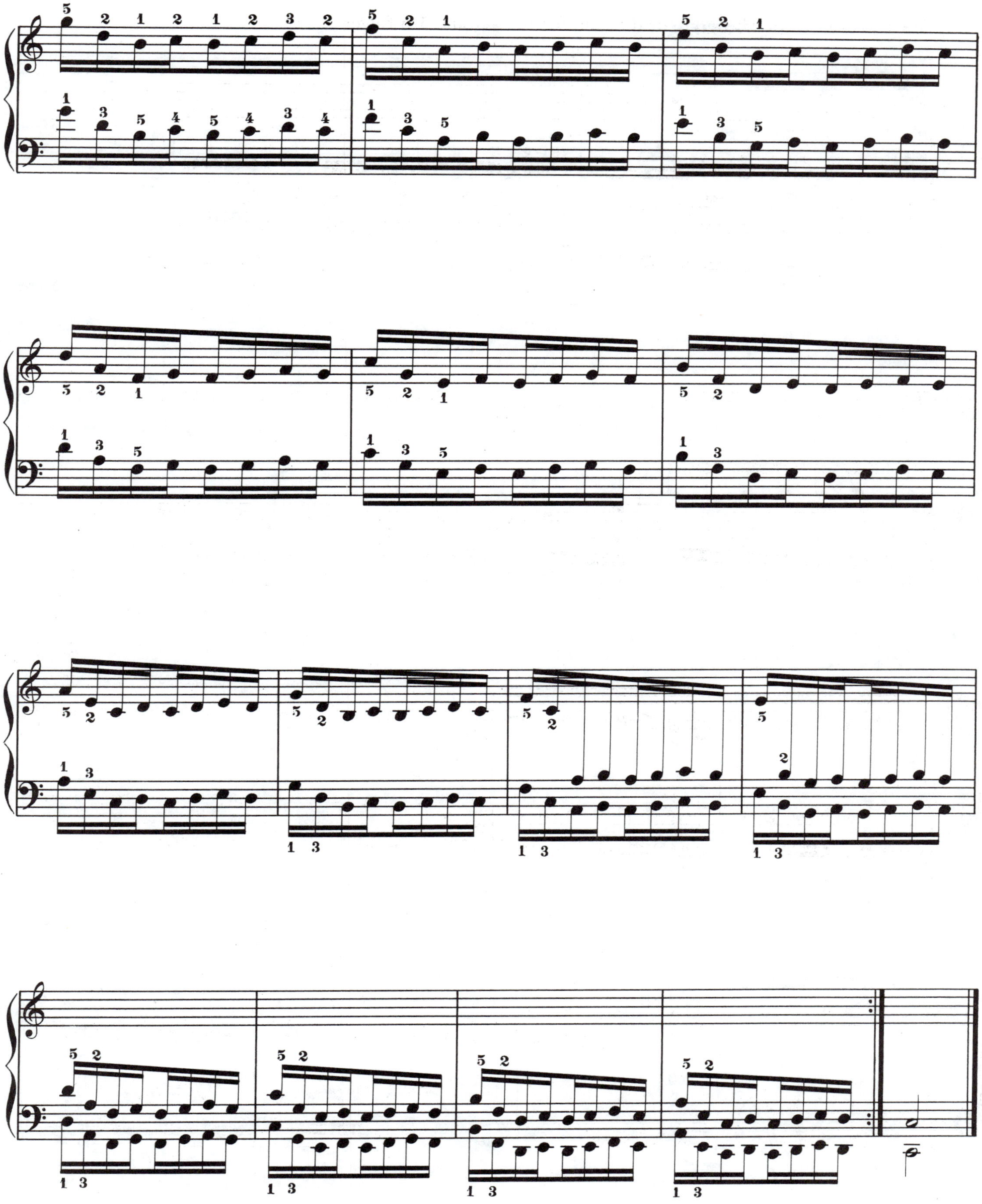

Extension of 1-5 and exercises for (3-4-5).

12.

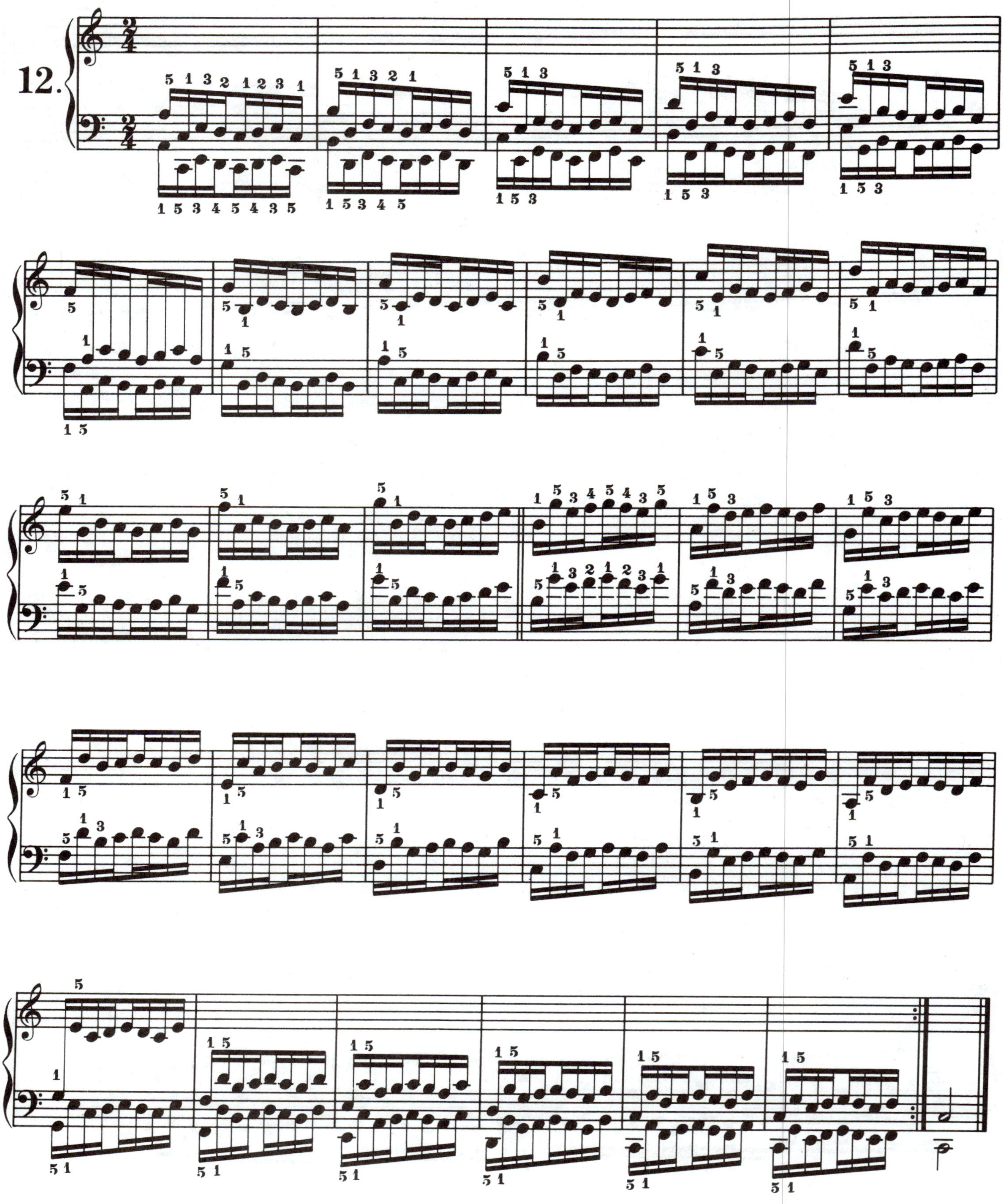

(3-4-5)

13.

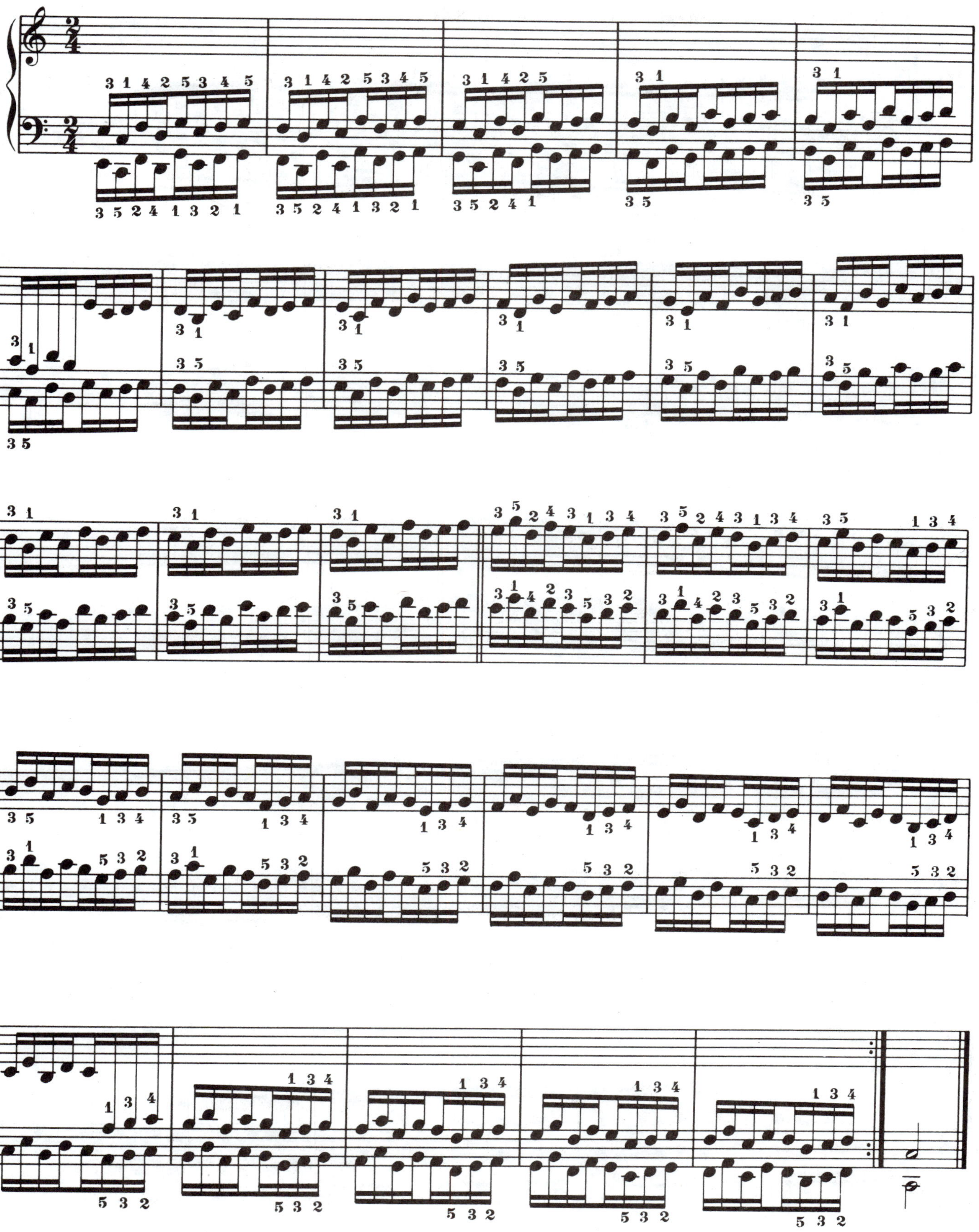

(3-4) Still another preparation for the trill, for the 3rd and 4th fingers.

14.

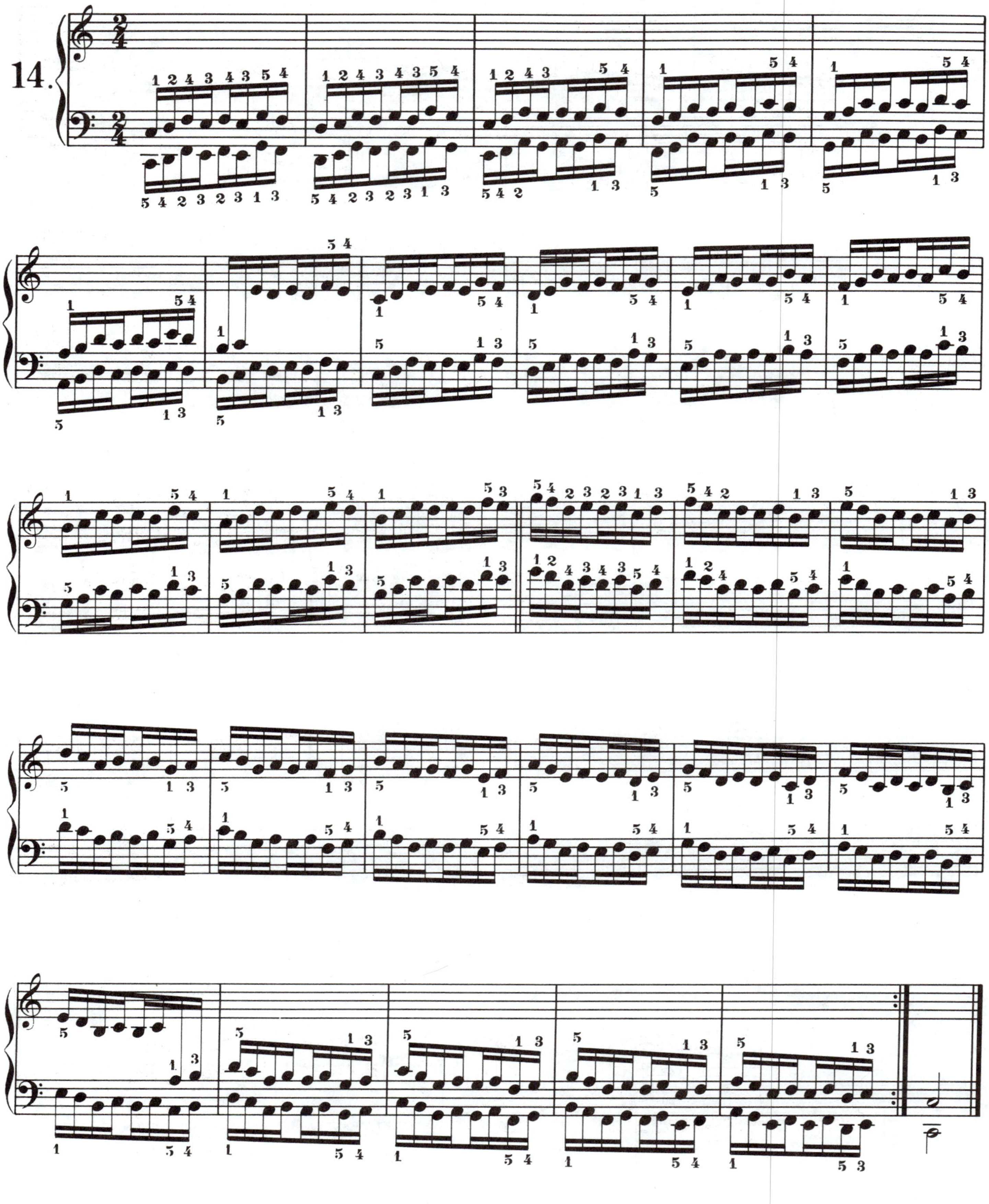

Extension of 1-2.

15.

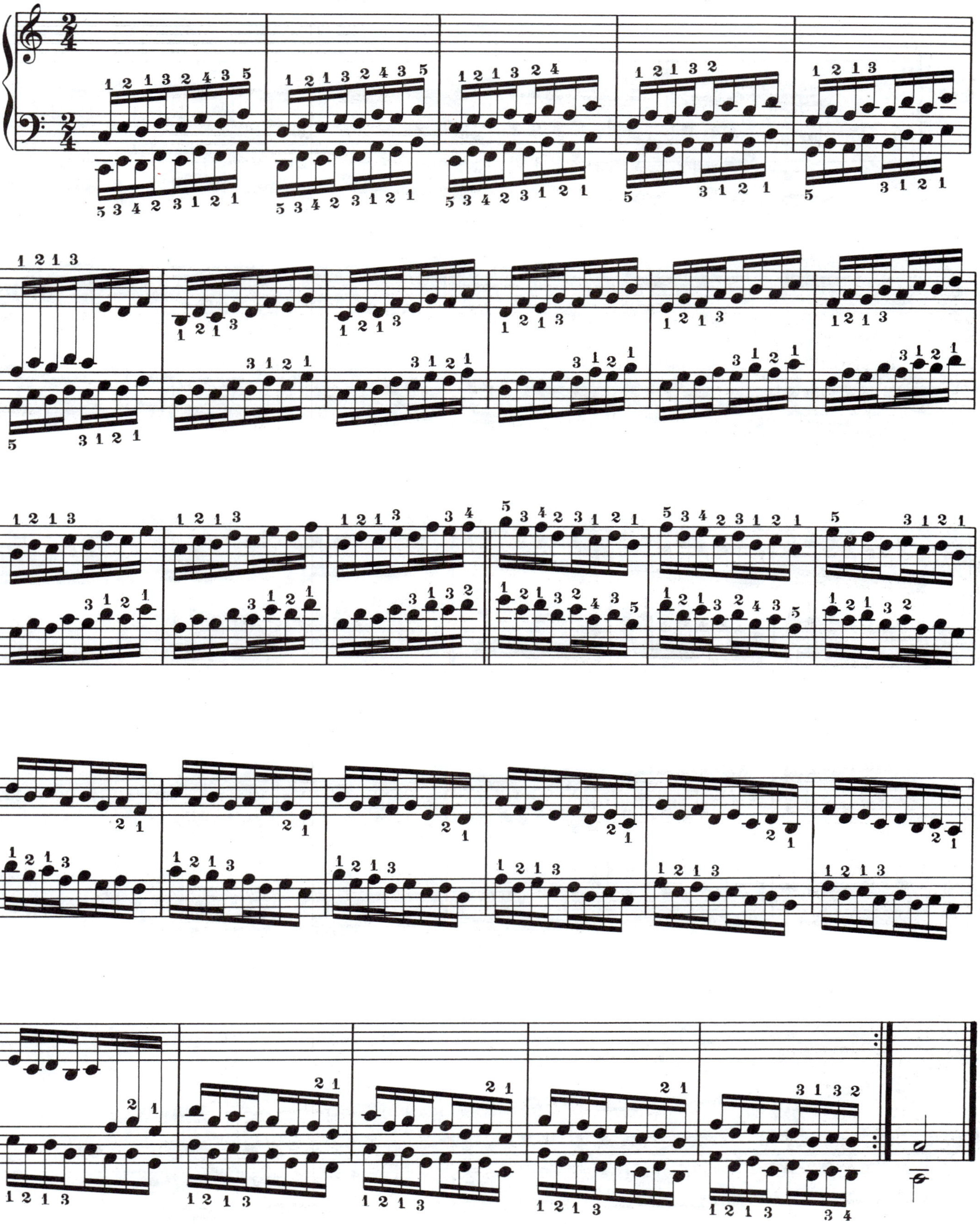

Extension of 3-5 and exercise for (3-4-5).

16.

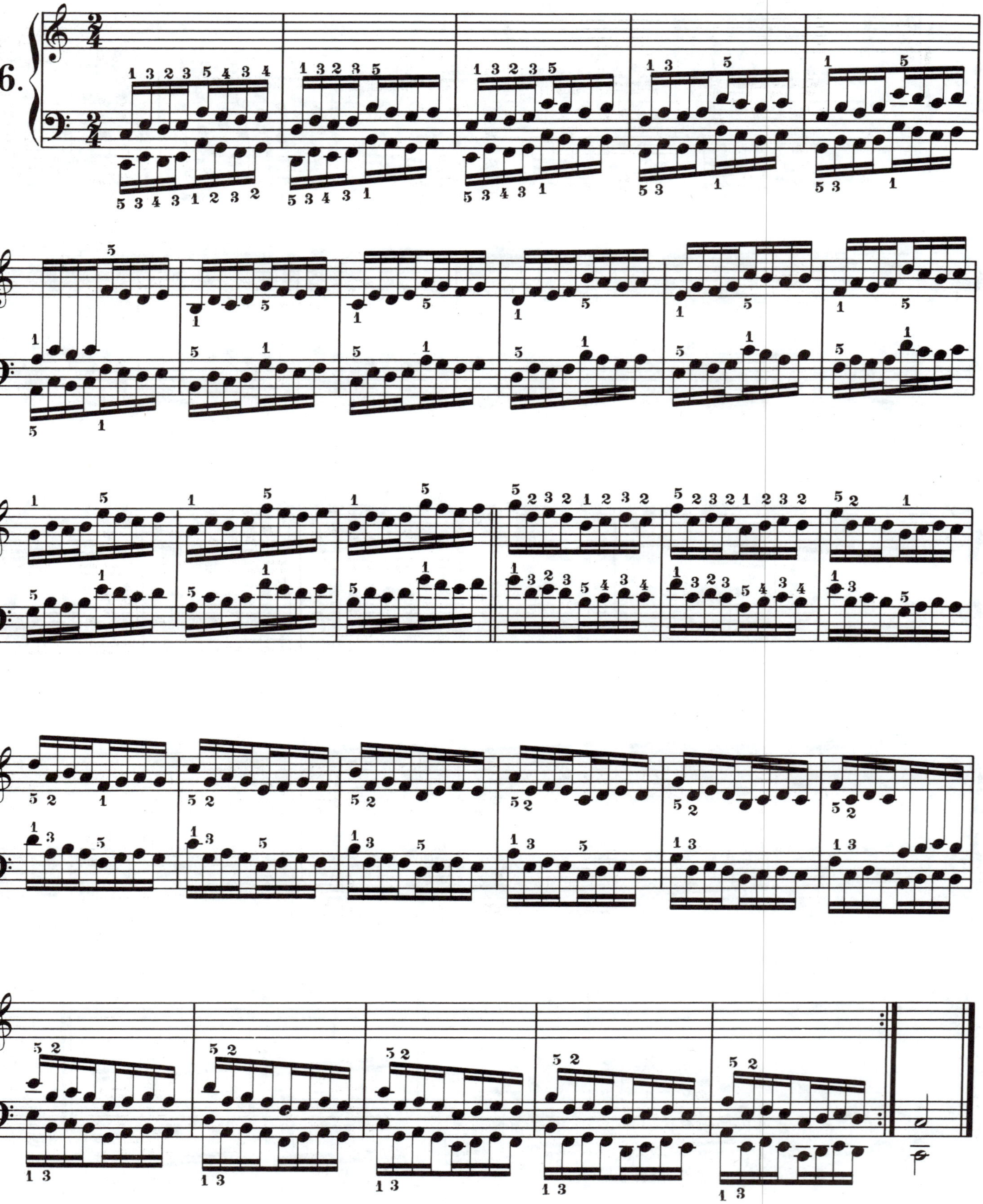

Extension of 1-2, 2-4, 4-5 and exercise for (3-4-5).

17.

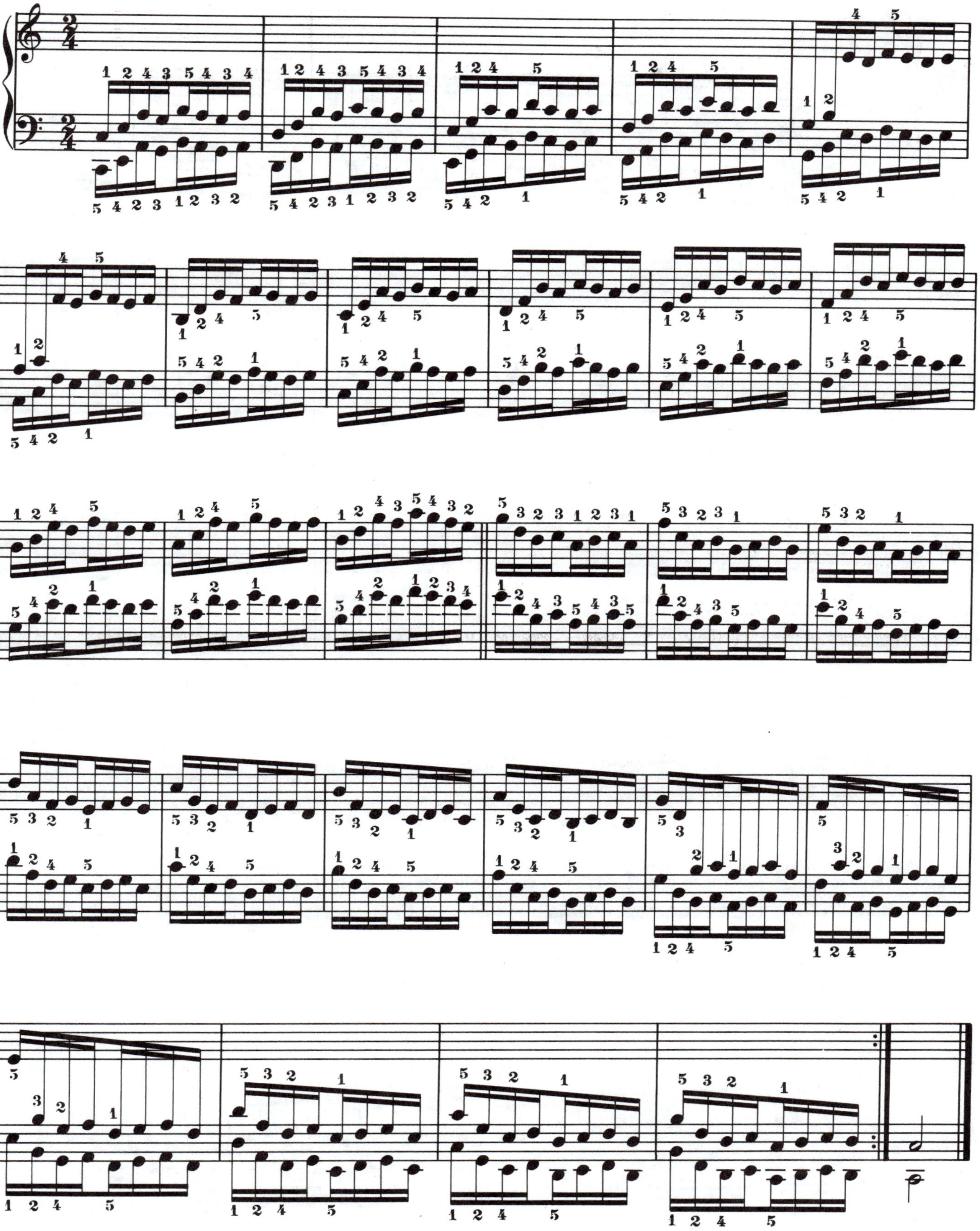

(1-2-3-4-5)

18.

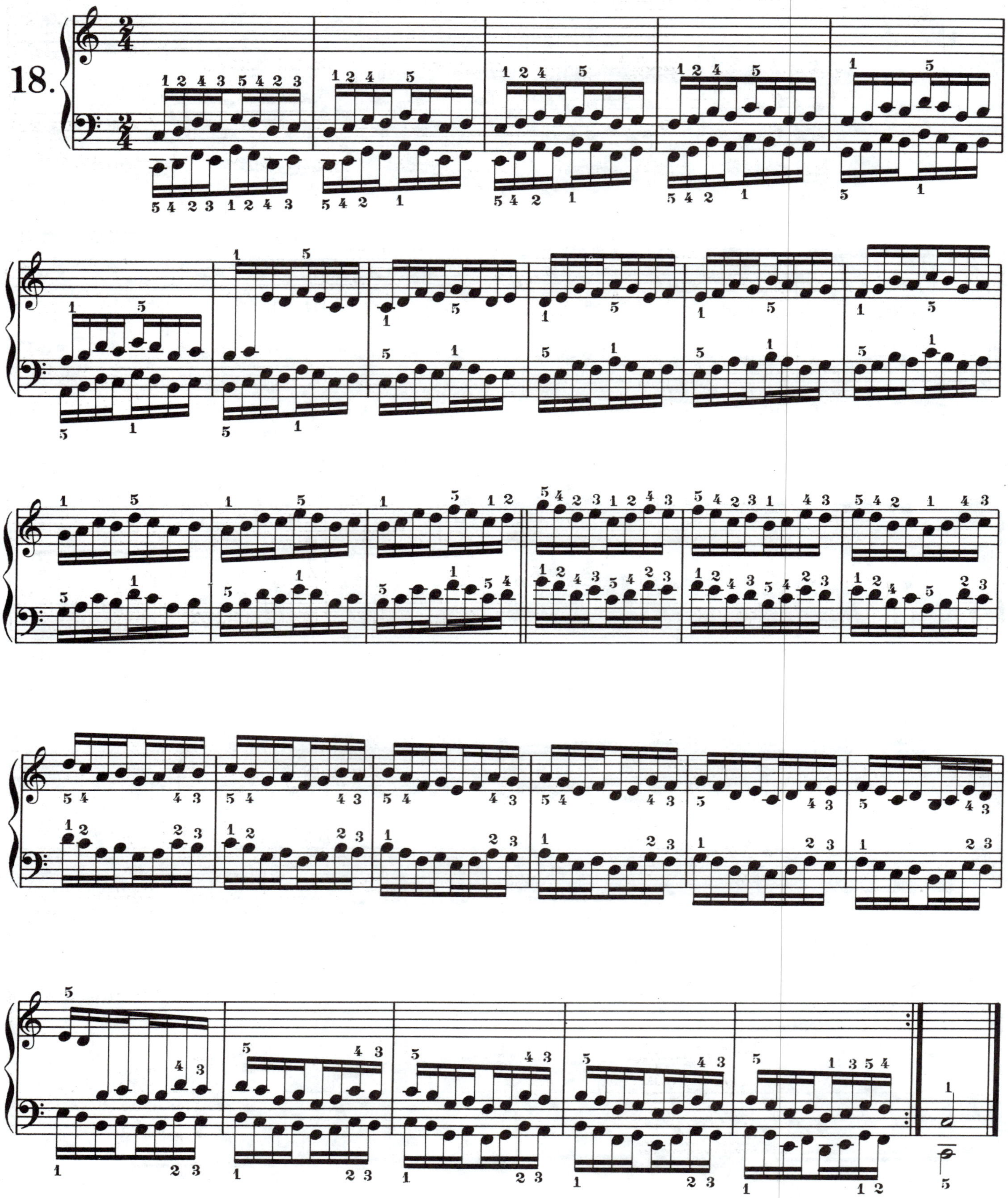

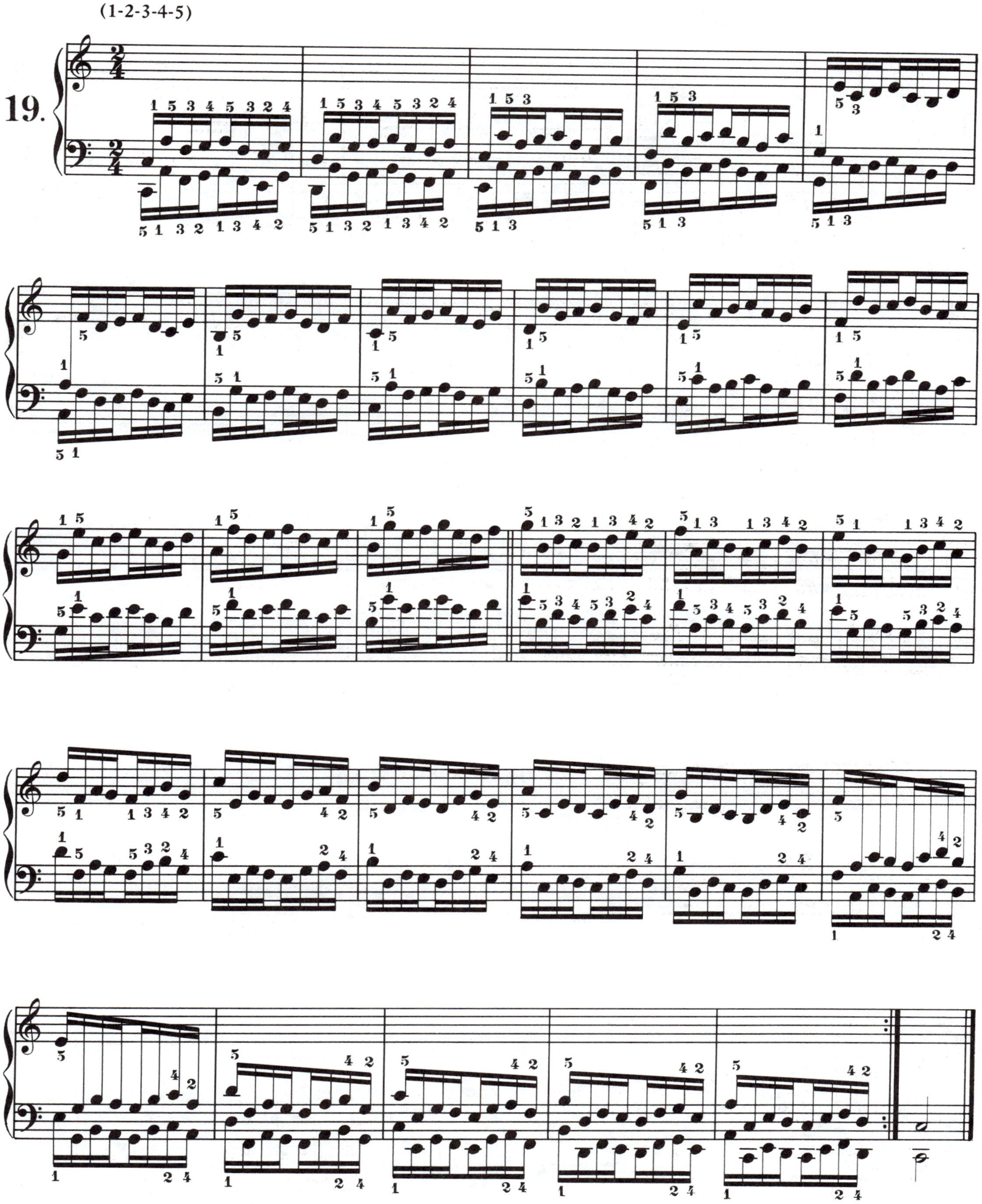
(1-2-3-4-5)
19.

Extension of **2-4**, **4-5** and exercise for **(2-3-4)**.

20.

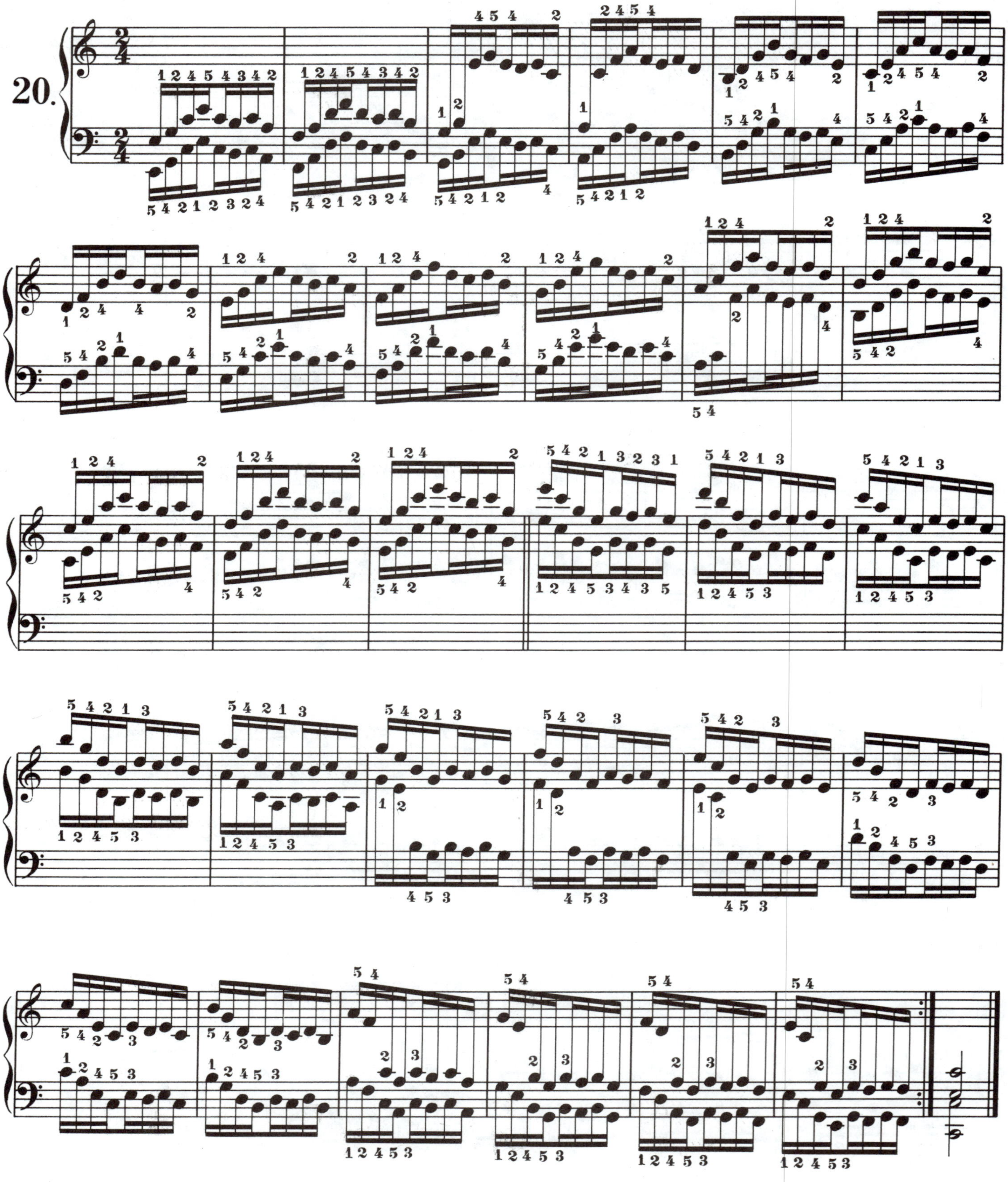

end of part 1

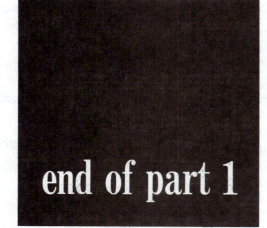

After having mastered Part 1, play it through once or twice daily for some time before beginning Part 2. By doing so, the pianist is sure to receive every possible advantage that these extraordinary exercises offer. Complete mastery of Part 1 provides the key towards overcoming the difficulties found in Part 2.

THE VIRTUOSO PIANIST, PART 2

Further Exercises for the Development of a Virtuoso Technique

What the 3rd, 4th and 5th fingers of the left hand play in the first beat of each measure (A), the corresponding fingers of the right hand inversely repeat in the third beat of the same measure (B).

(3-4-5)

M. M. ♩ = 60 to 108

C. L. HANON

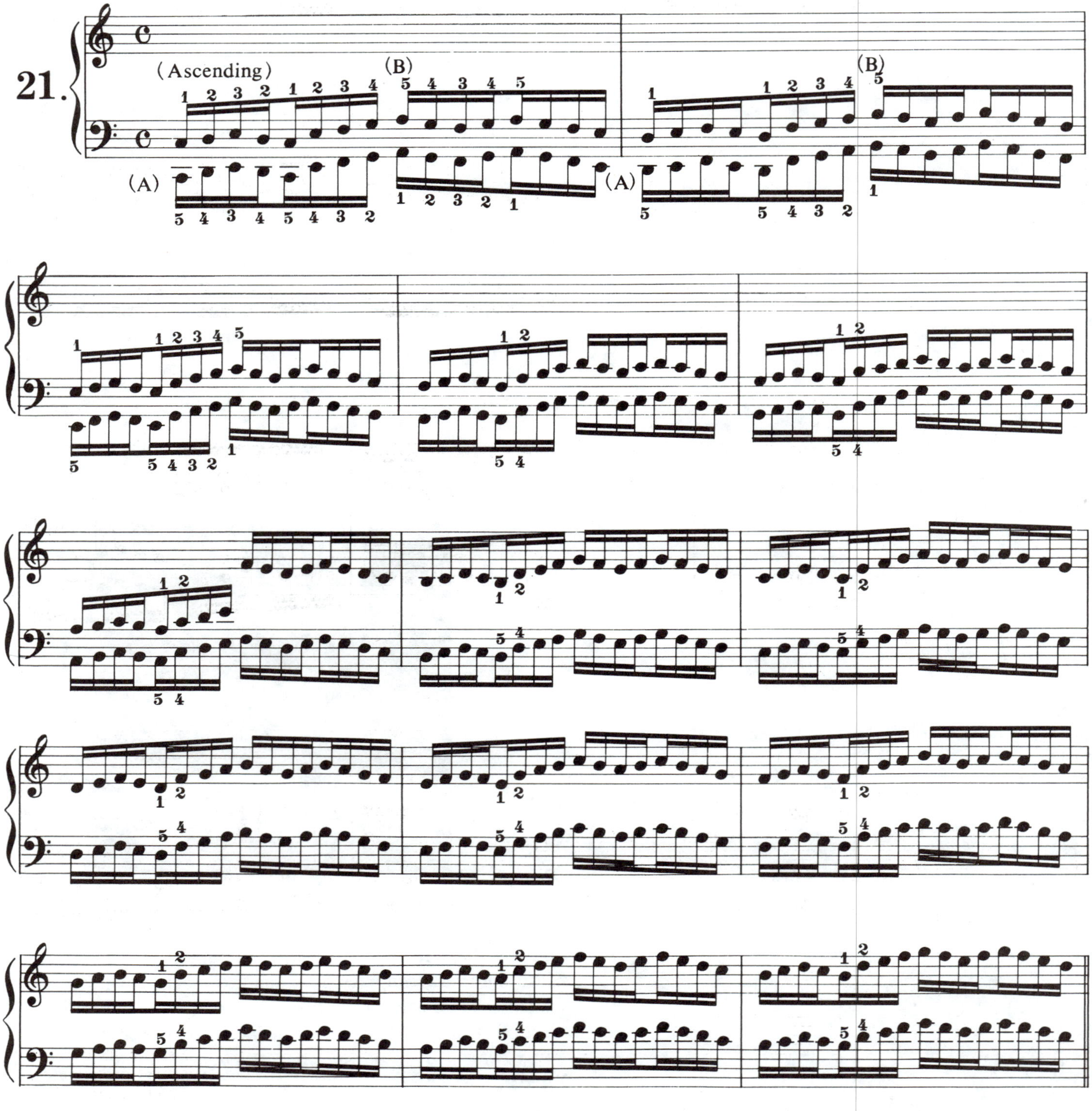

Practice the exercises in Part 2 at the same tempos as in Part 1. Where no Metronome Mark is indicated, begin at 60 and gradually increase the speed to 108. When a different tempo is required, it will be indicated at the head of the exercise.

(Descending)

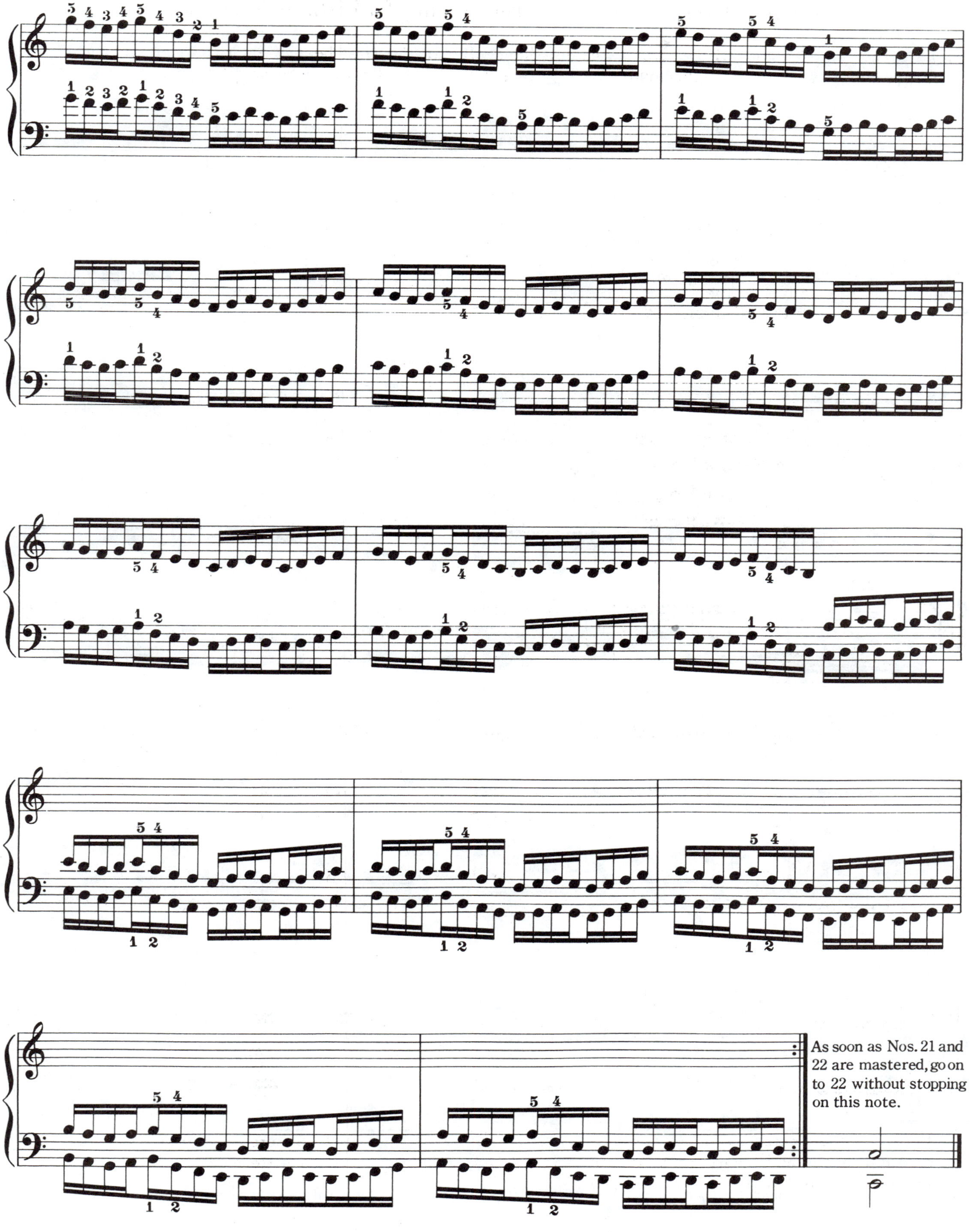
As soon as Nos. 21 and 22 are mastered, go on to 22 without stopping on this note.

(3-4-5)

22.

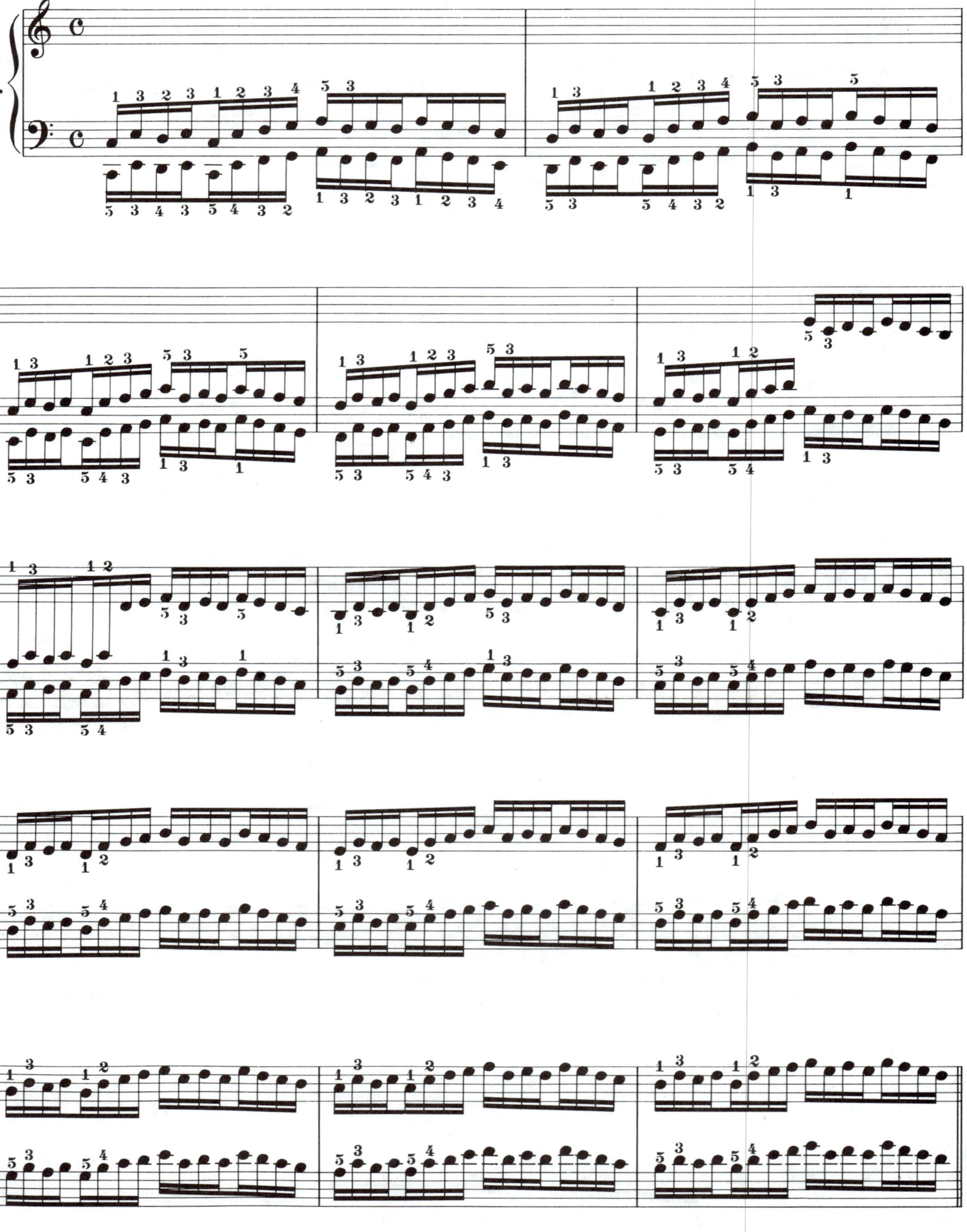

Practice the exercises one after another as in Part 1. In playing through the exercises, stop only on the last note on pages 37, 41, 45, 49, 53, 56, 58 and 61.

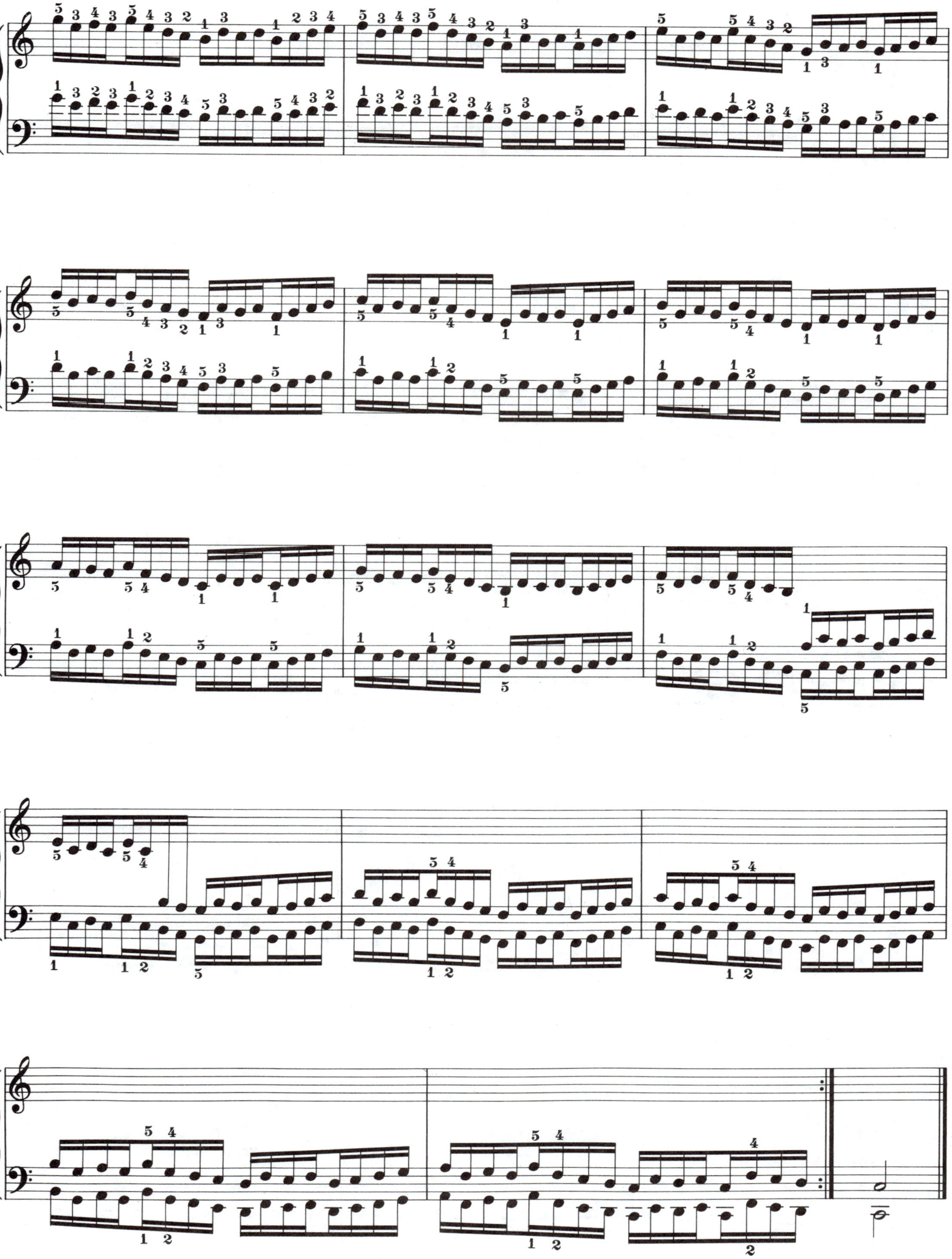

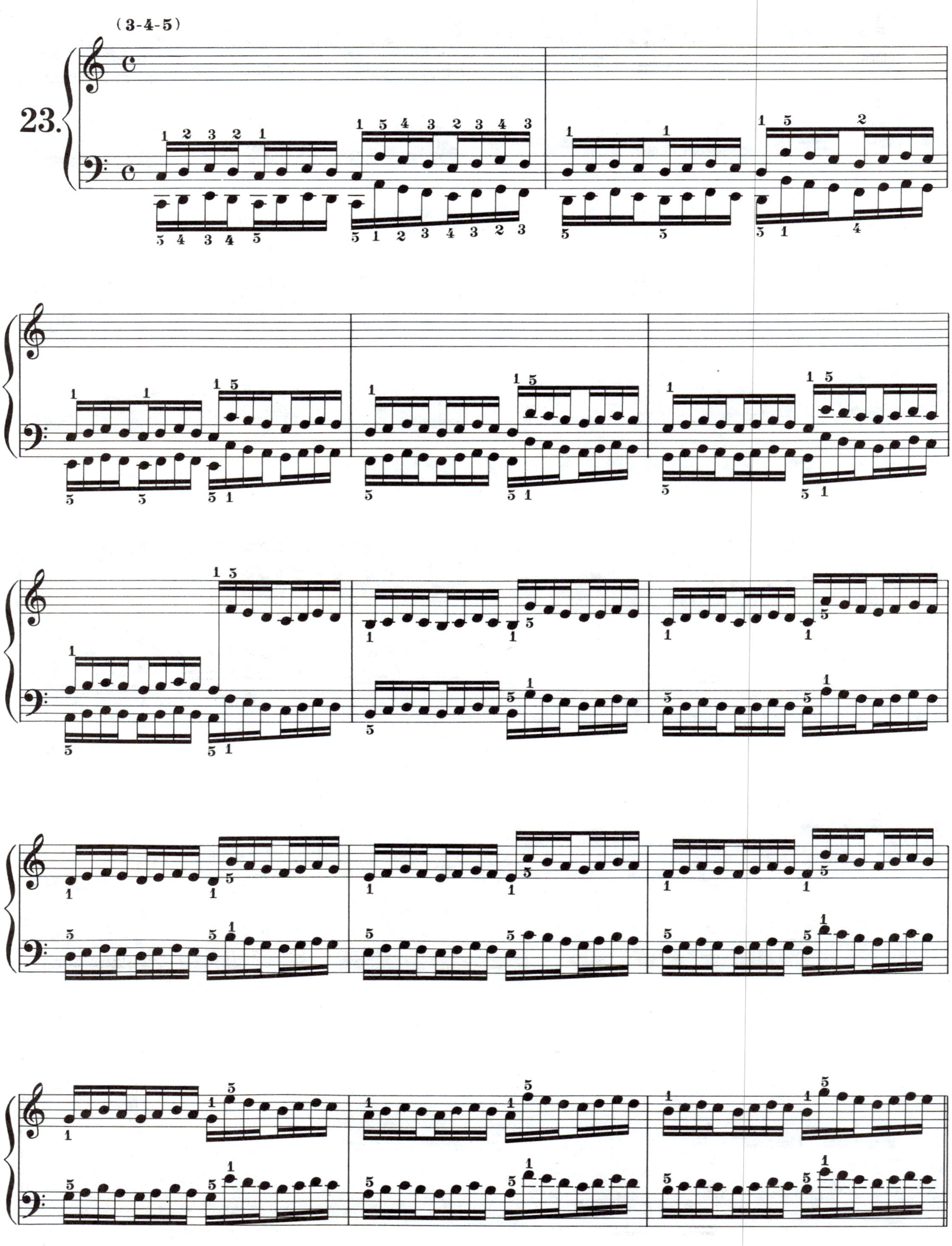
(3-4-5)
23.

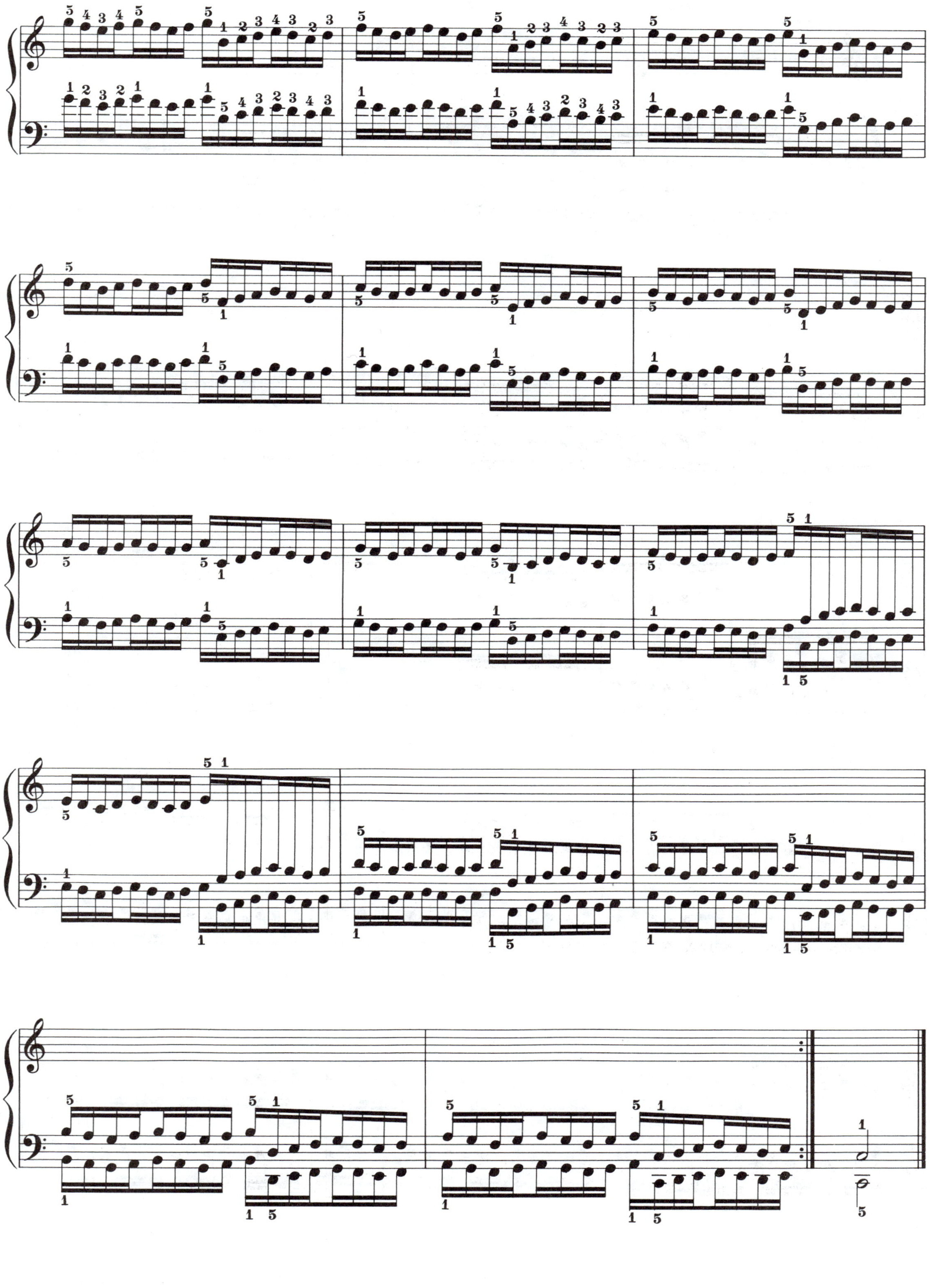

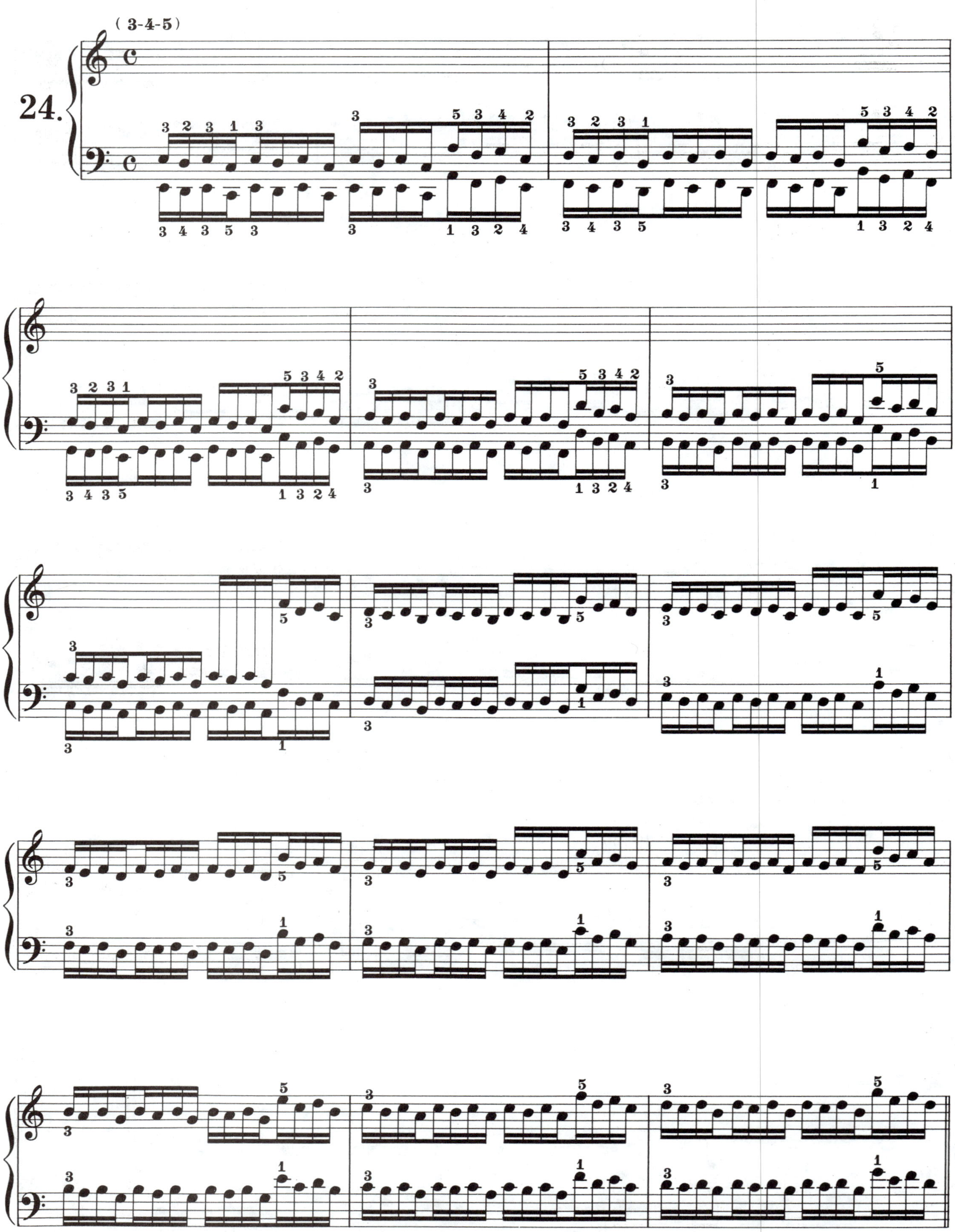
(3-4-5)
24.

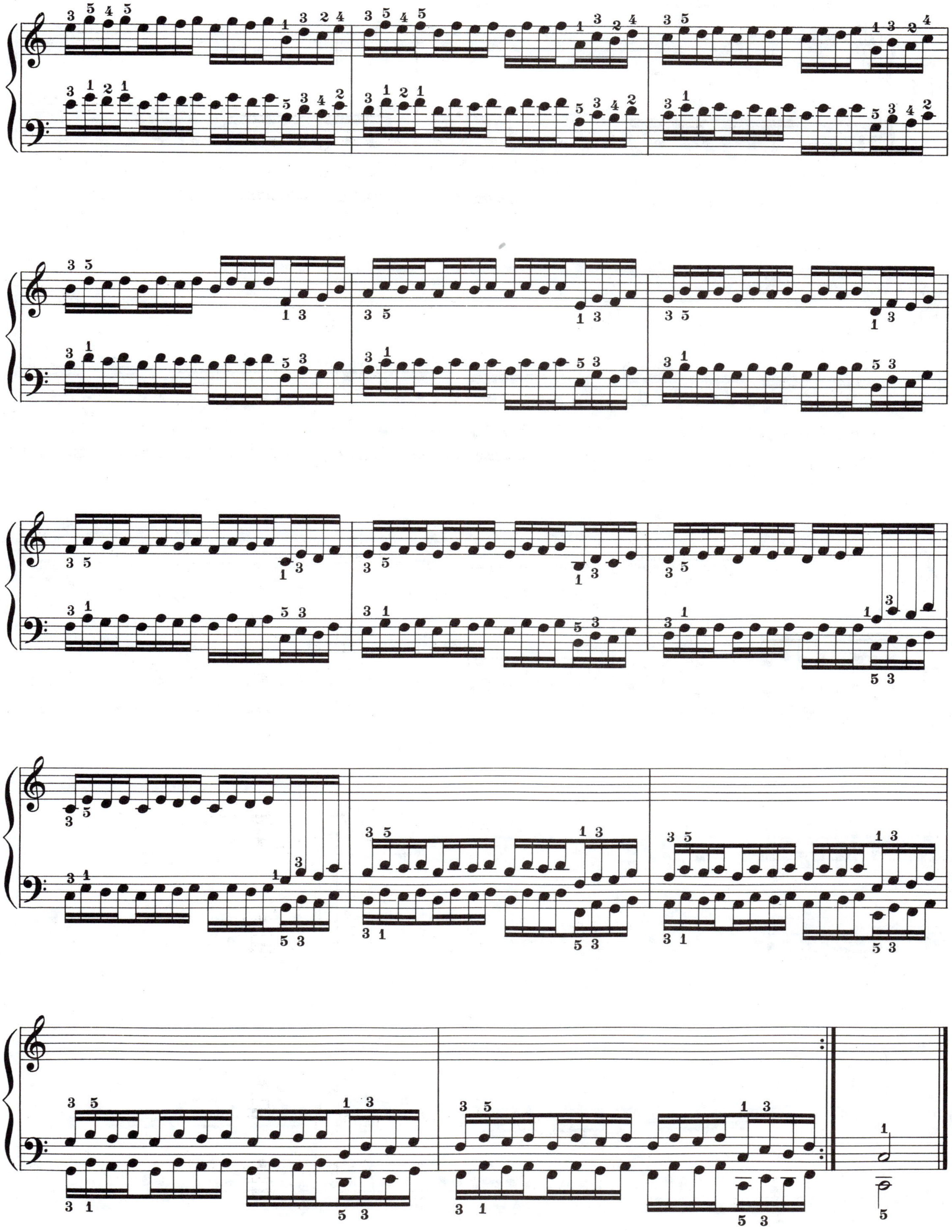

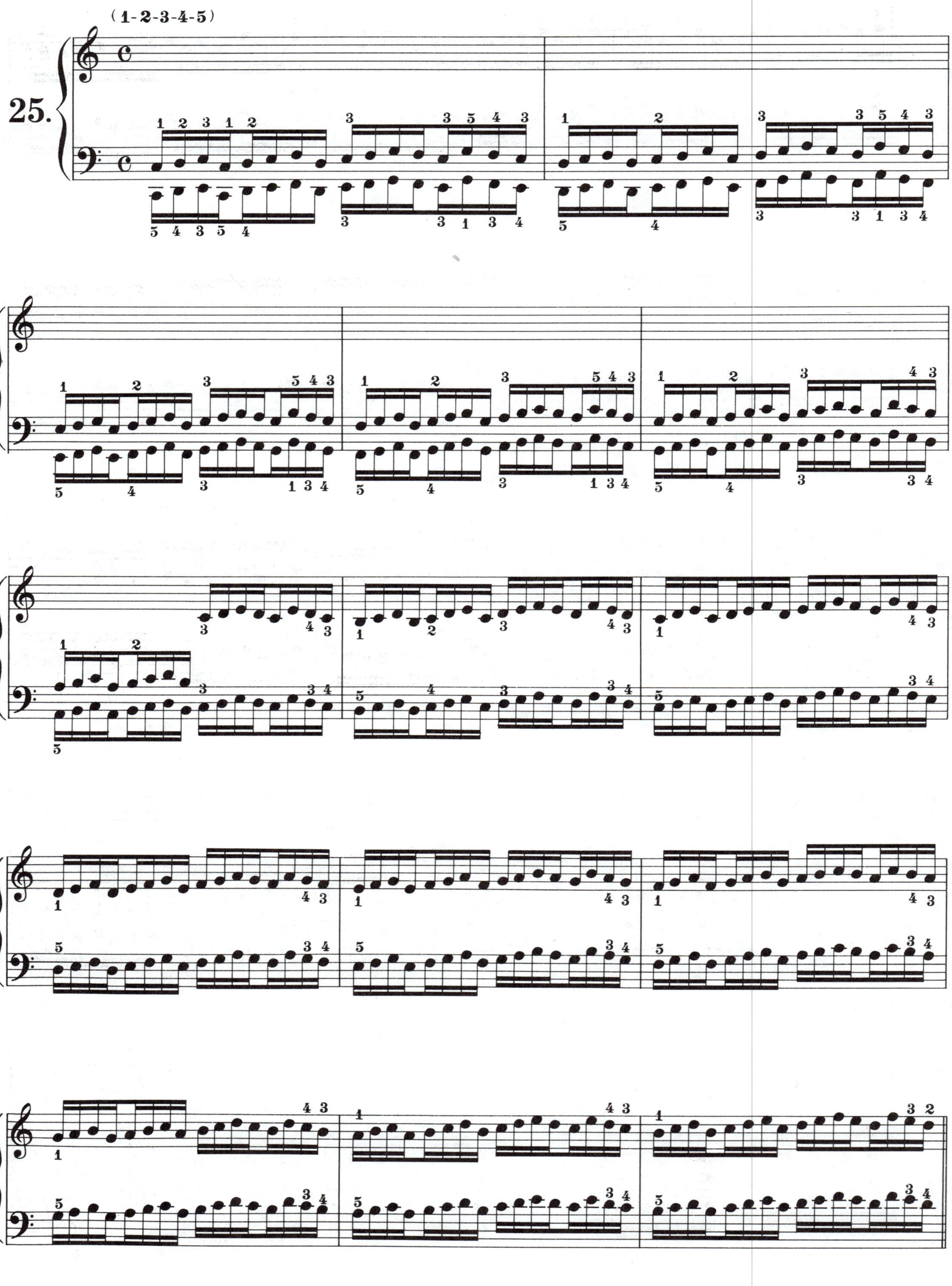
(1-2-3-4-5)
25.

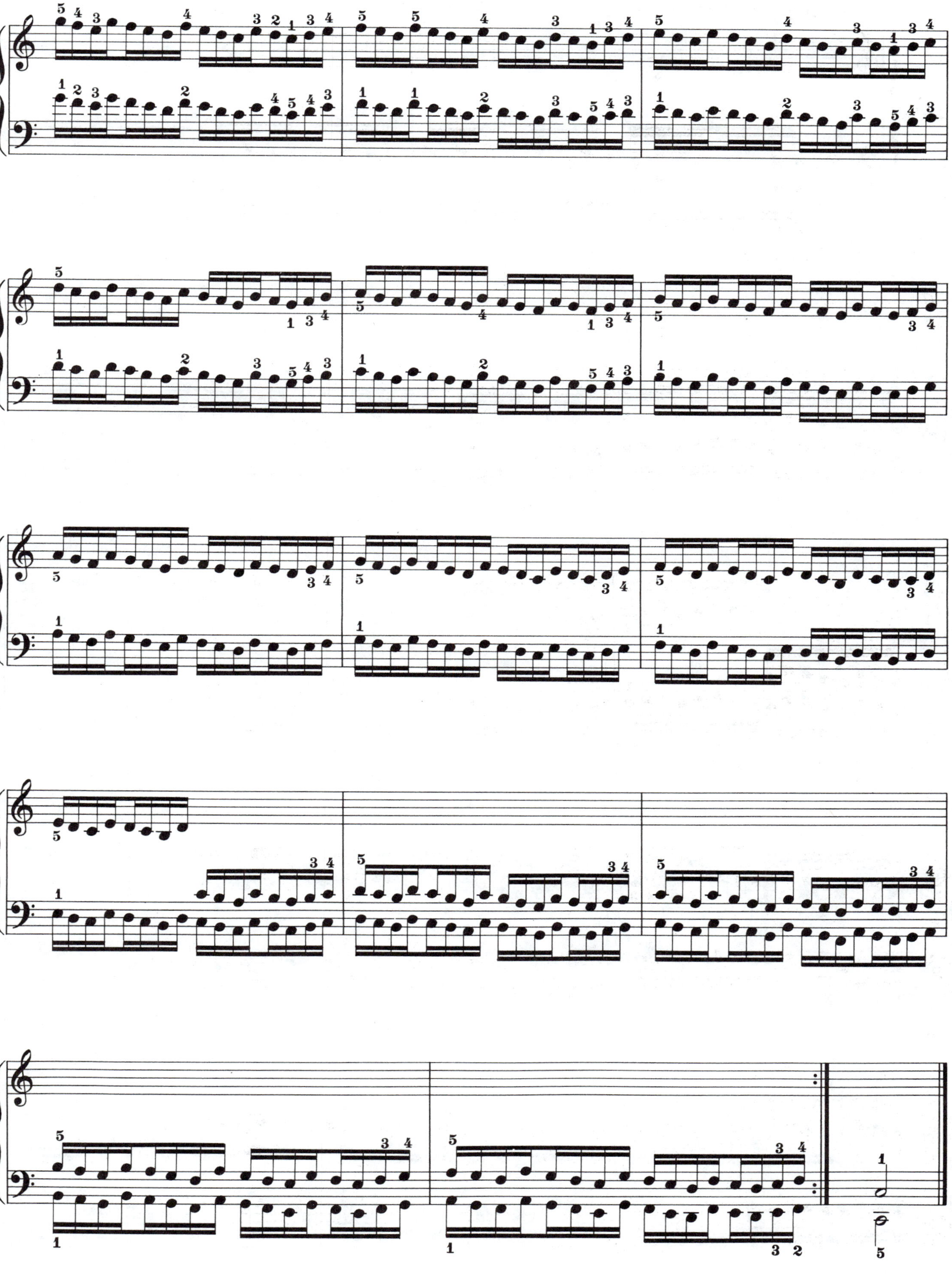

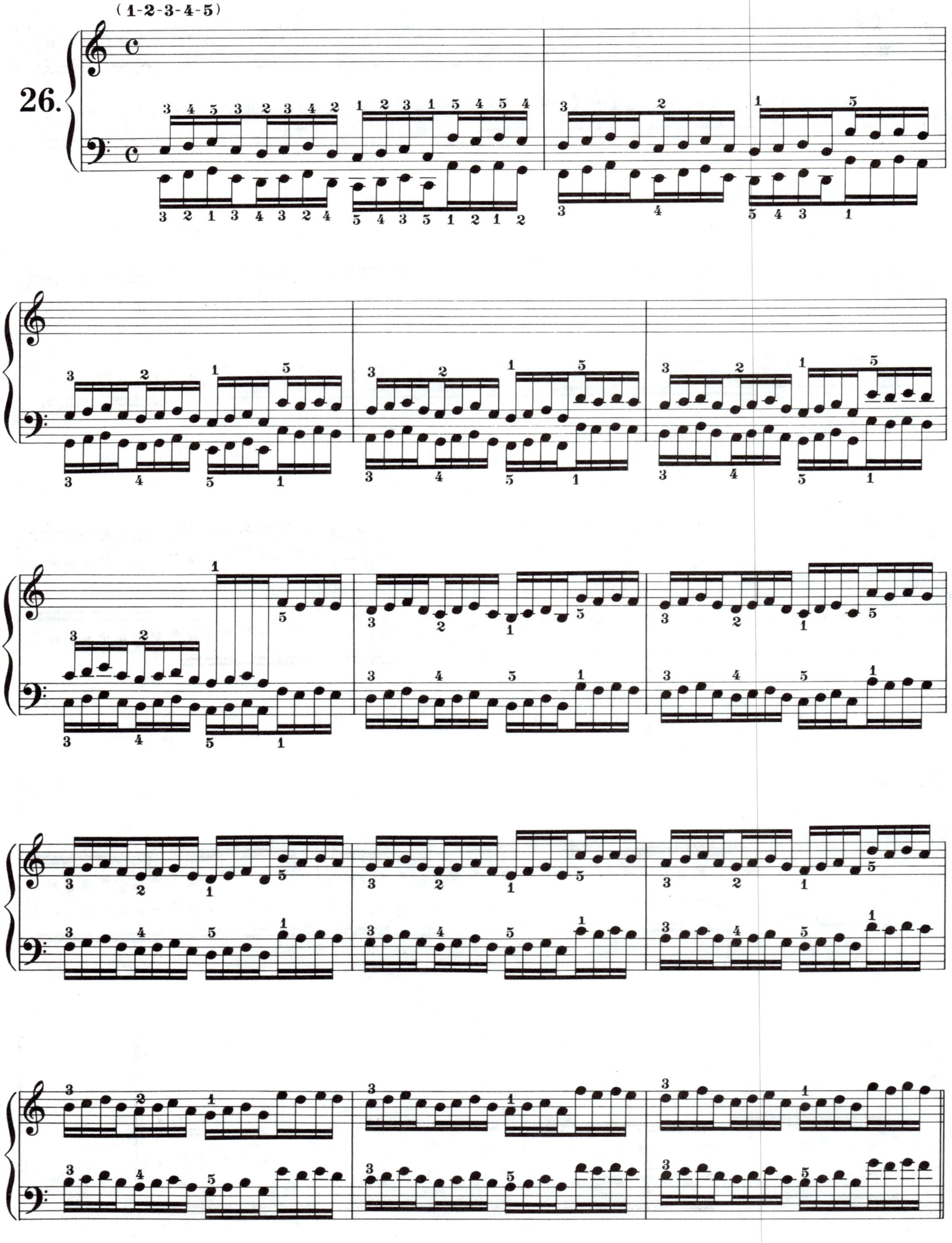
(1-2-3-4-5)
26.

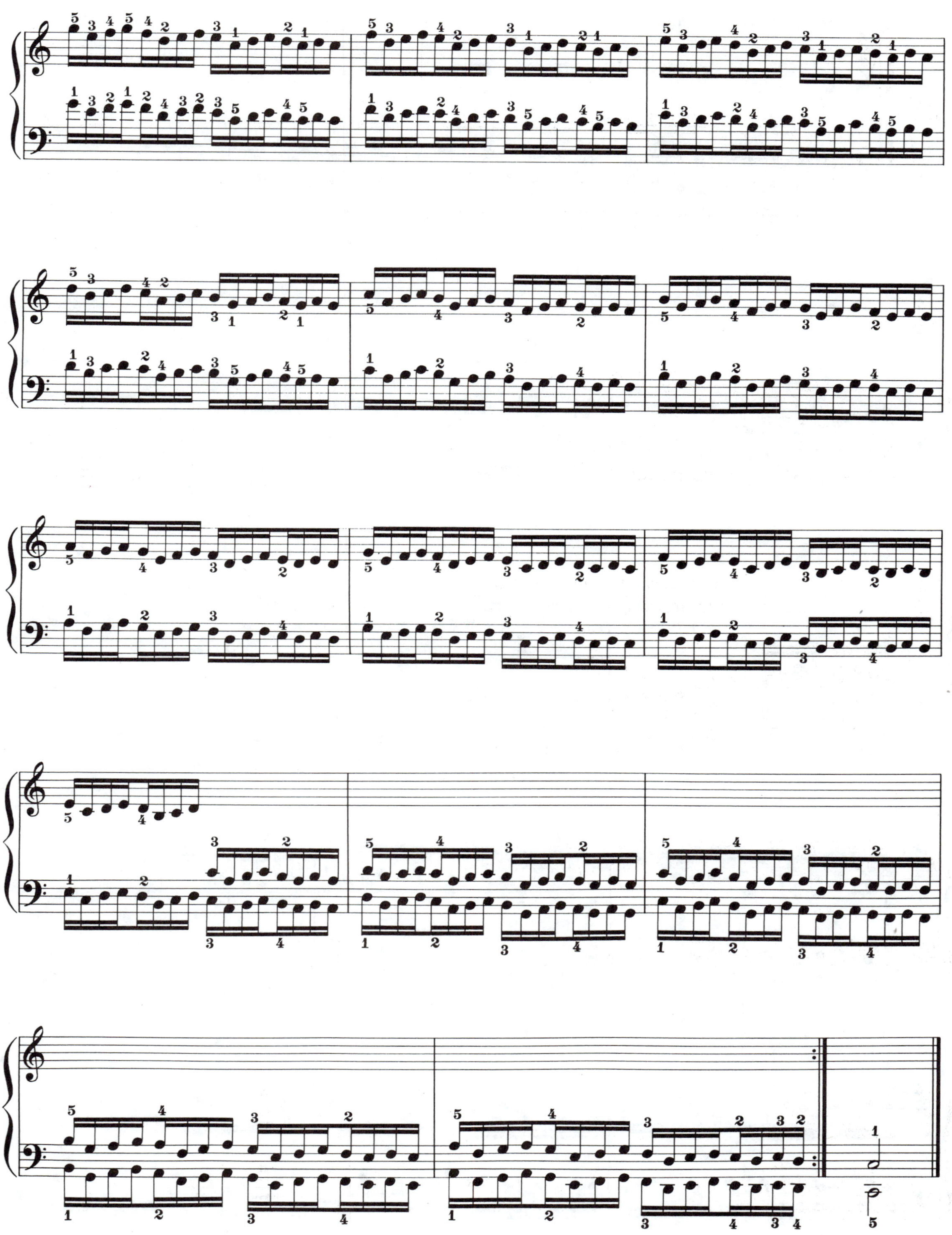

(1-2-3-4-5) Prepares the 4th and 5th fingers for the trill given further on.

27.

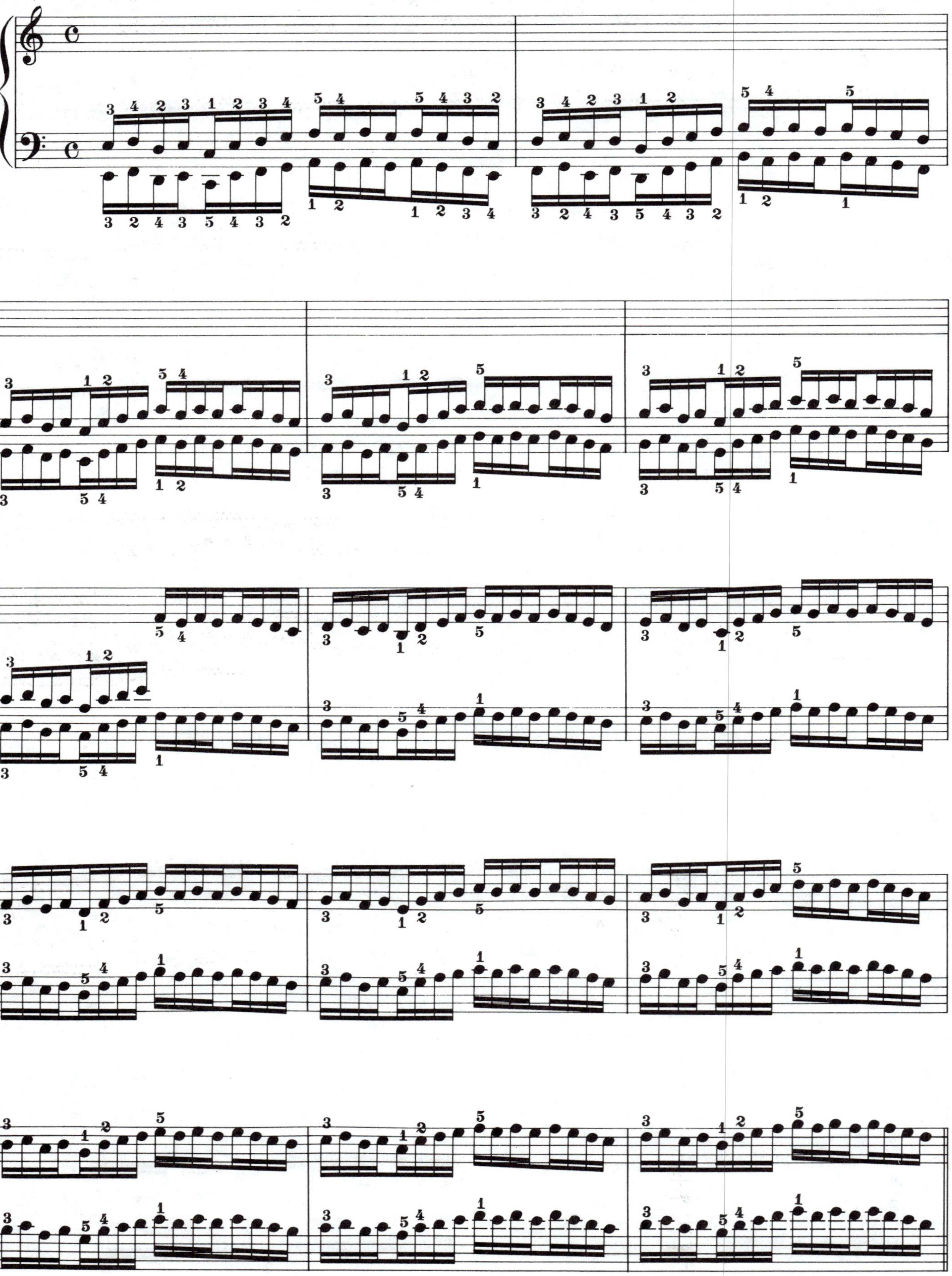

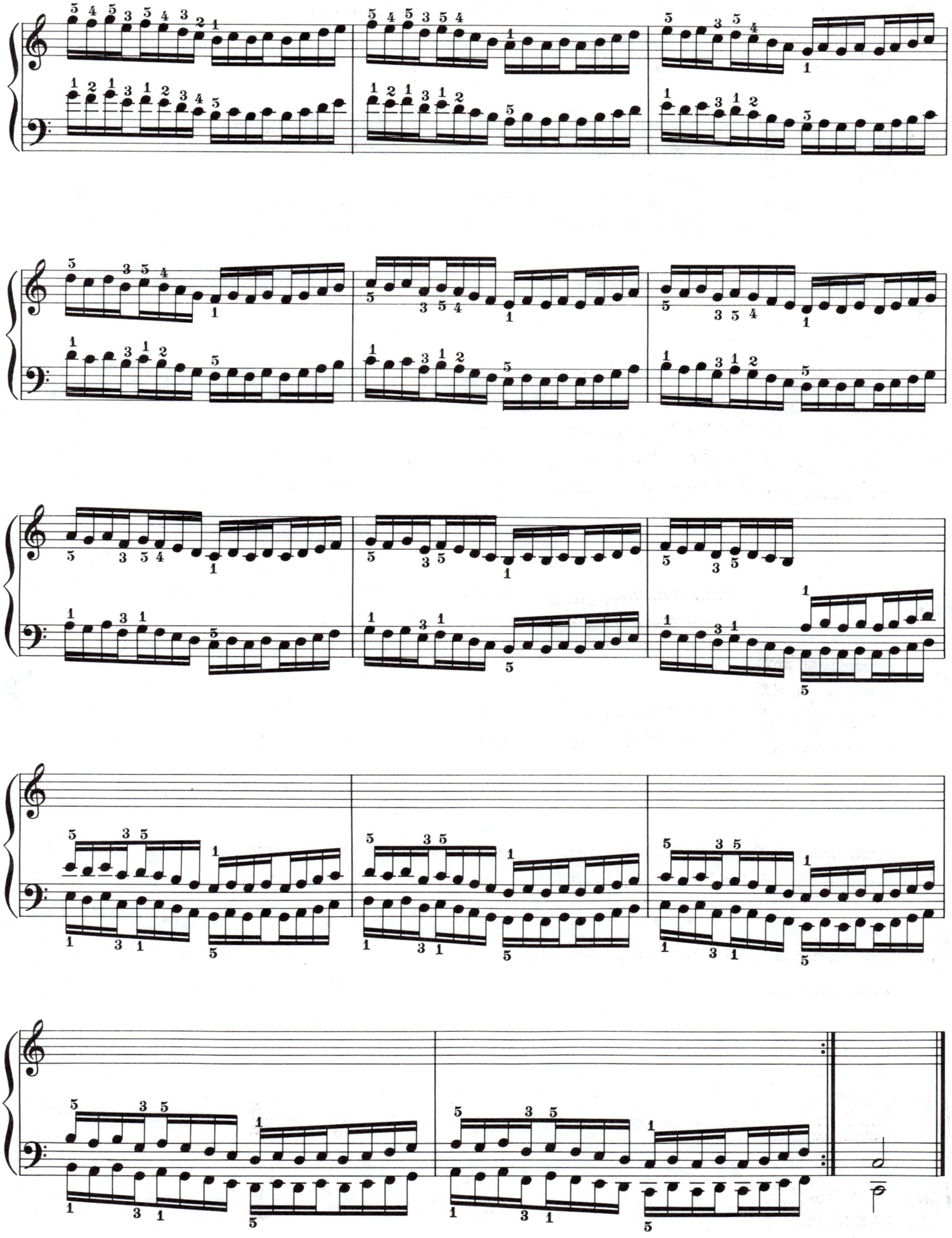

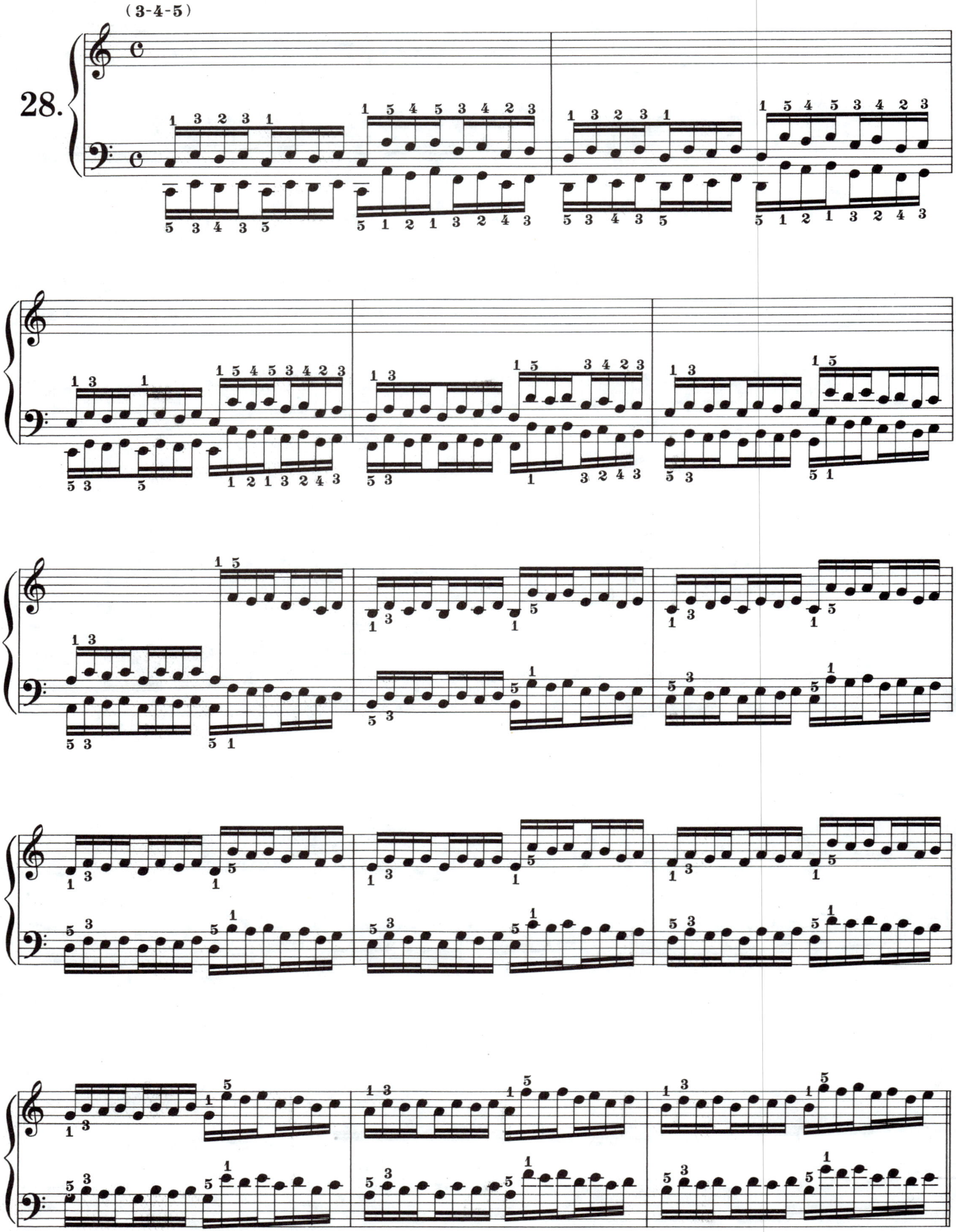
(3-4-5)
28.

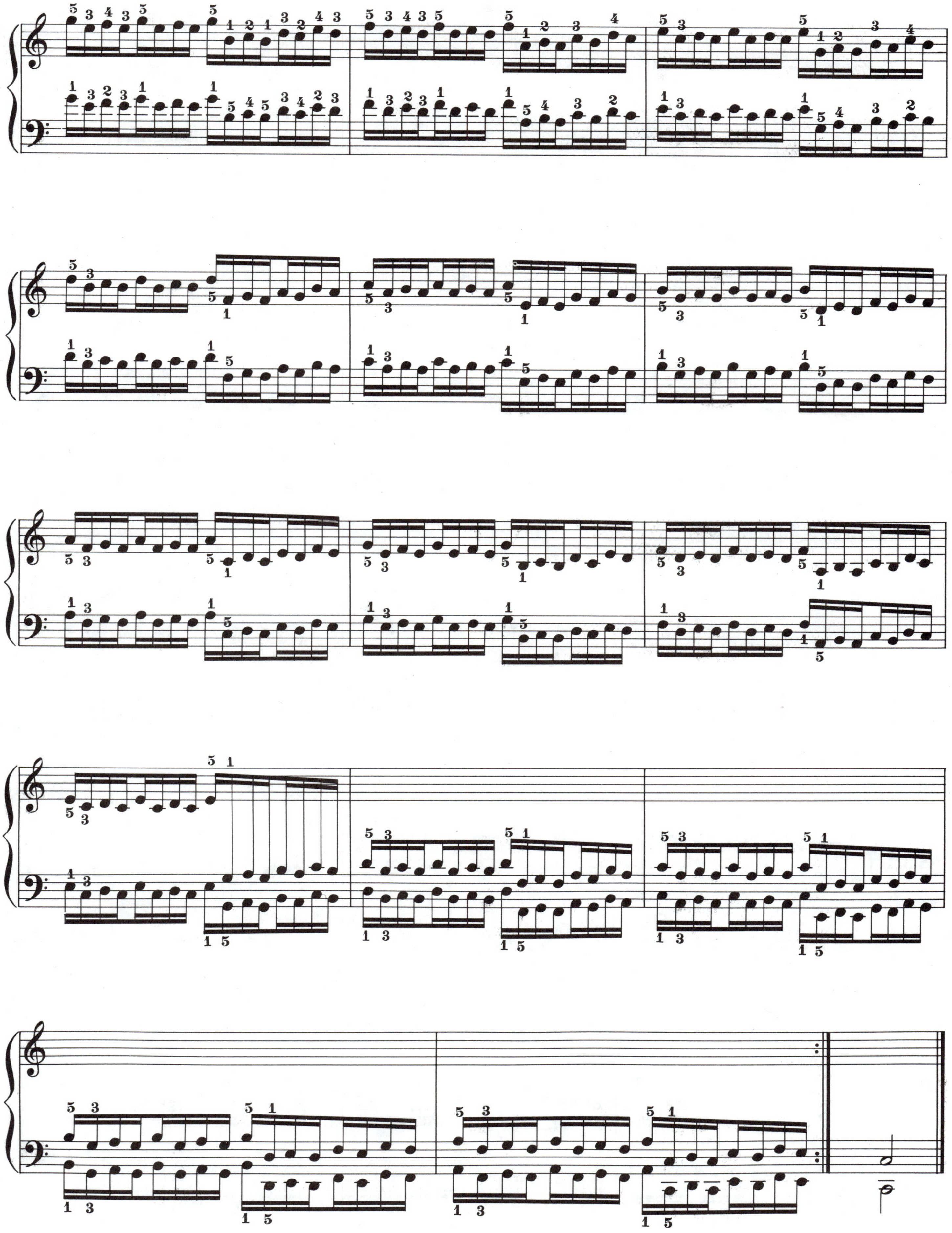

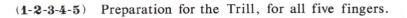

(**1-2-3-4-5**) Preparation for the Trill, for all five fingers.

29.

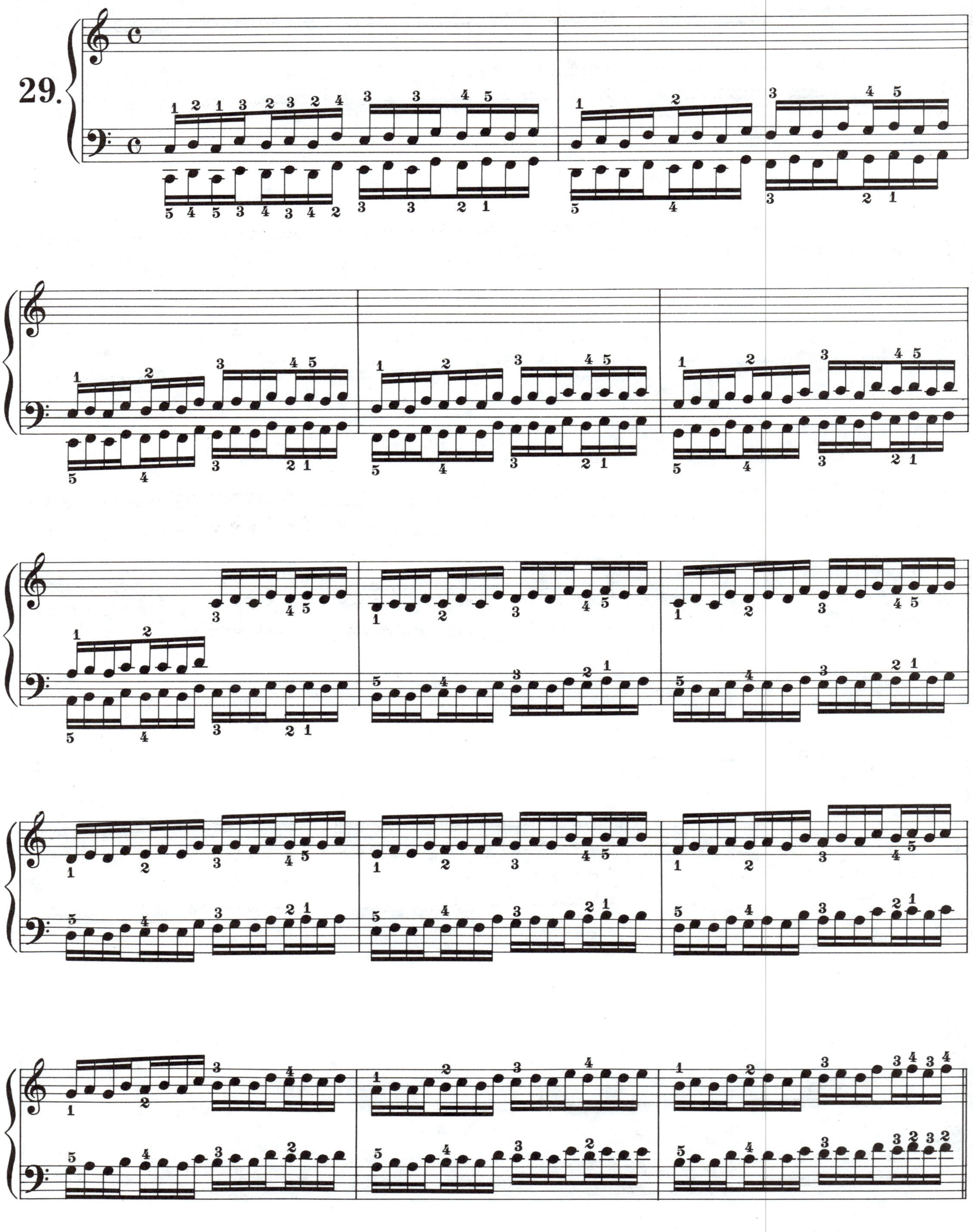

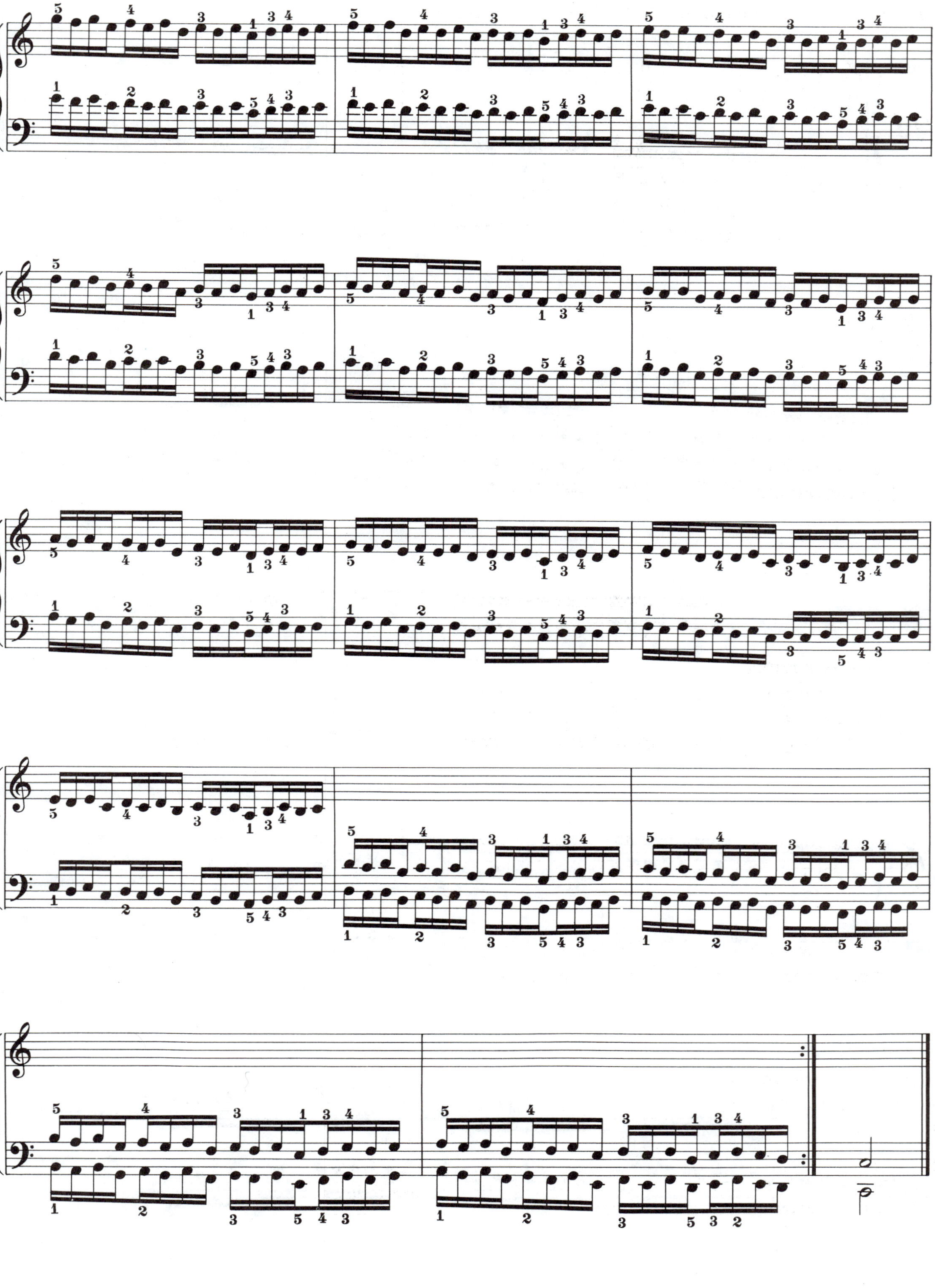

Trill alternating between **1-2** and **4-5**.

30.

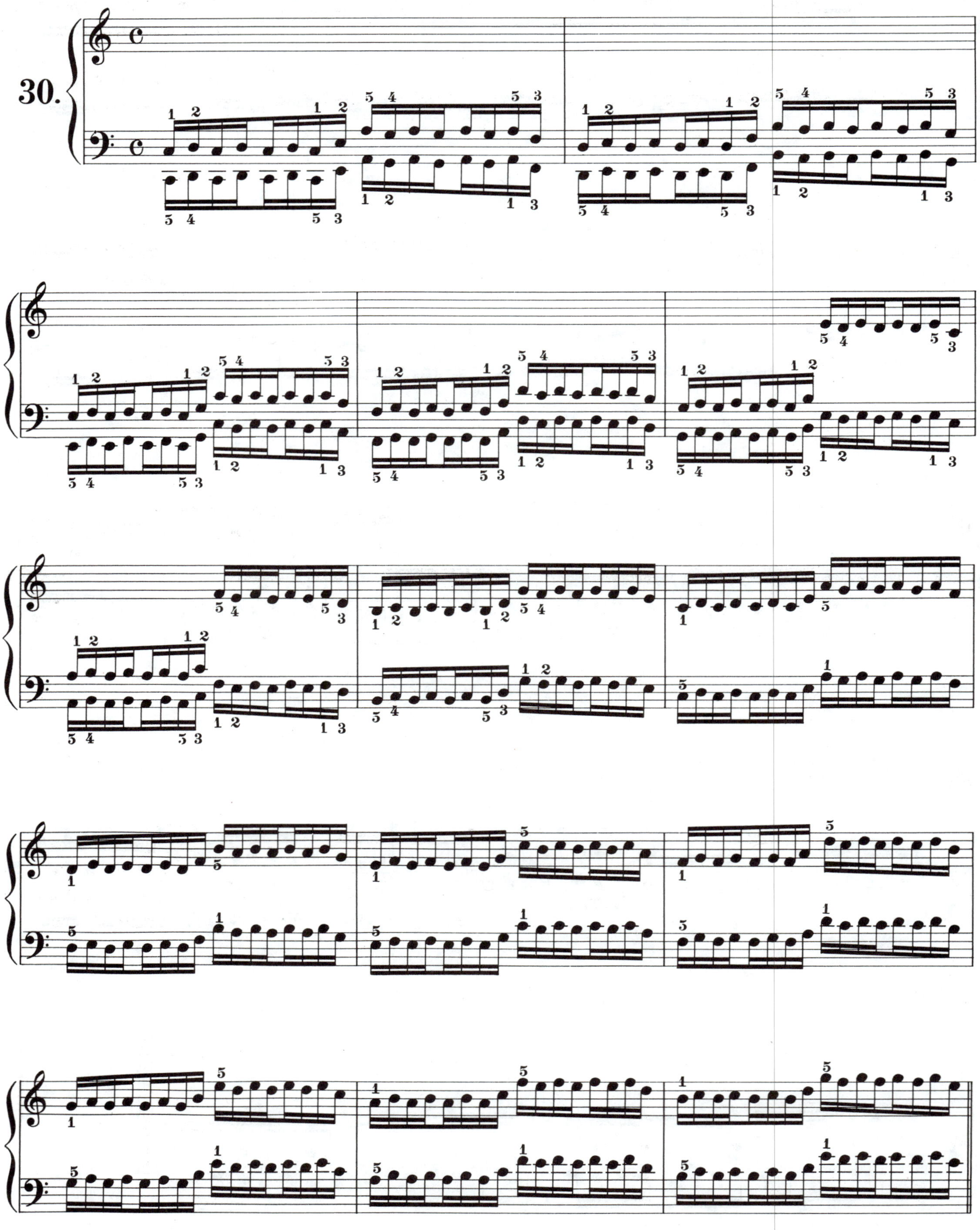

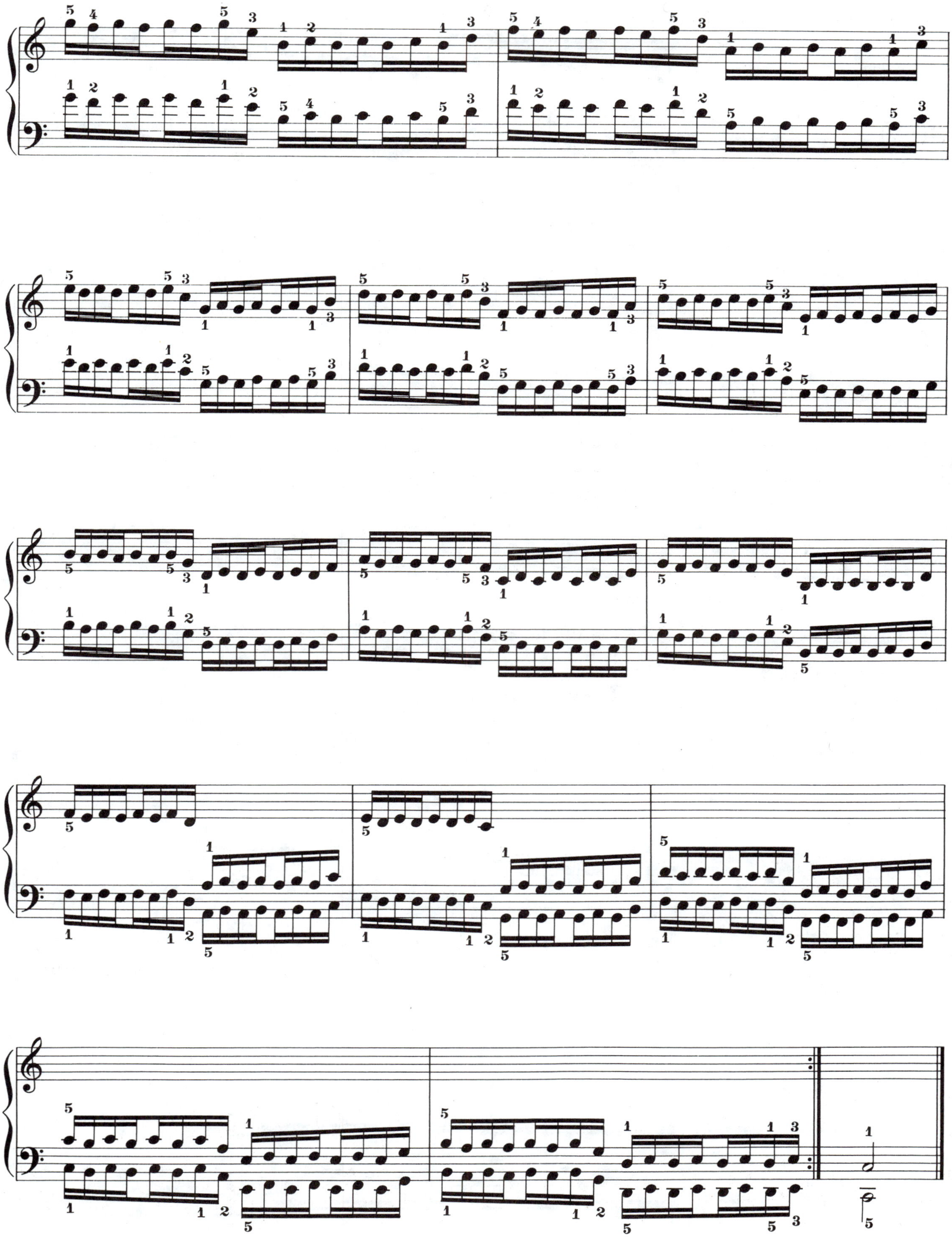

(1-2-3-4-5, and extensions).

31.

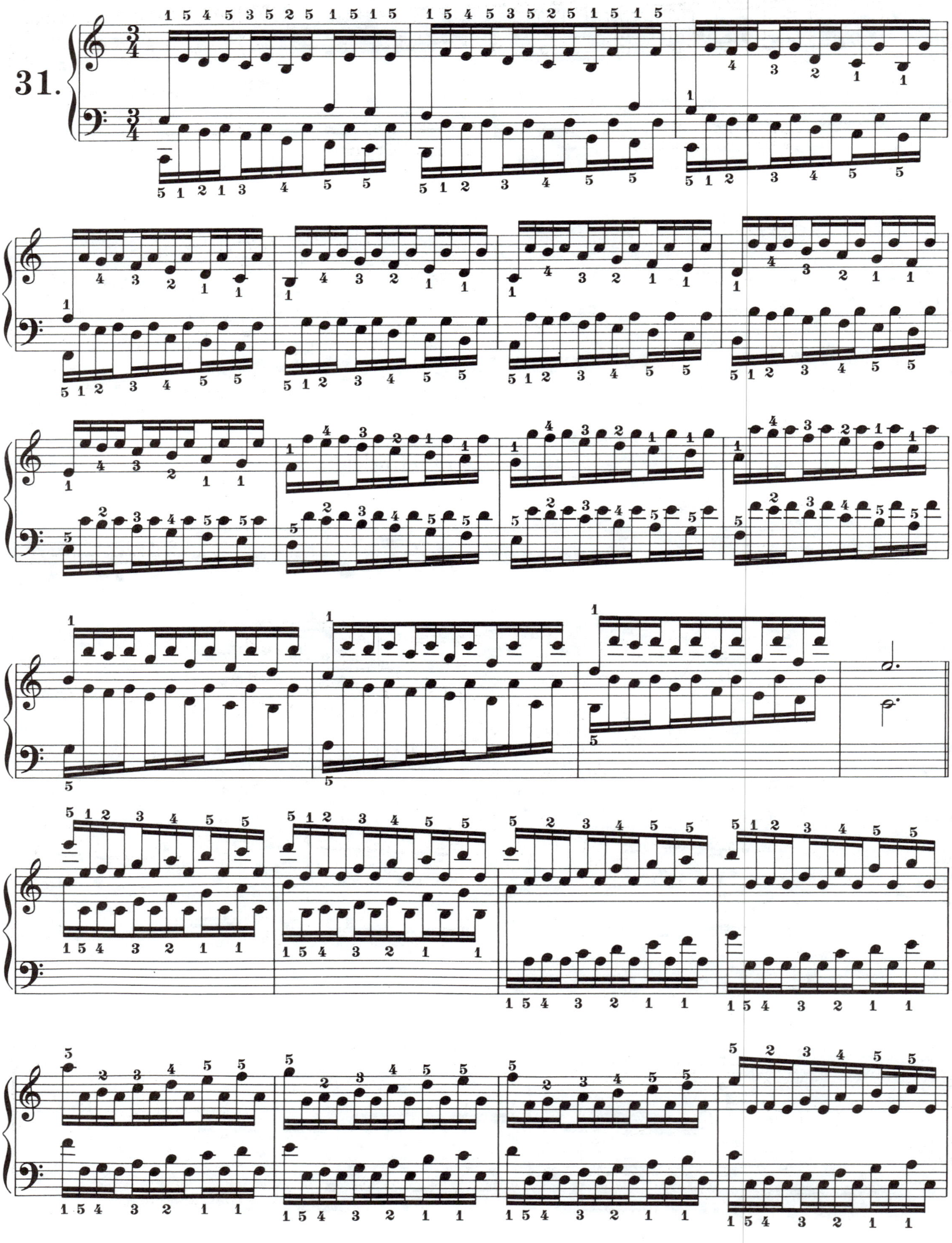

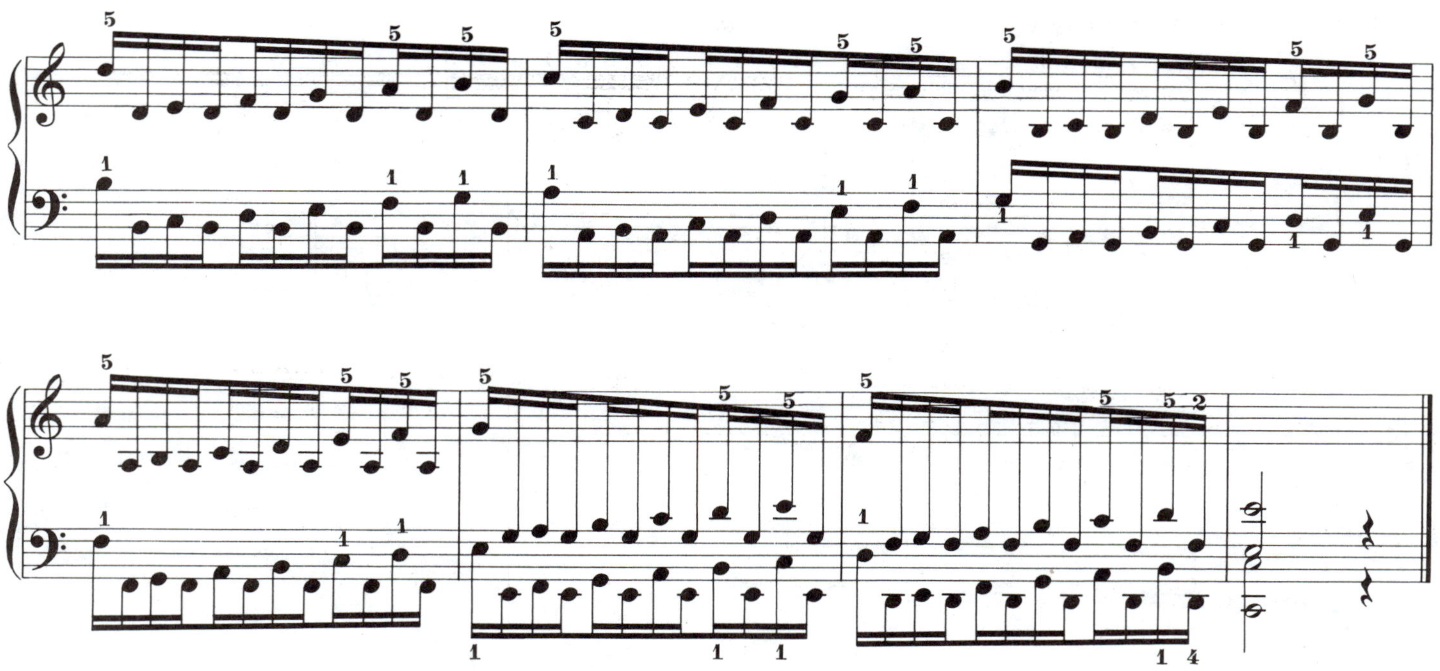

Passing the Thumb Under

Passing the thumb under the 2nd finger.

32.

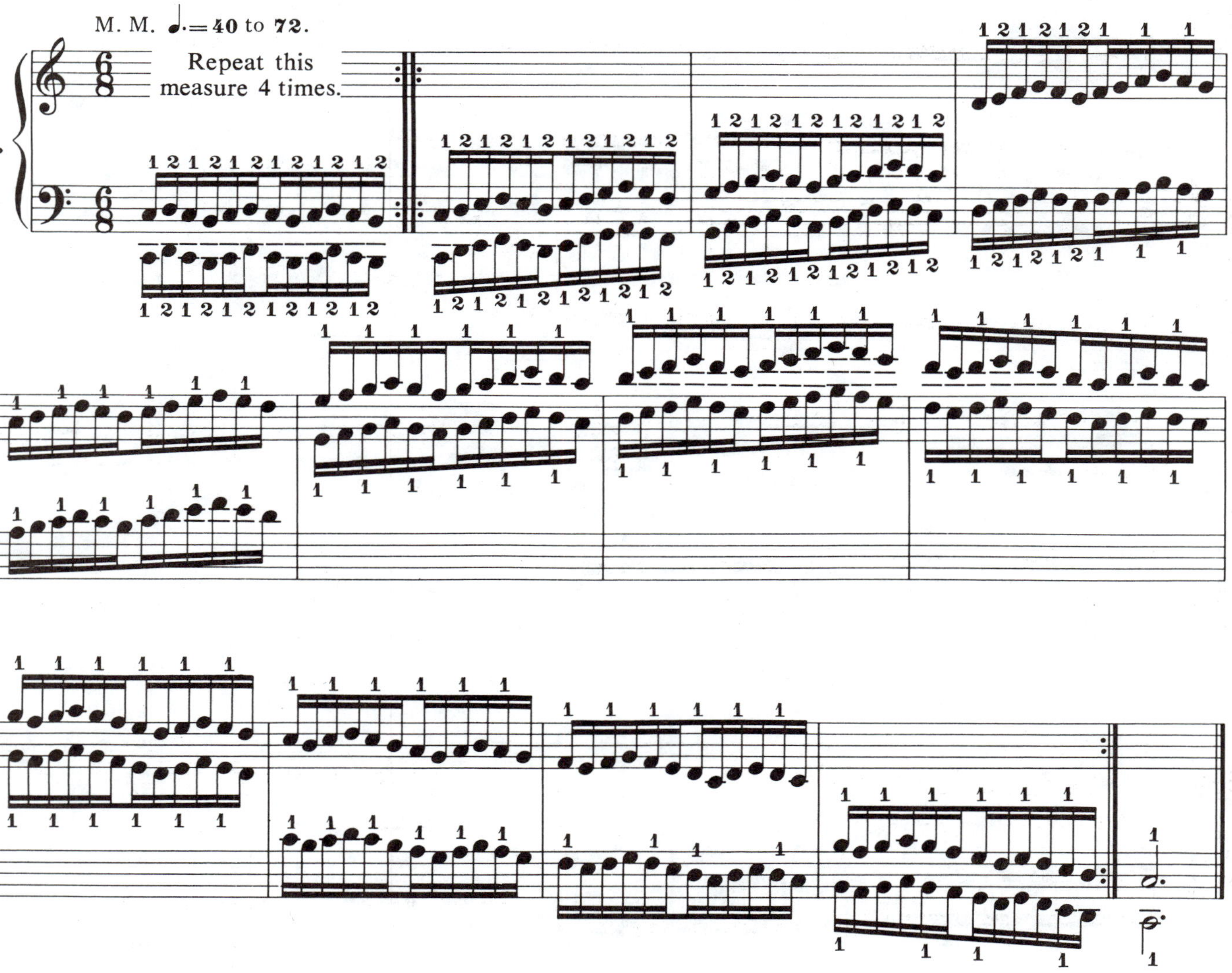

Passing the thumb under the 3rd finger.

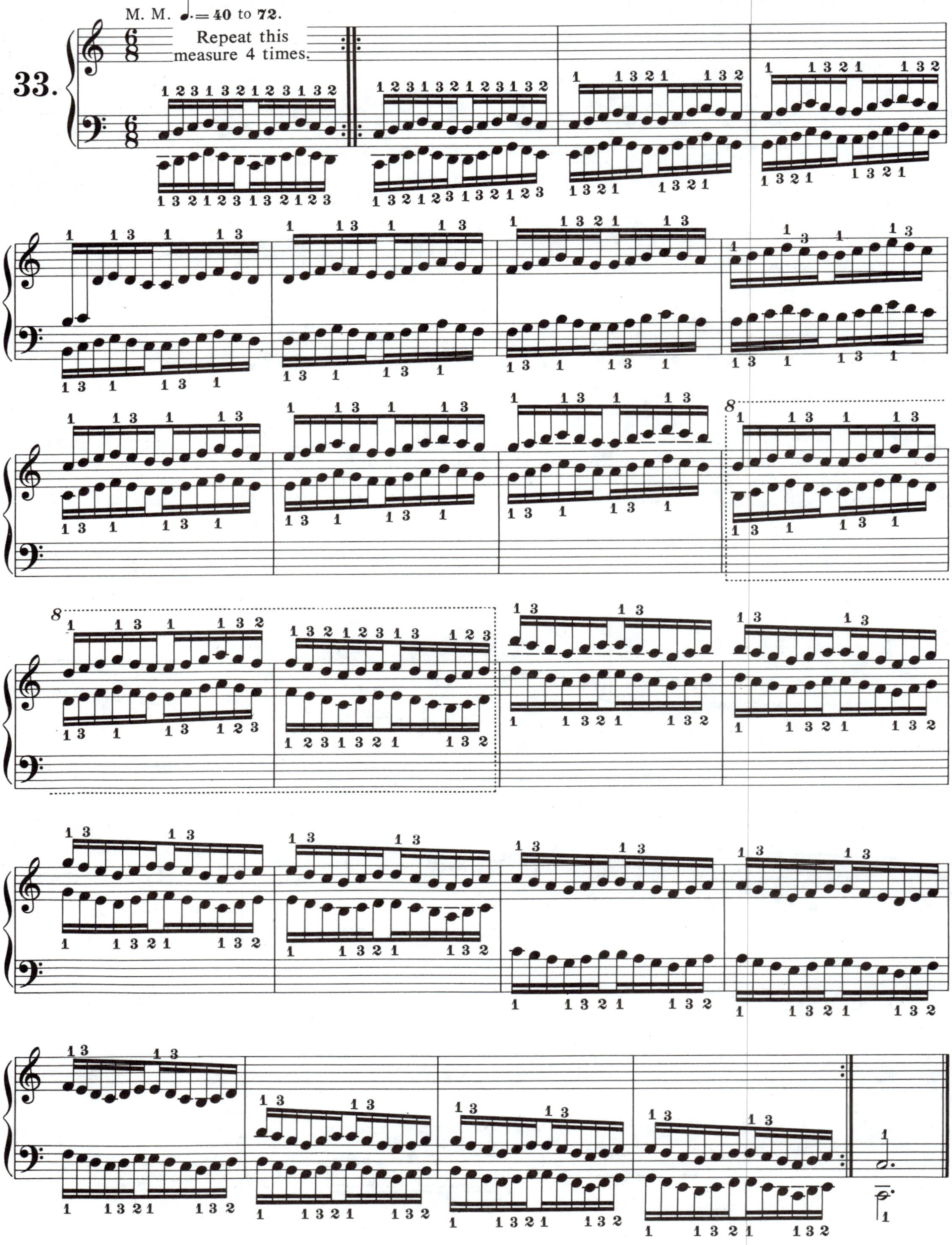

Passing the thumb under the 4th finger.

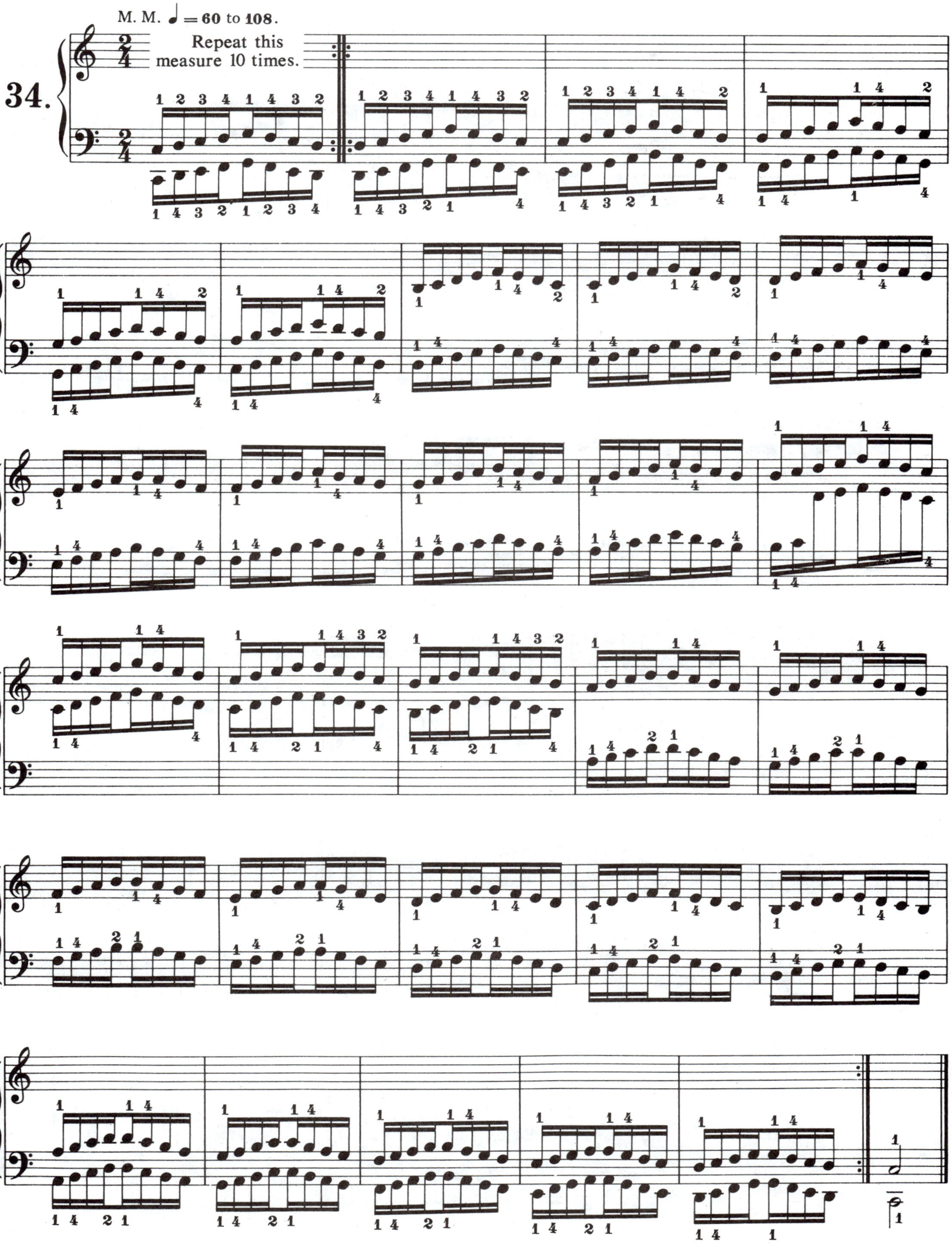

Passing the thumb under 5th finger.

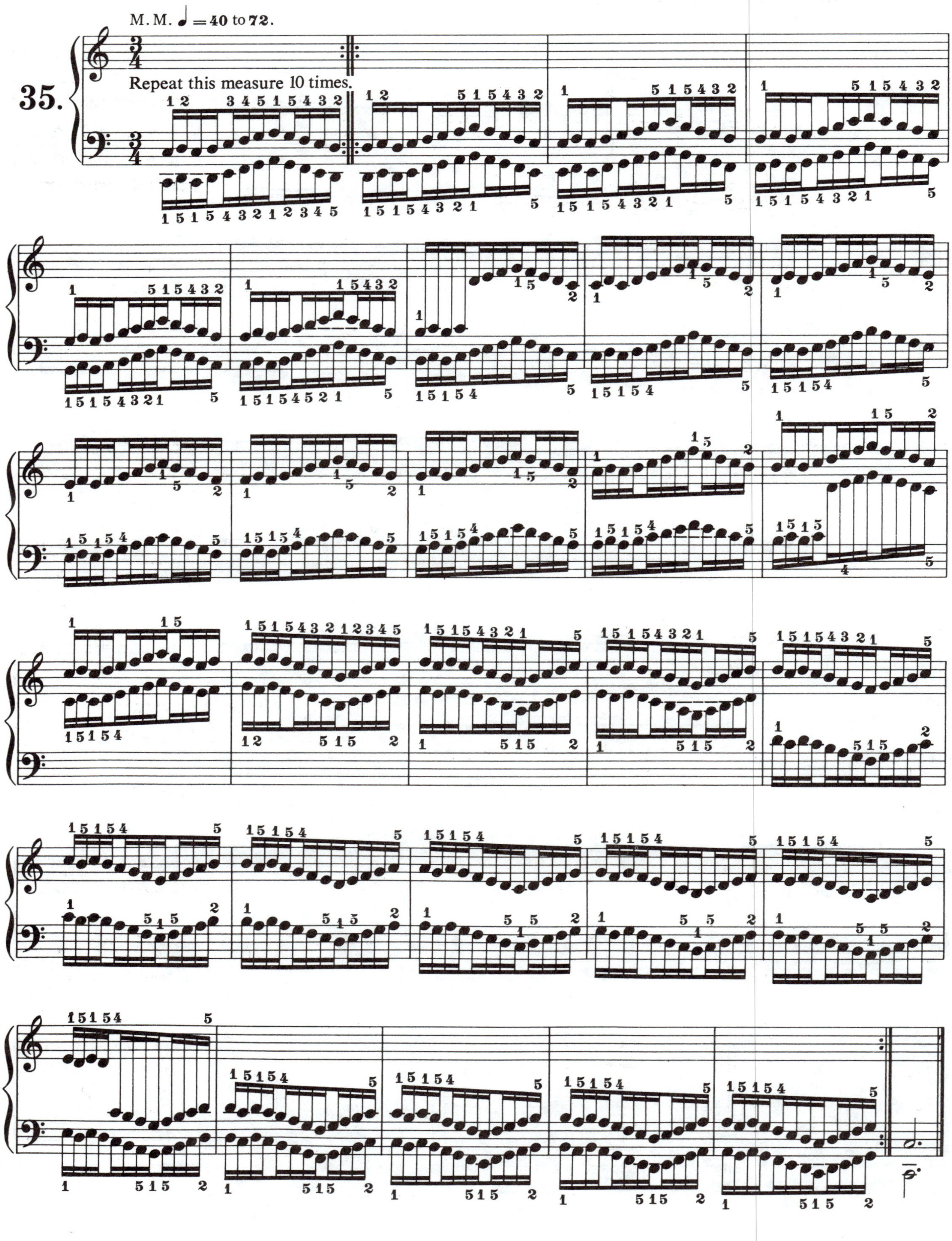

Another example of passing the thumb under.

36.

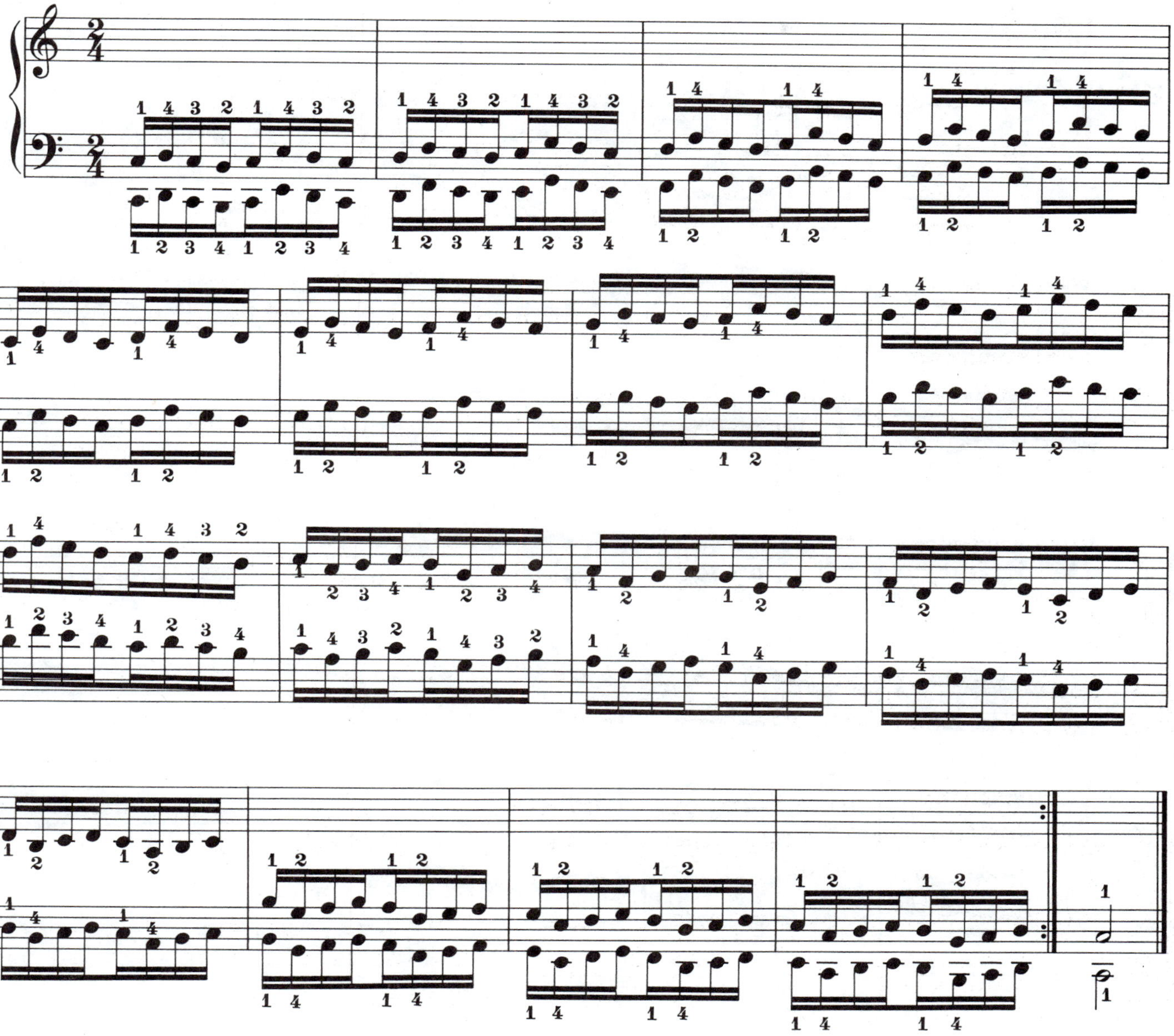

37.

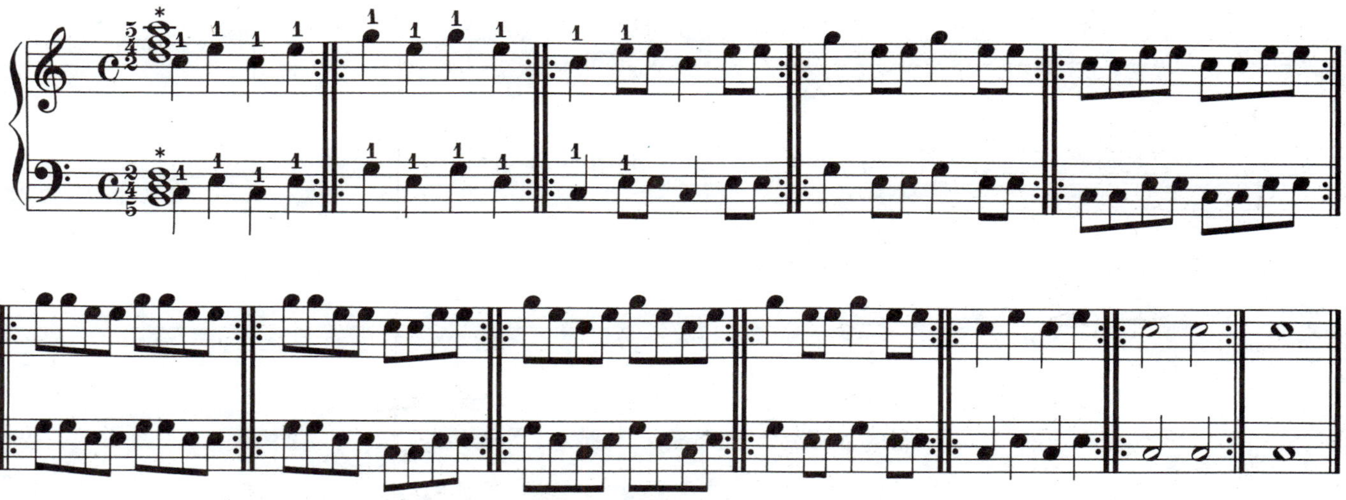

* Hold down these three notes with each hand while executing the 12 measures.

Preparatory exercise for the study of scales.

38.

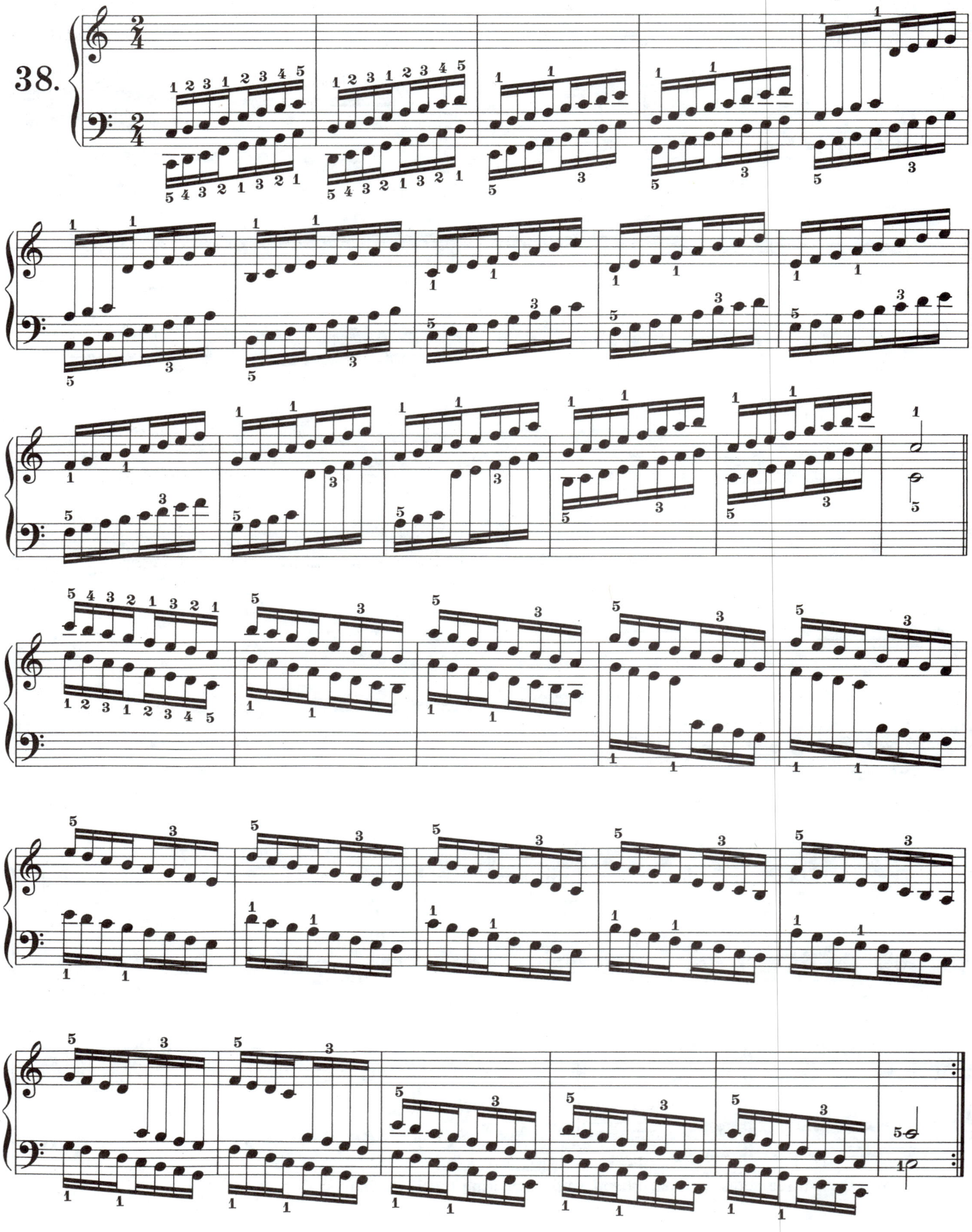

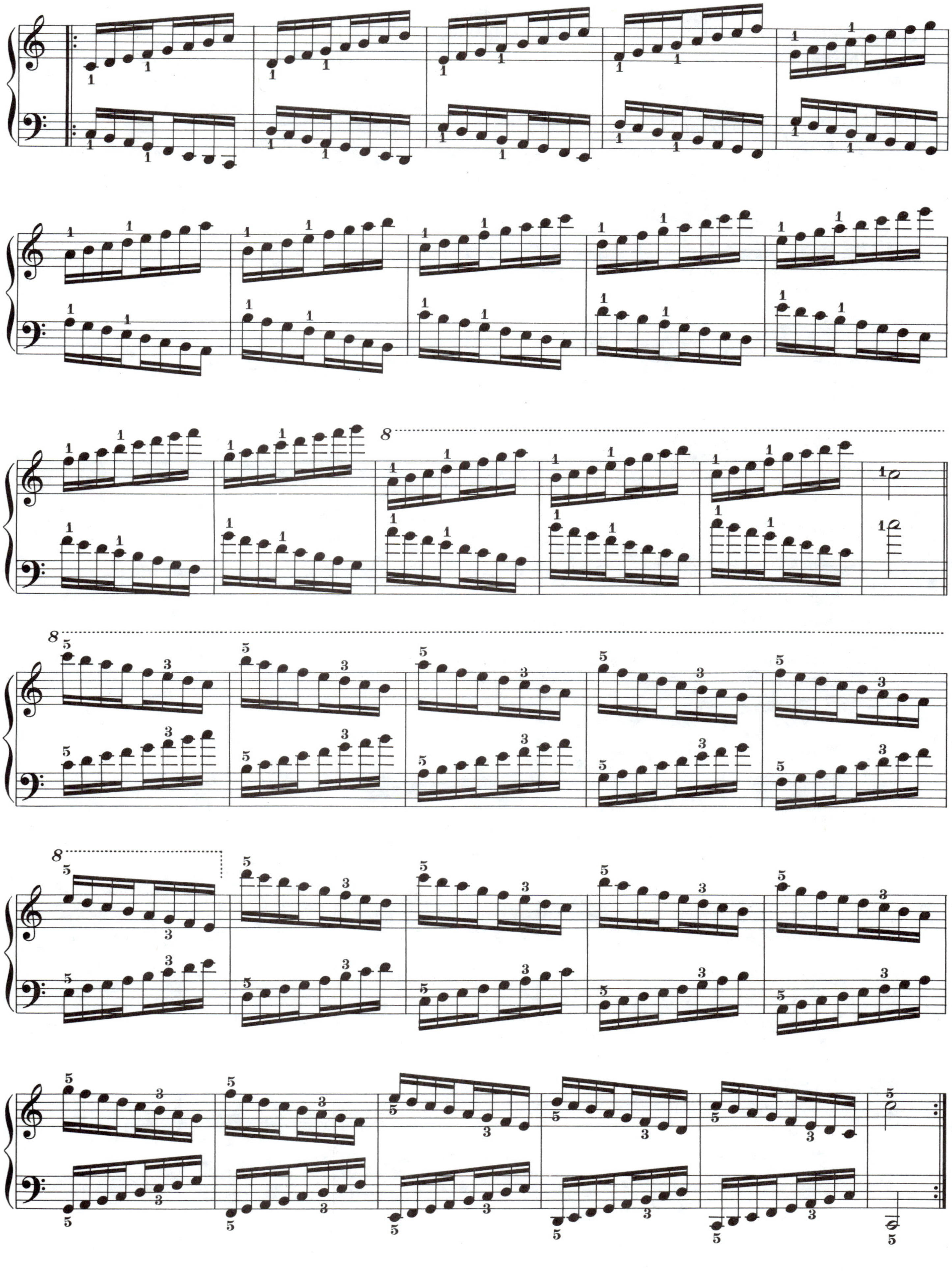

The 12 Major and Minor Scales

Each major scale is shown with two related minor scales. One is the "harmonic minor scale" (see 1, below), the other is the "melodic minor scale" (see 2, below).

The "harmonic minor" has a minor sixth and the leading-note both ascending and descending. The "melodic minor" has a major sixth and the leading-note ascending, but a minor seventh and a minor sixth descending.

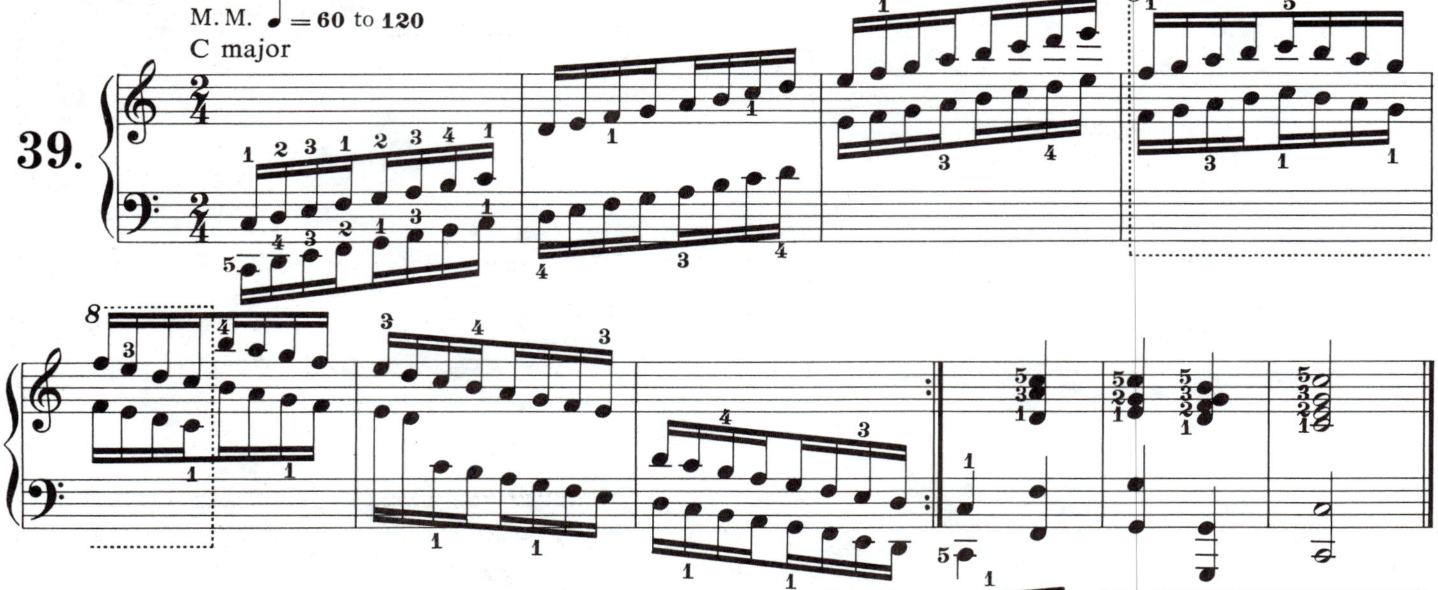

1. A minor (harmonic), relative to C major.

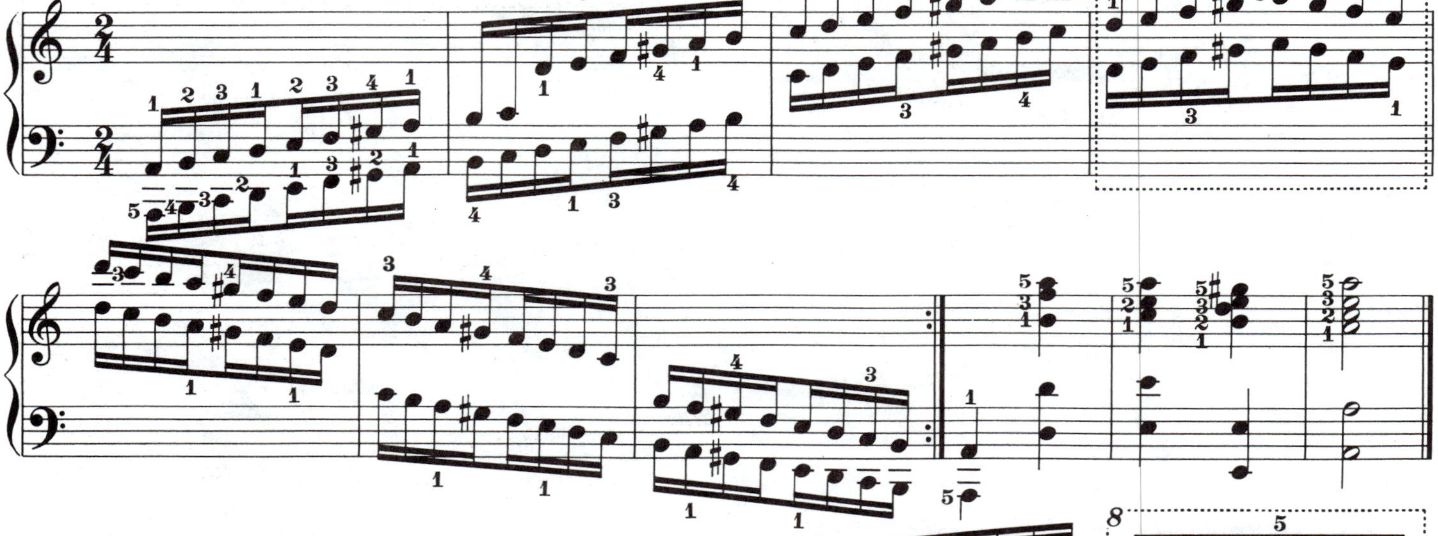

2. A minor (melodic), relative to C major.

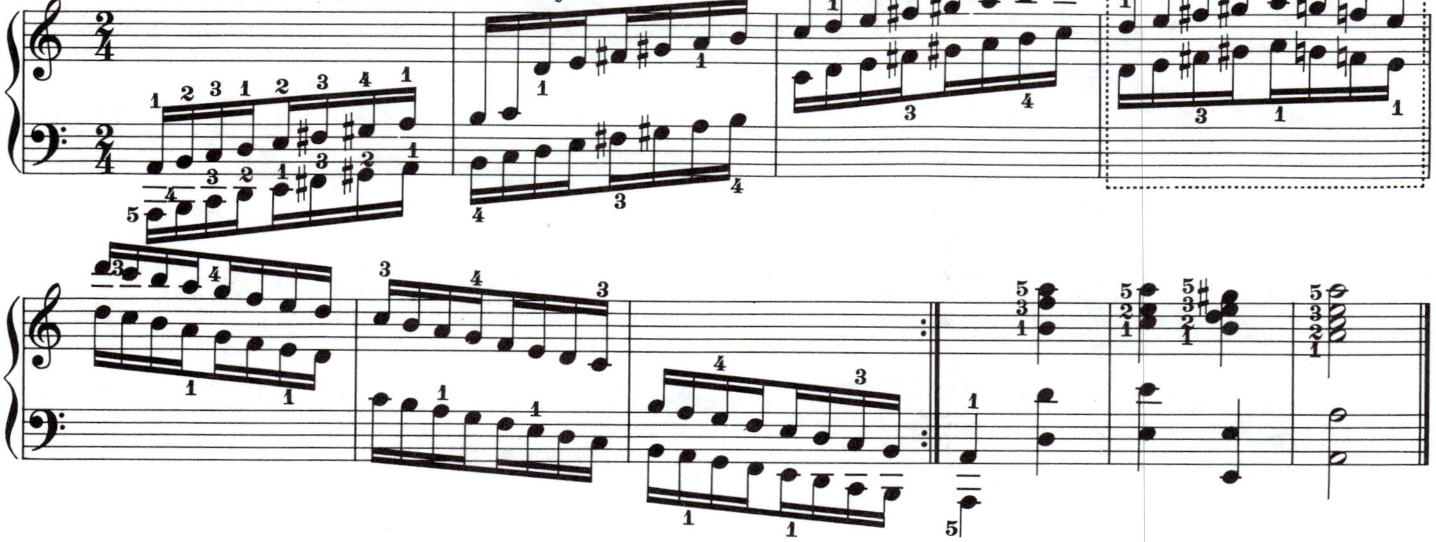

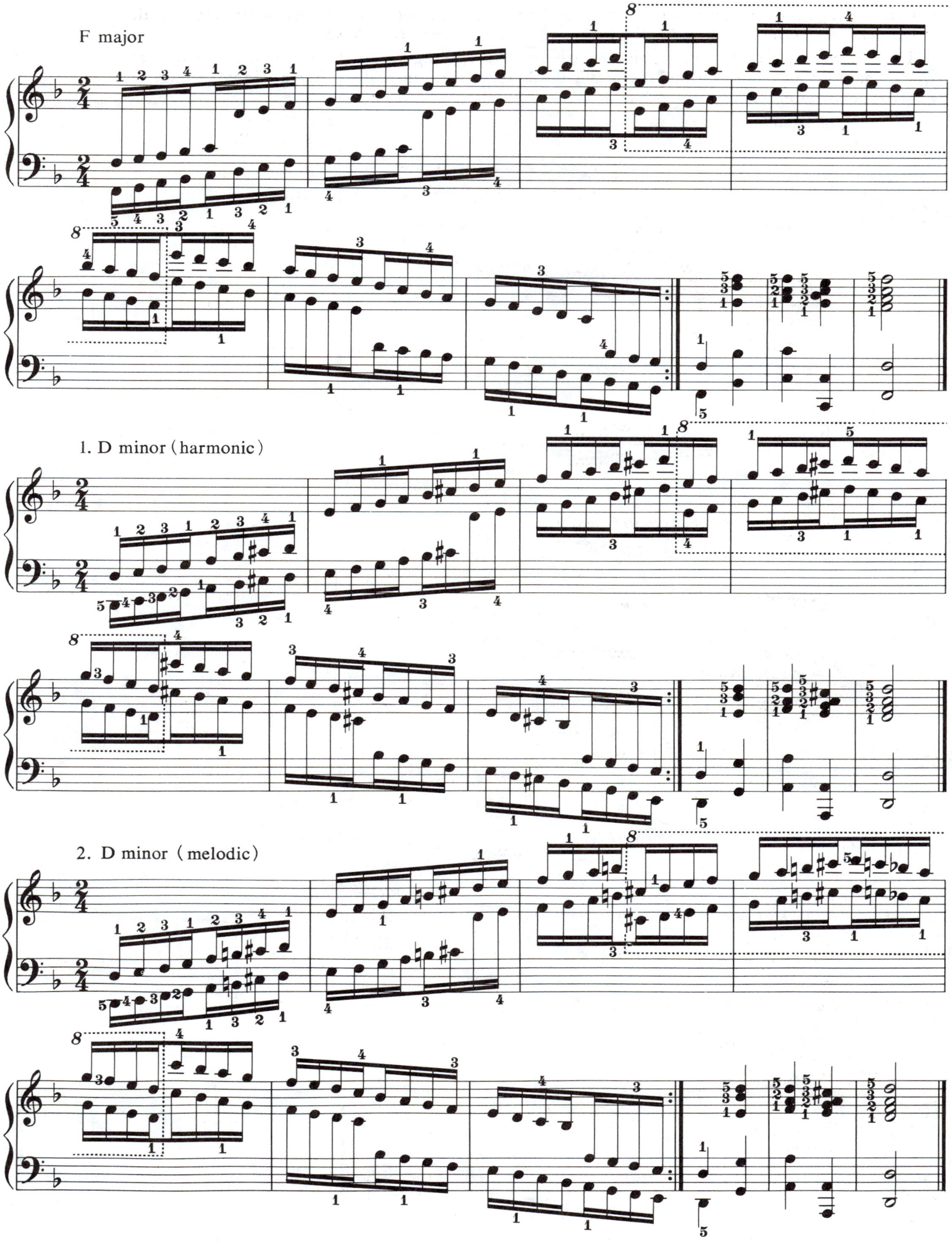
F major
1. D minor (harmonic)
2. D minor (melodic)

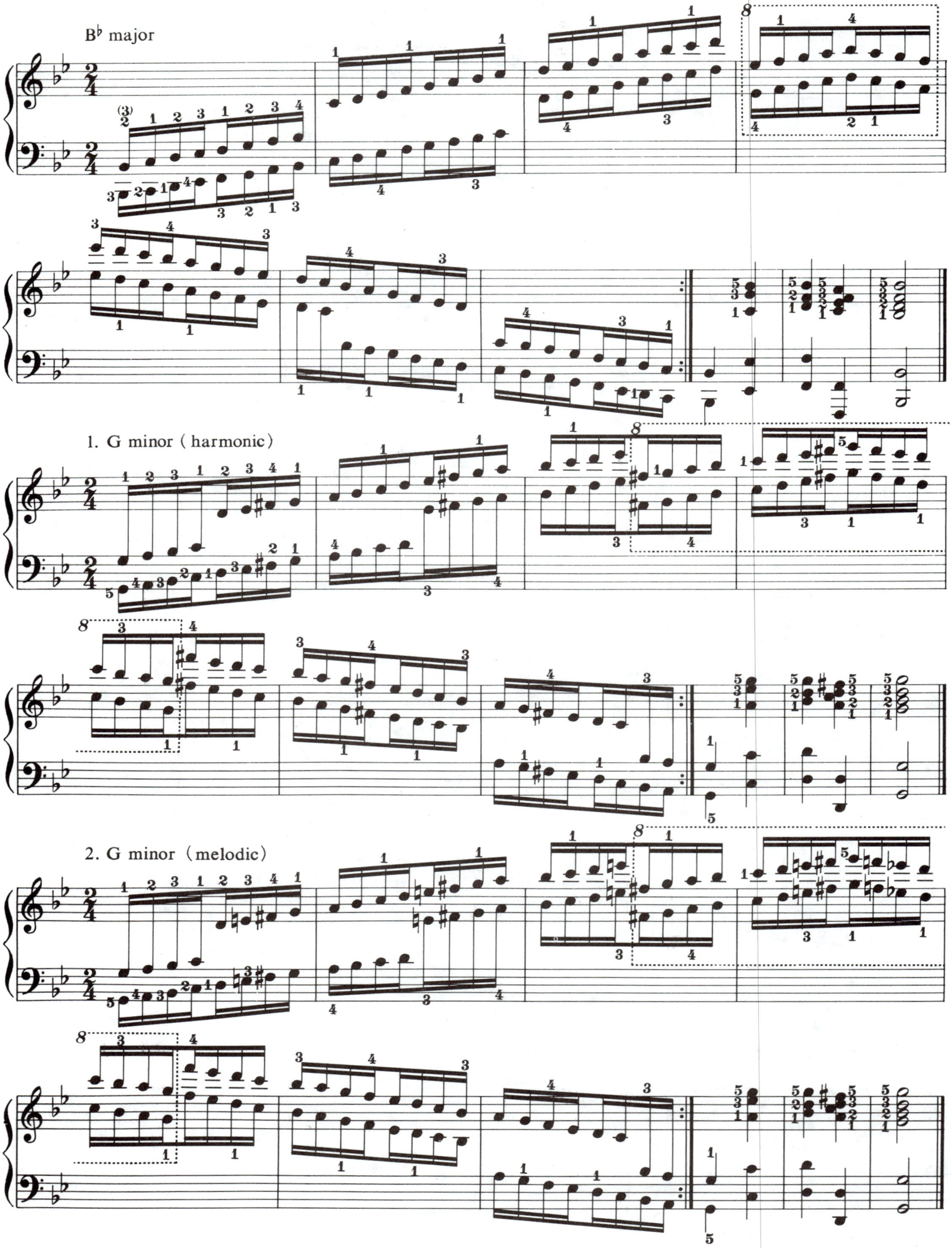
B♭ major
1. G minor (harmonic)
2. G minor (melodic)

E♭ major.

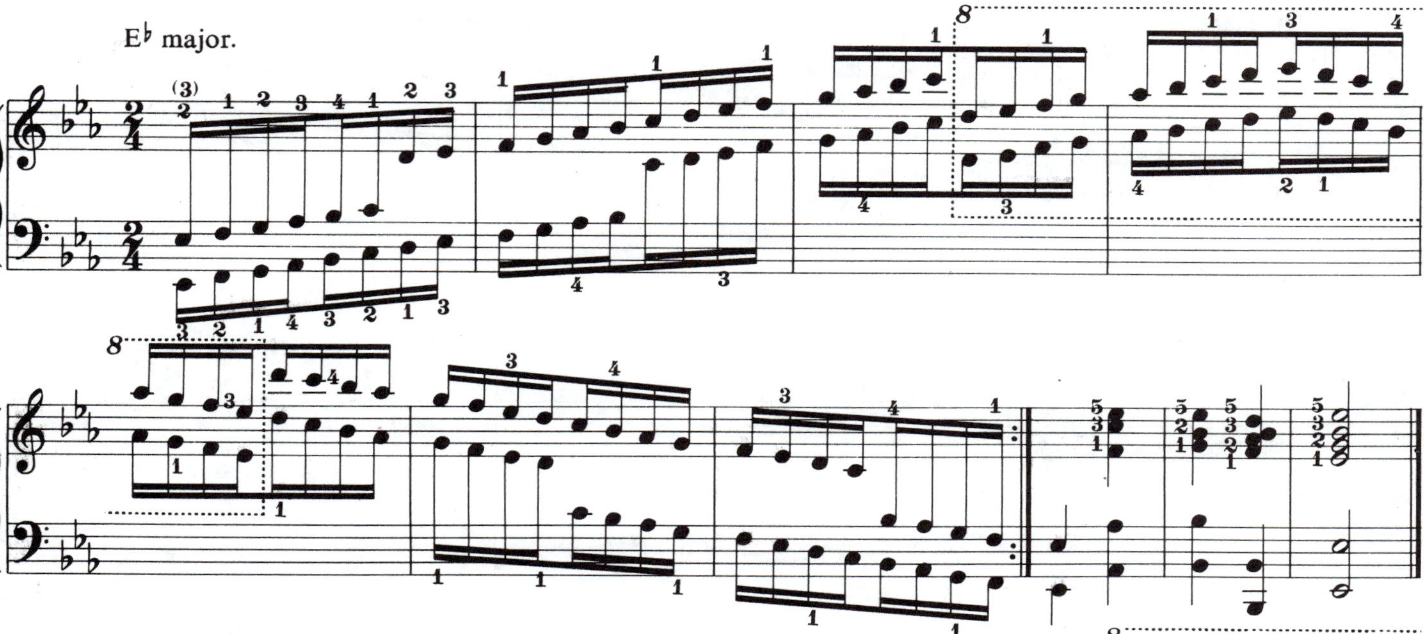

1. C minor (harmonic).

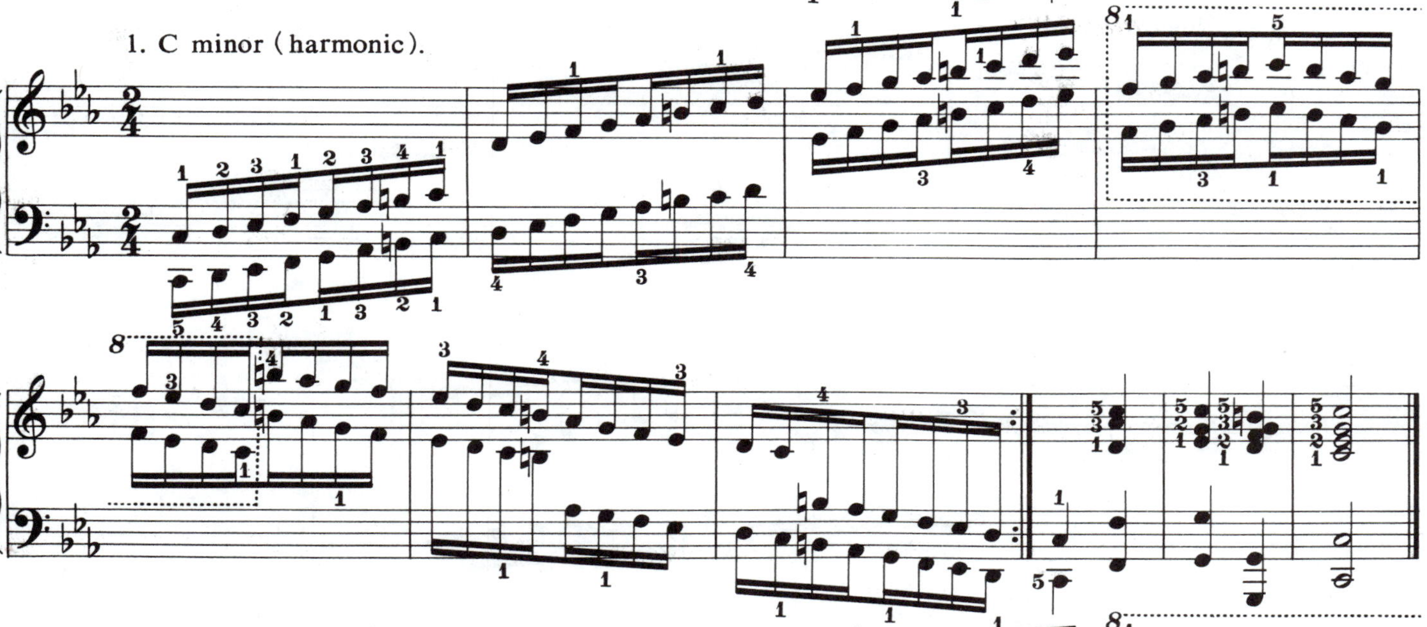

2. C minor (melodic).

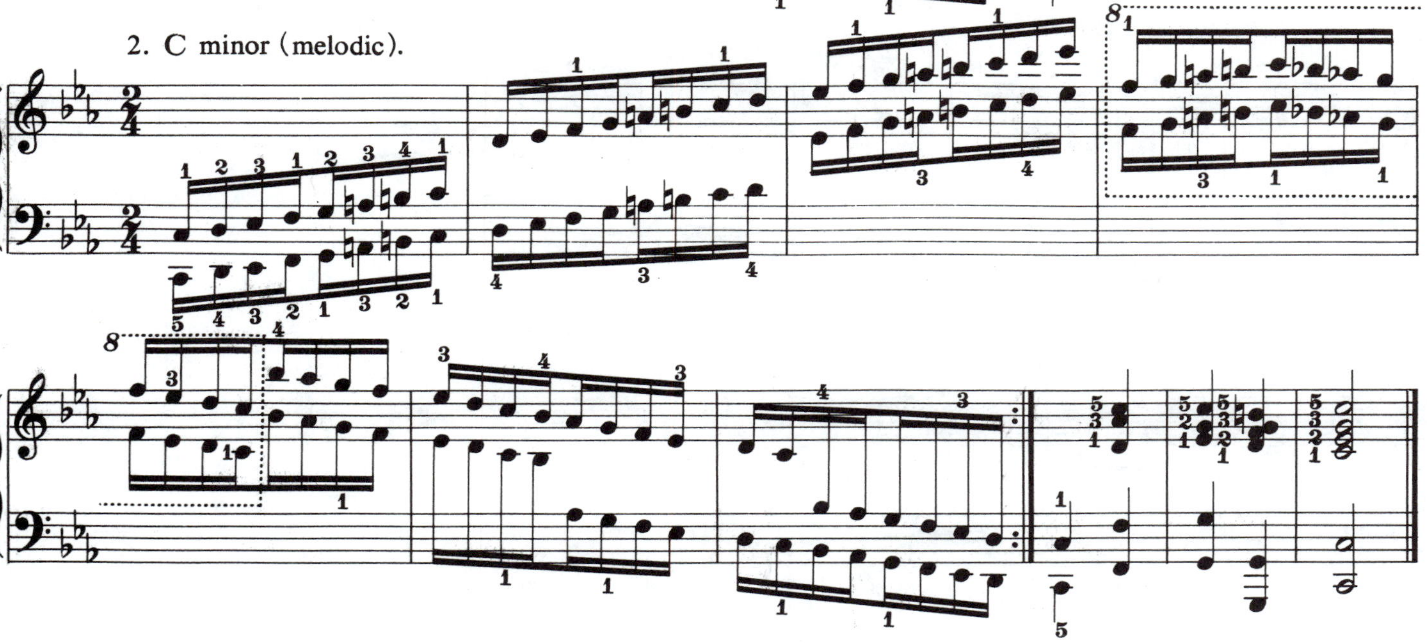

A♭ major

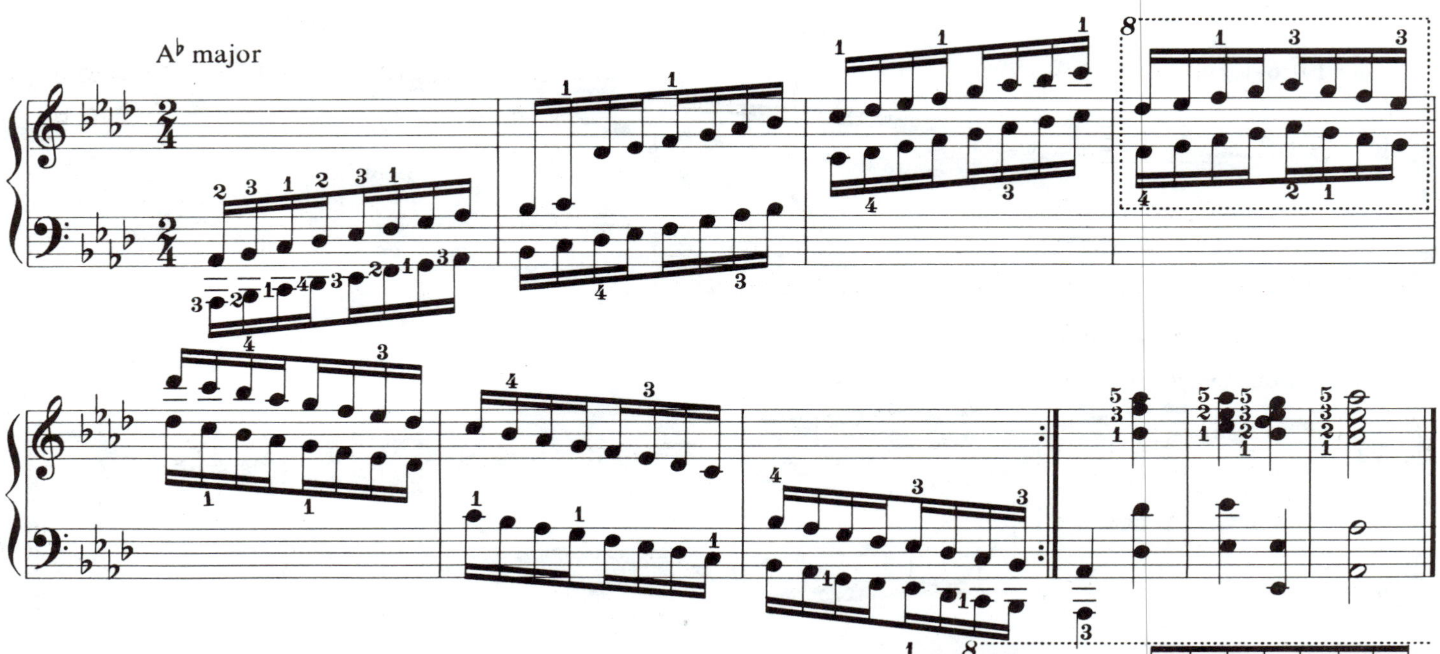

1. F minor (harmonic)

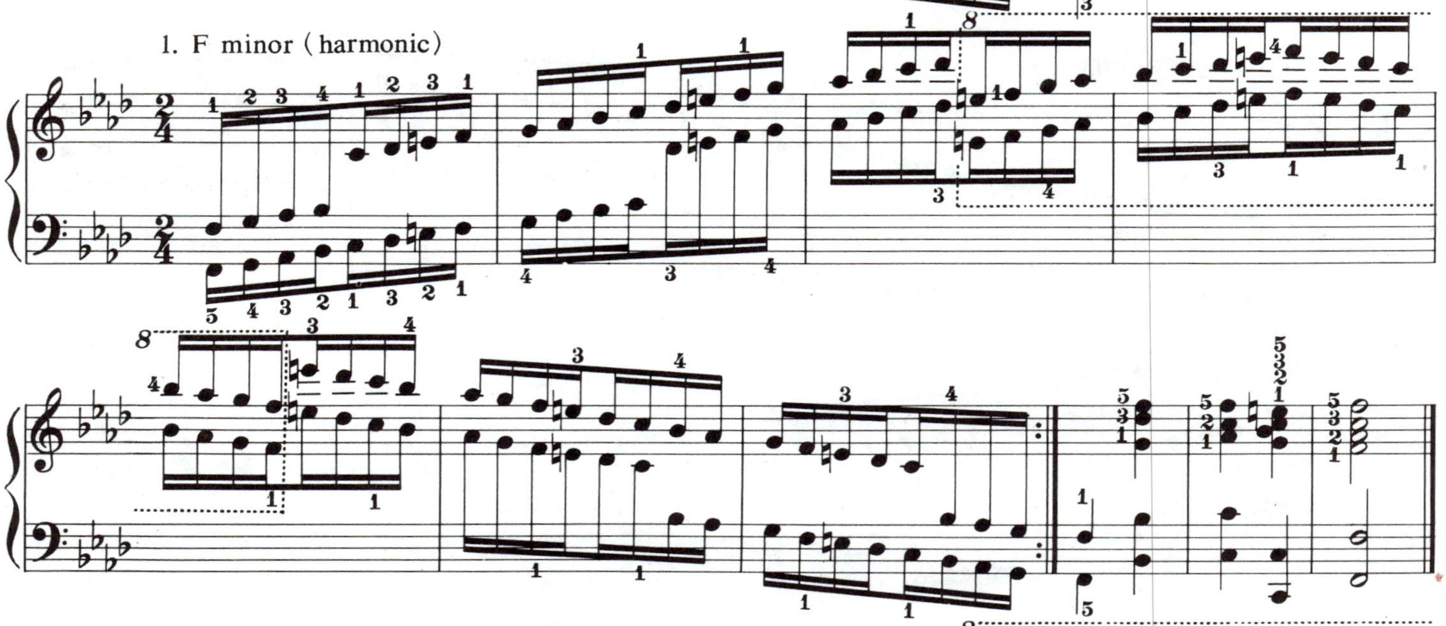

2. F minor (melodic)

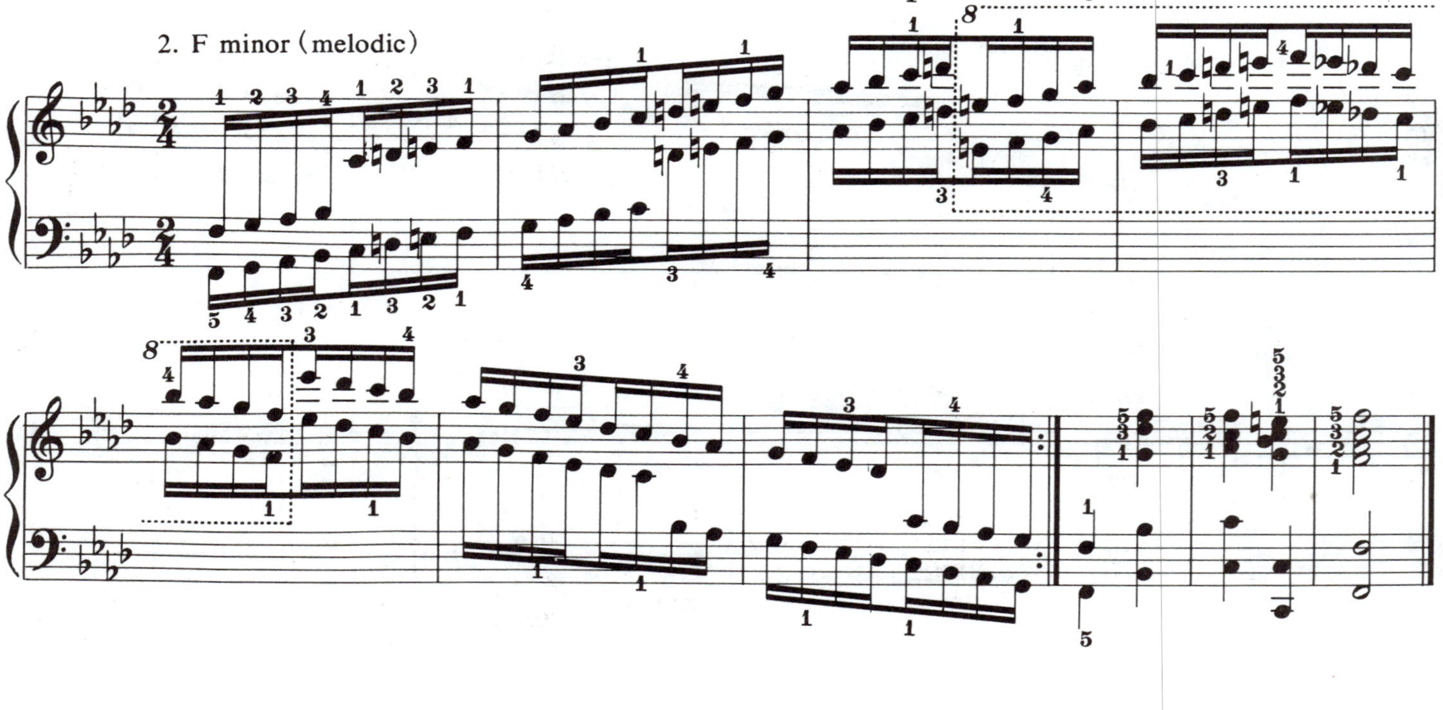

D♭ major

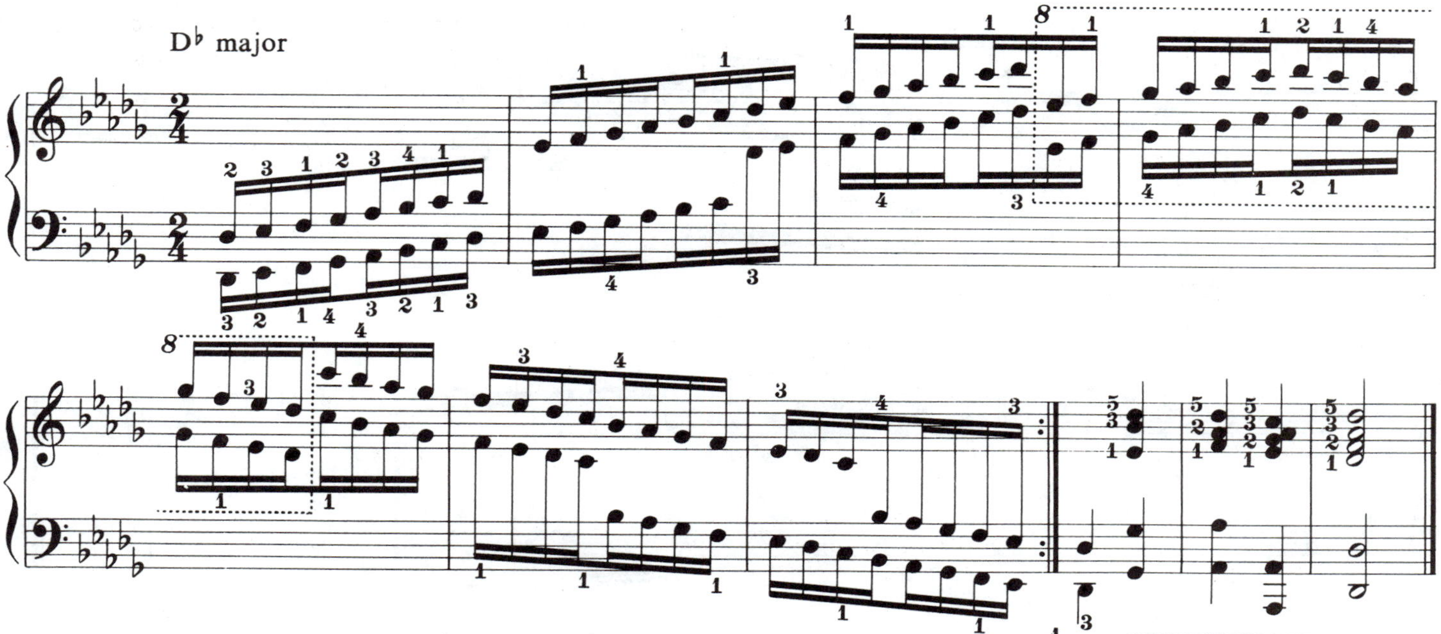

1. B♭ minor (harmonic)

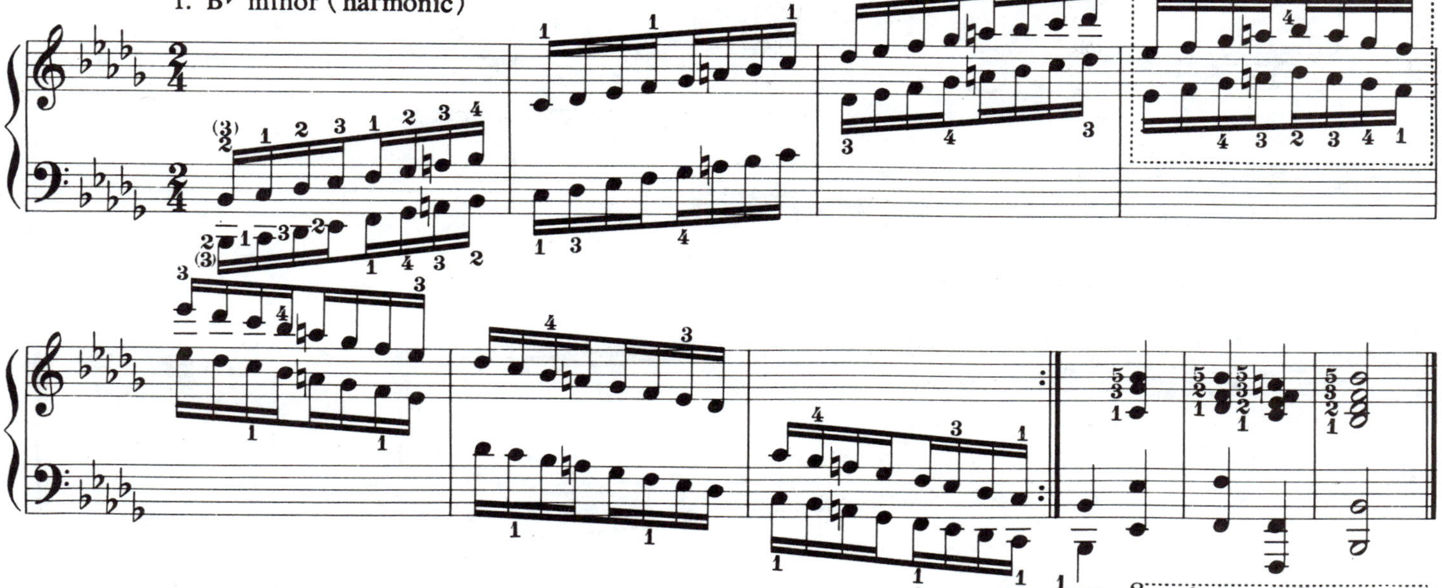

2. B♭ minor (melodic)

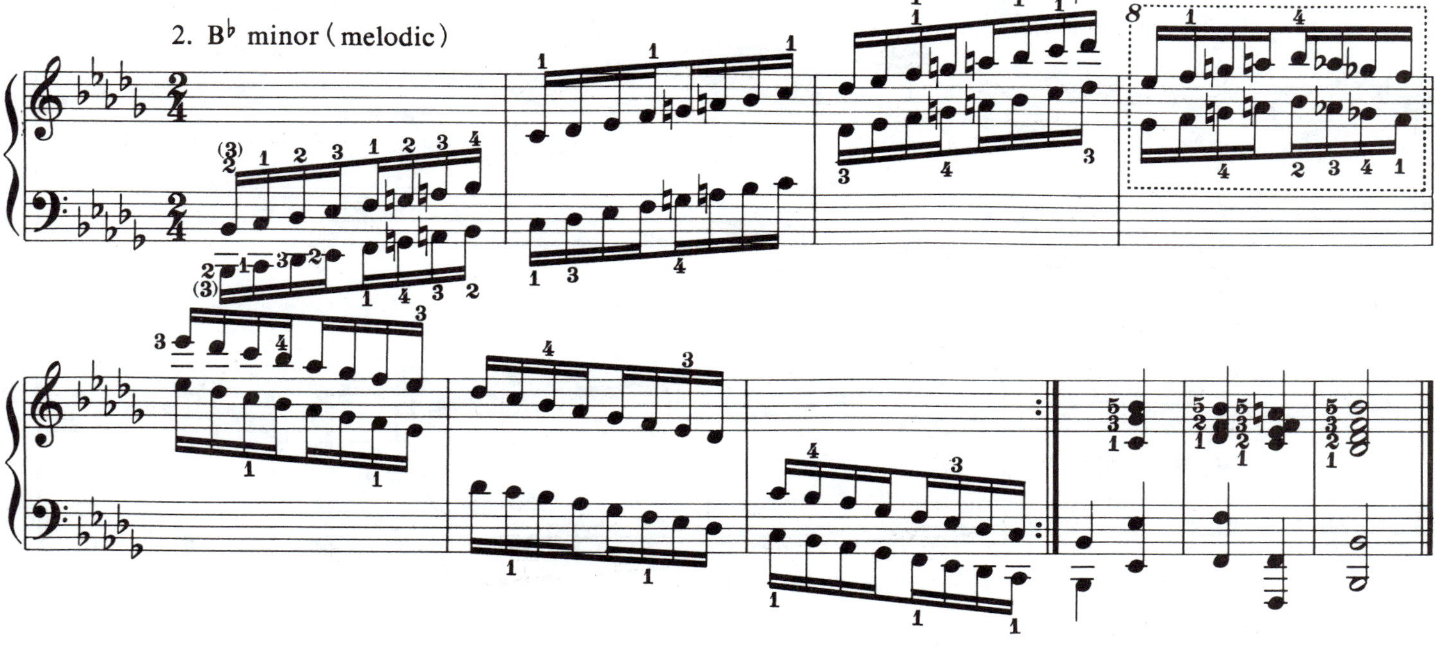

G♭ major

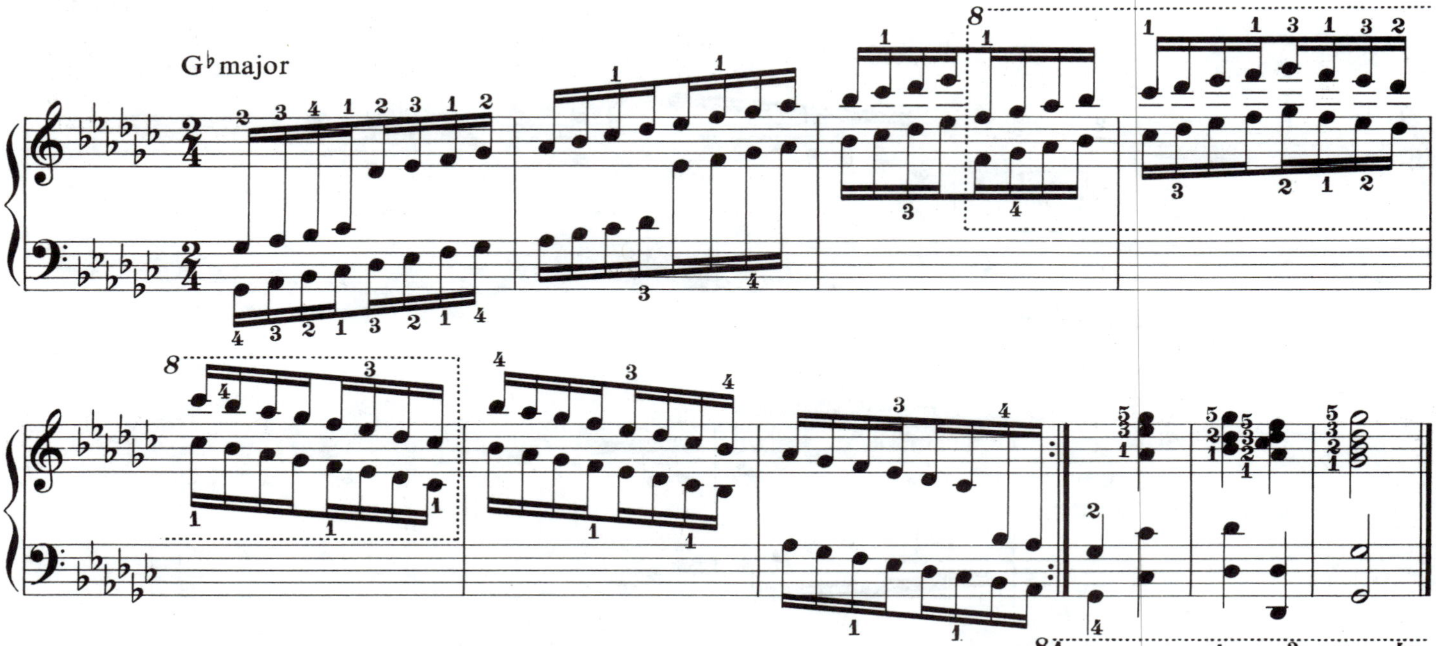

1. E♭ minor (harmonic).

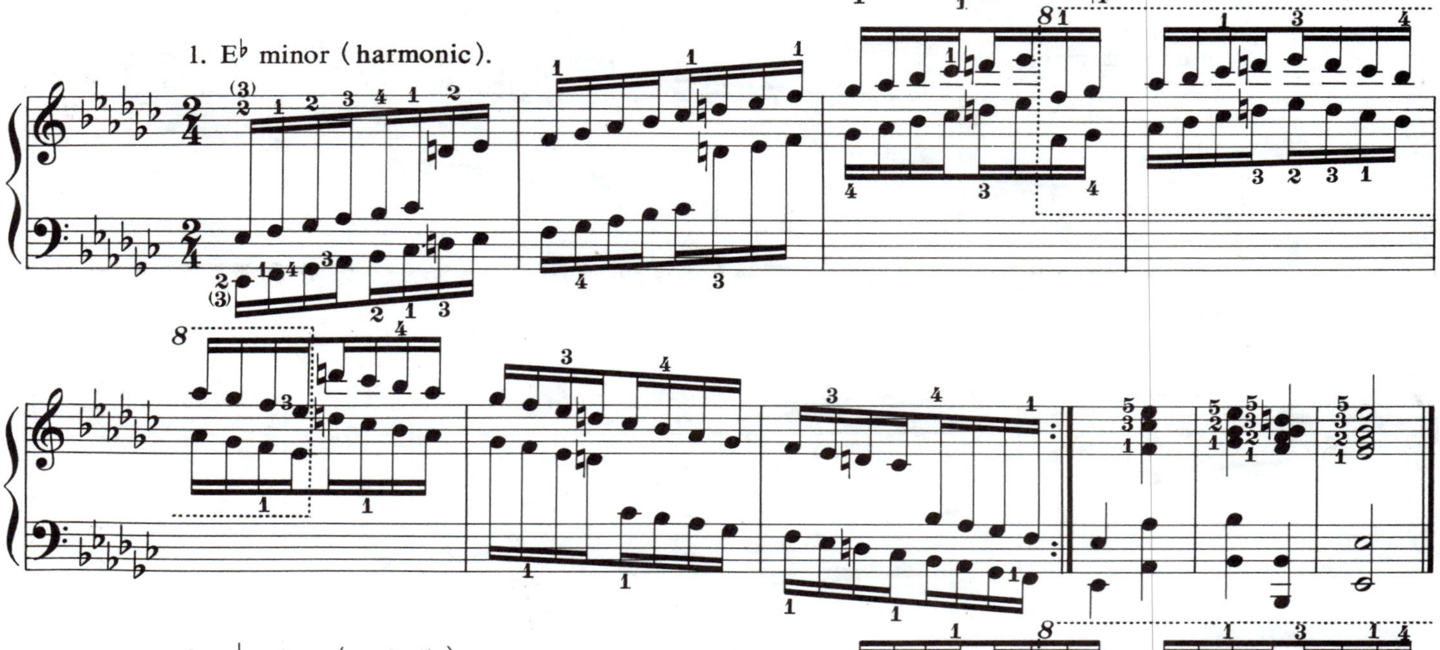

2. E♭ minor (melodic)

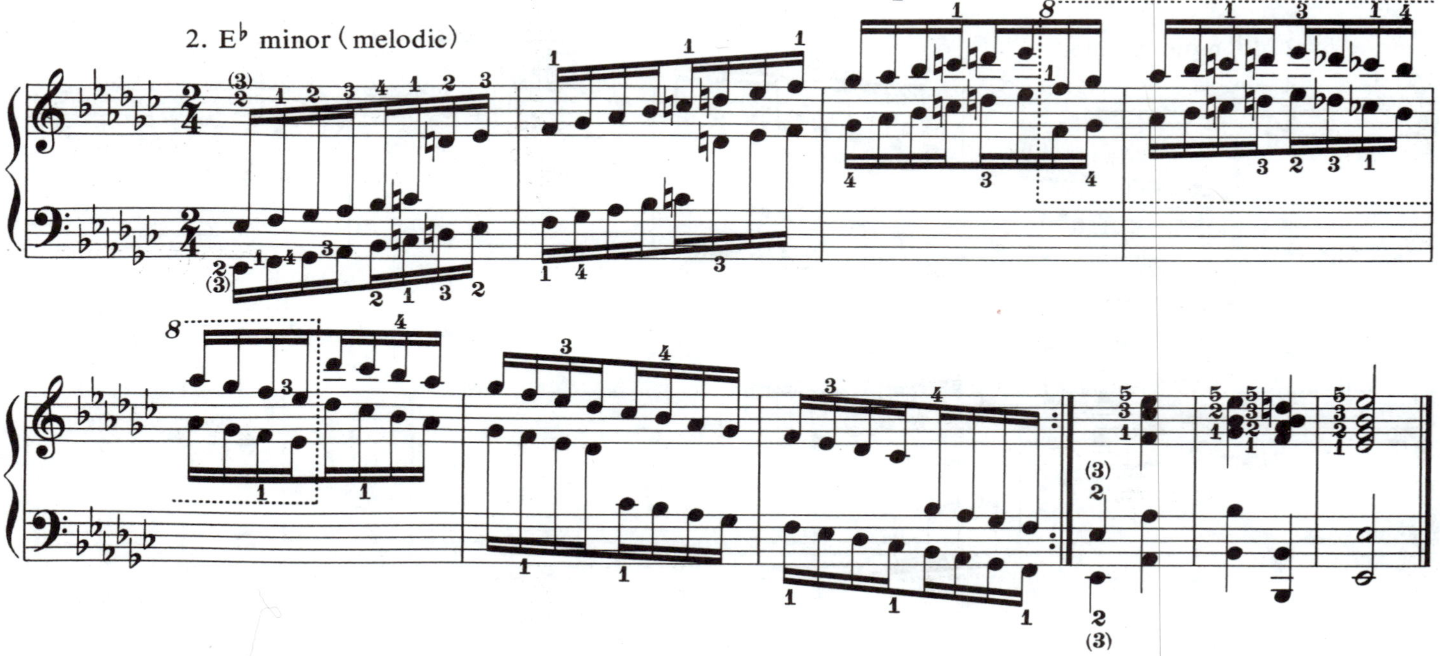

B major.

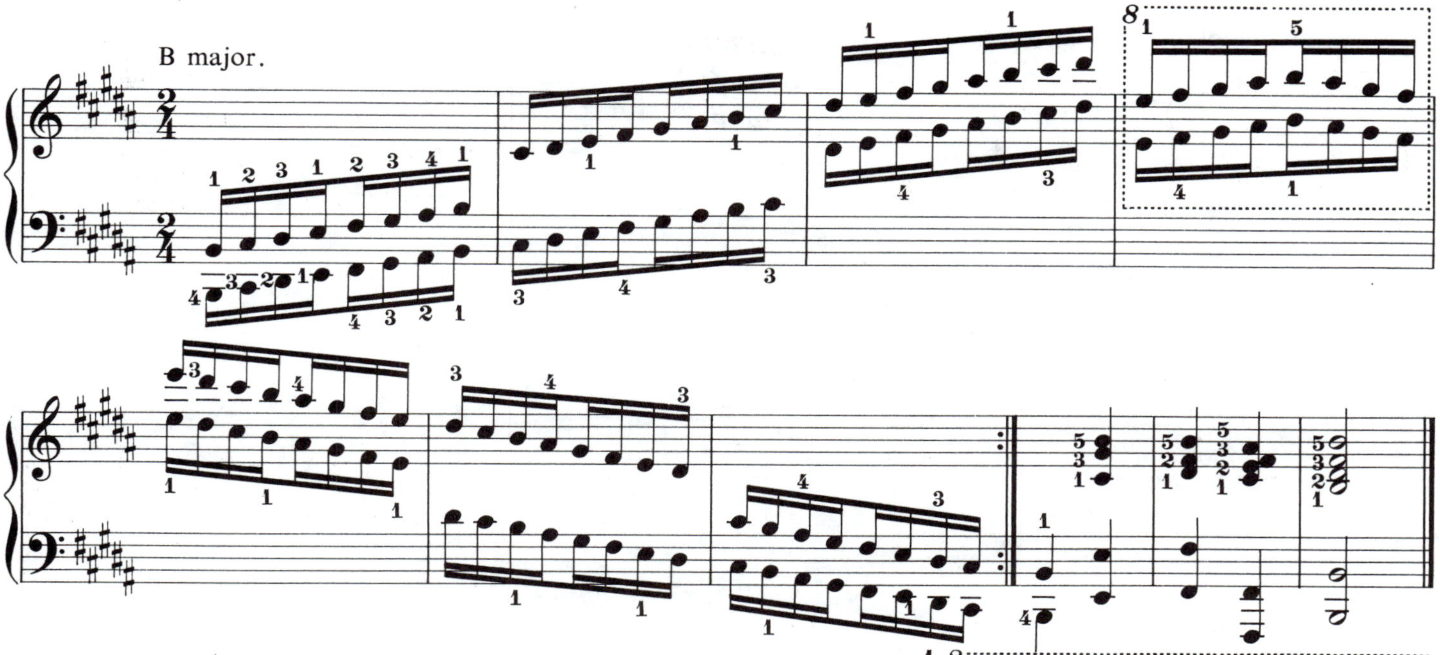

1. G♯ minor (harmonic).

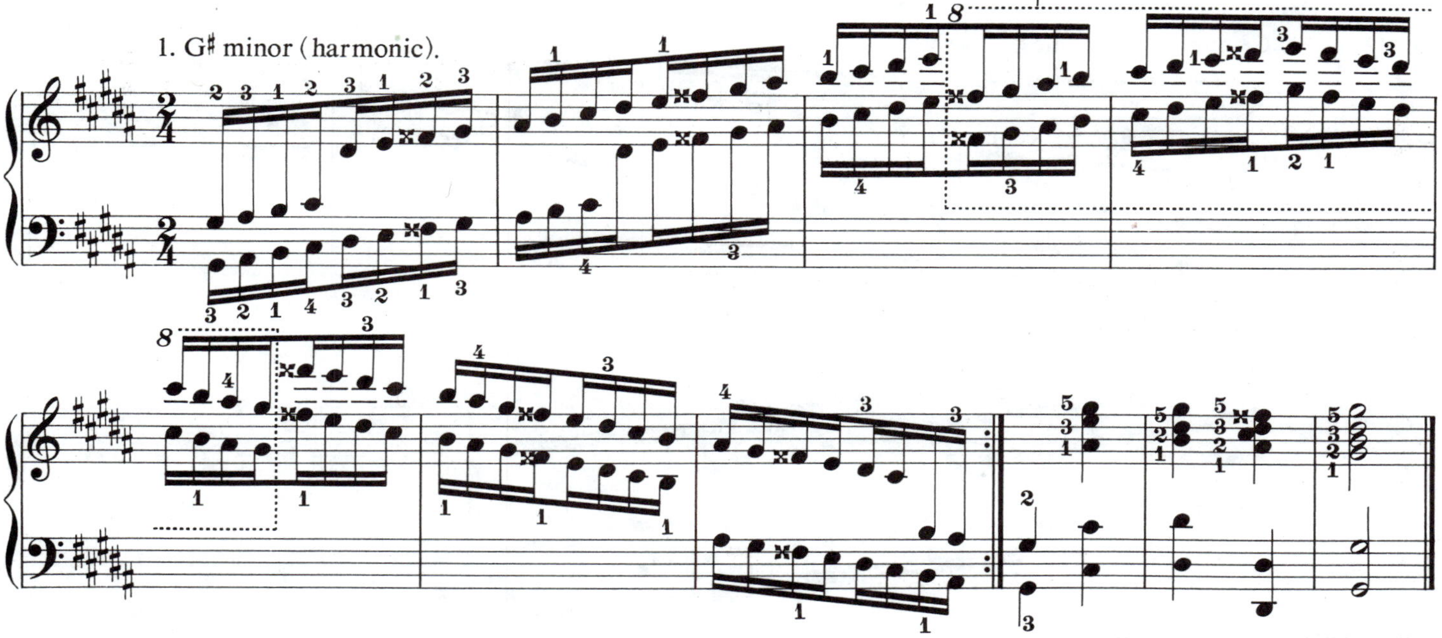

2. G♯ minor (melodic).

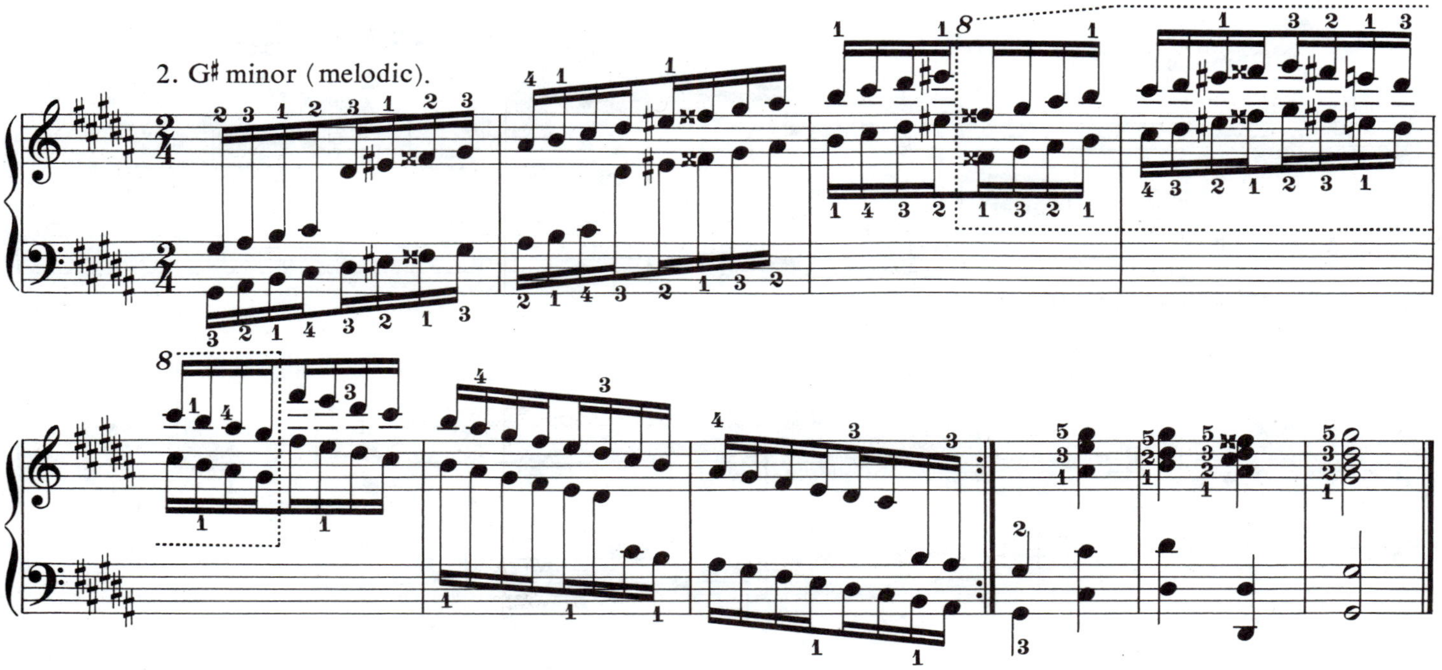

E major.

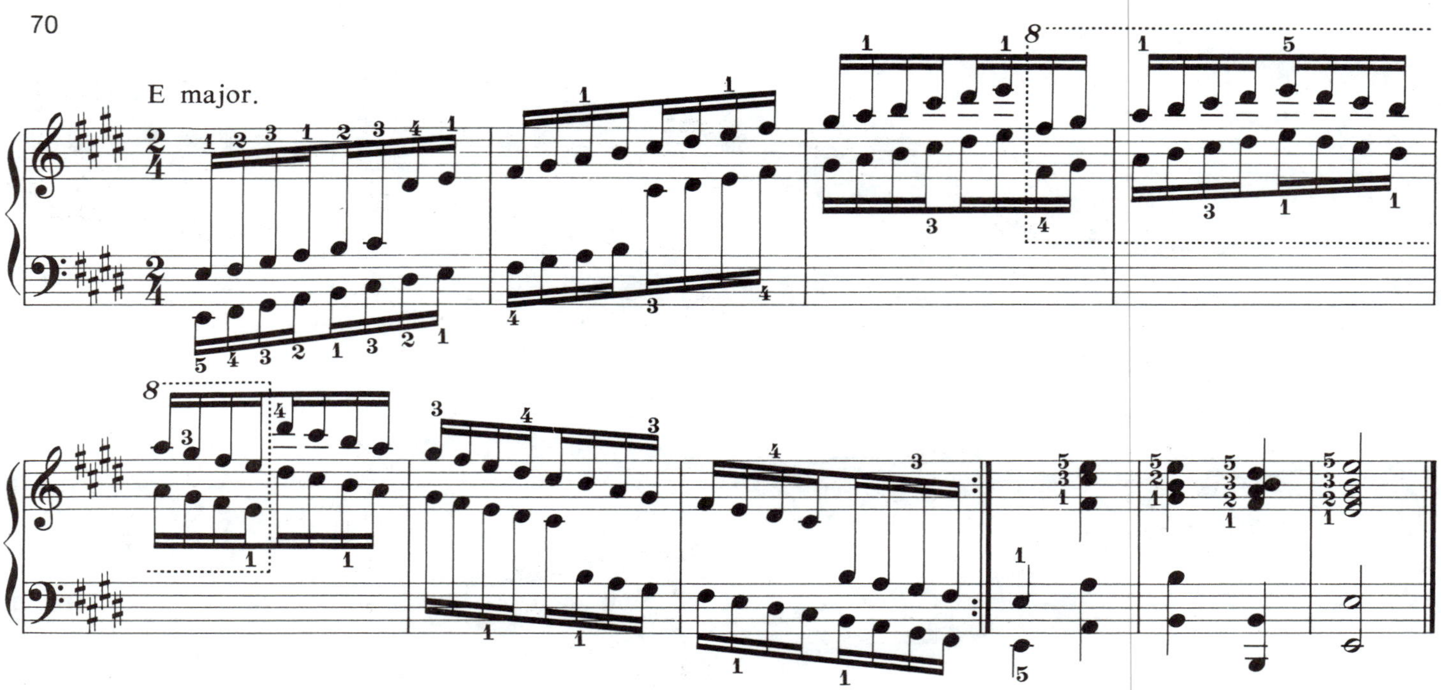

1. C♯ minor (harmonic).

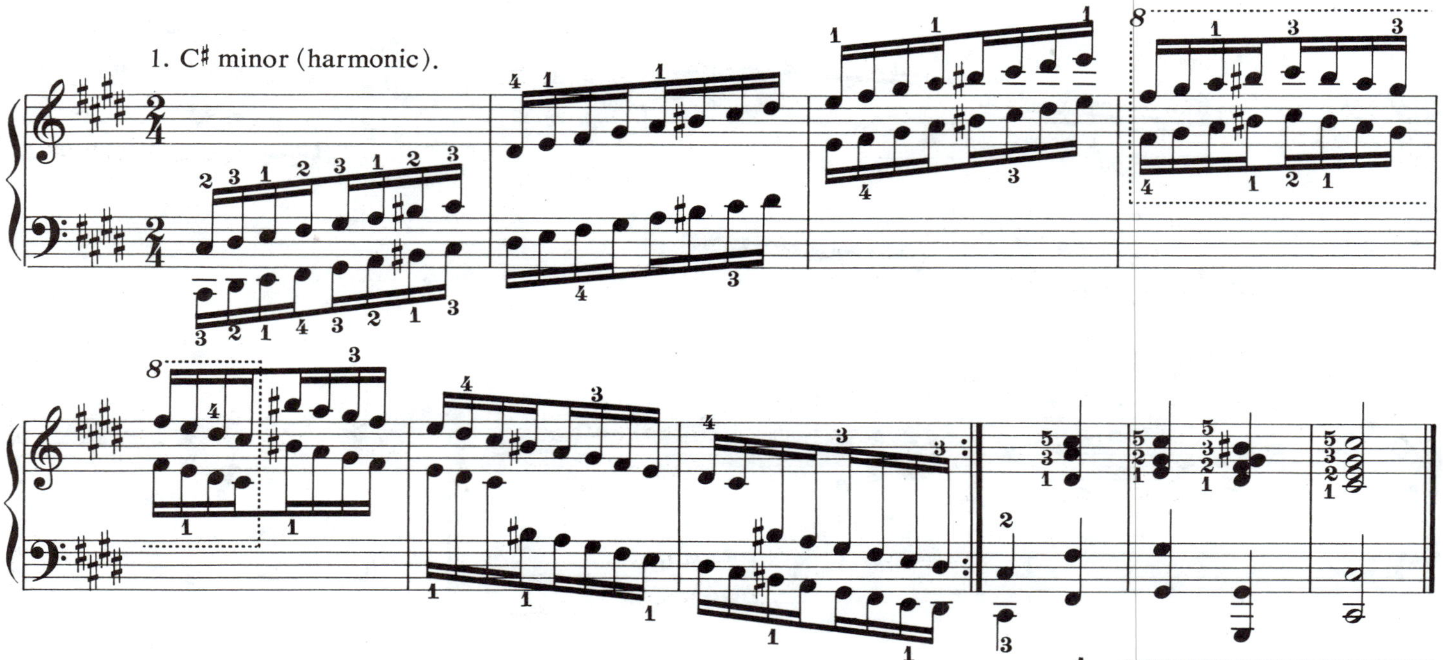

2. C♯ minor (melodic).

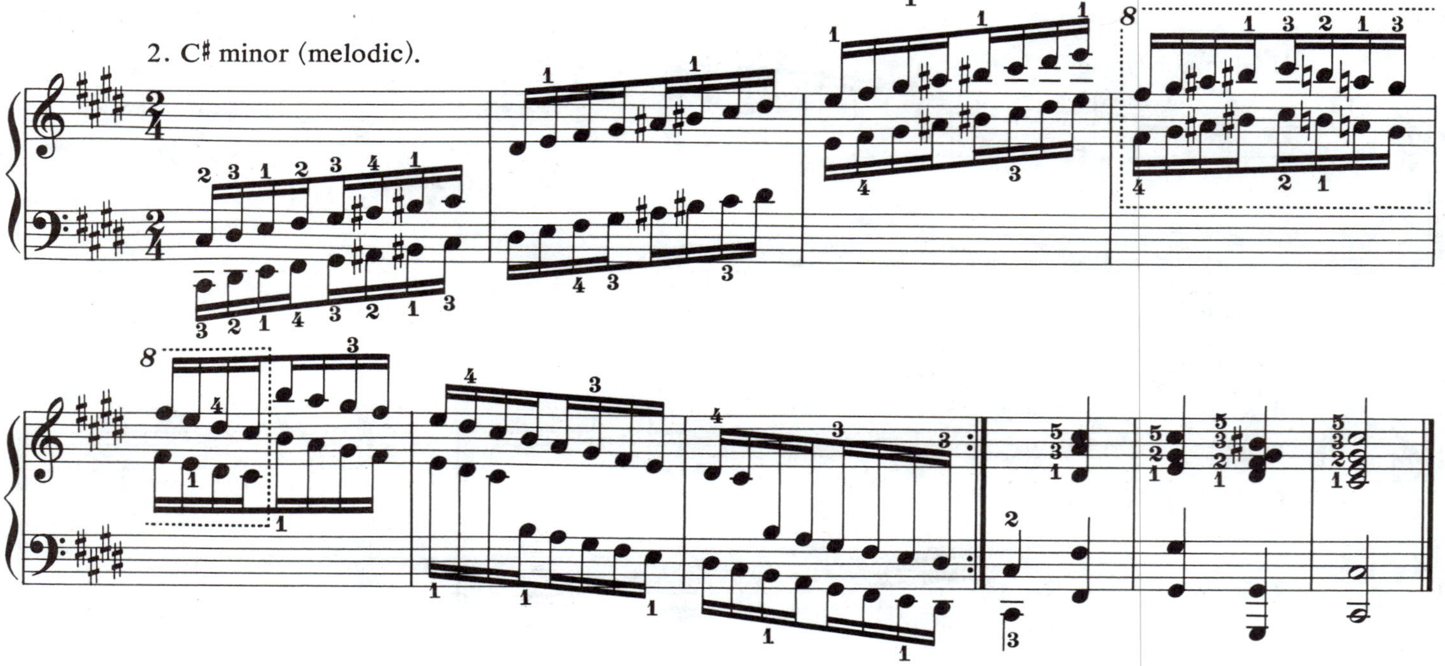

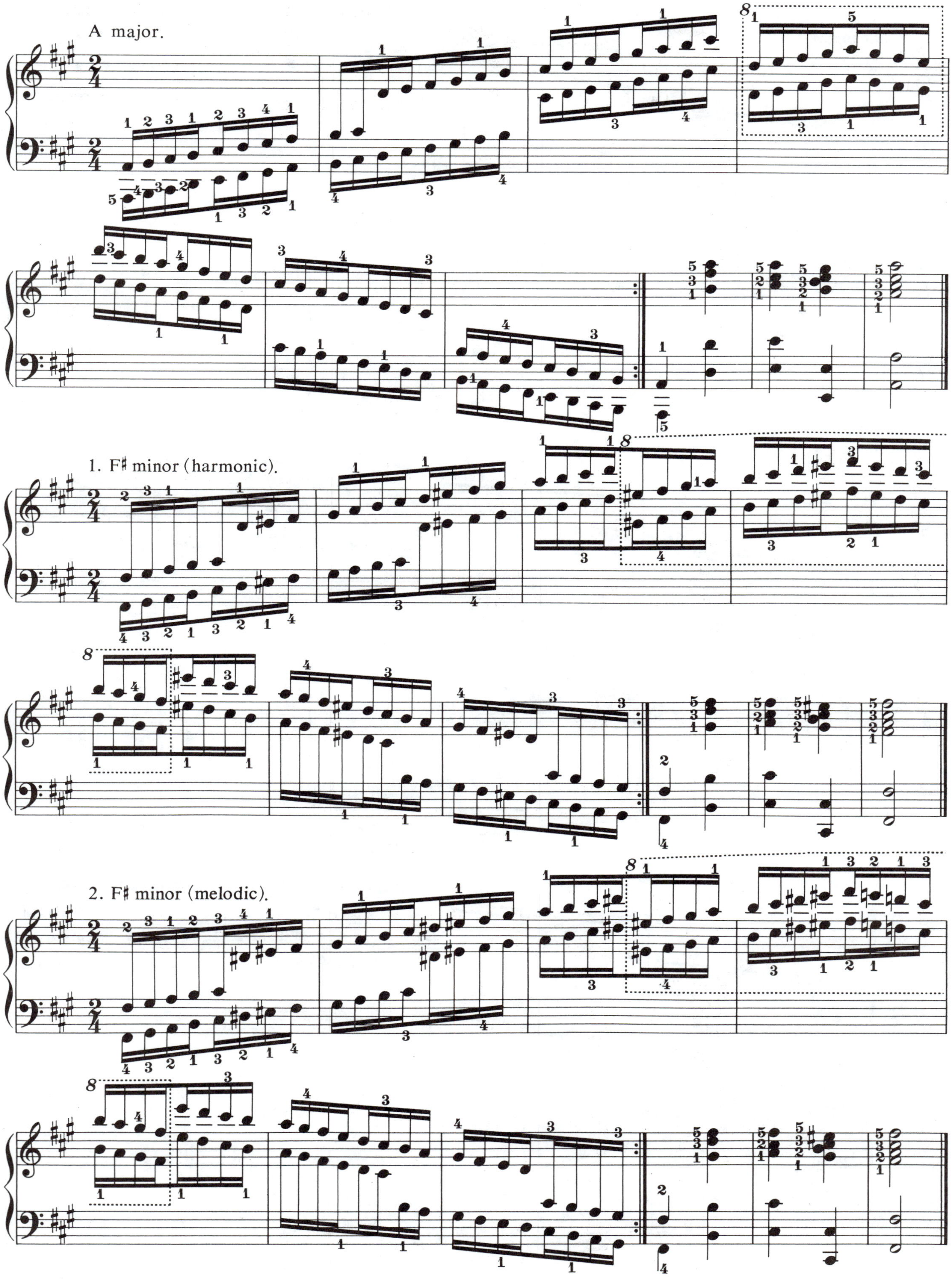
A major.
1. F♯ minor (harmonic).
2. F♯ minor (melodic).

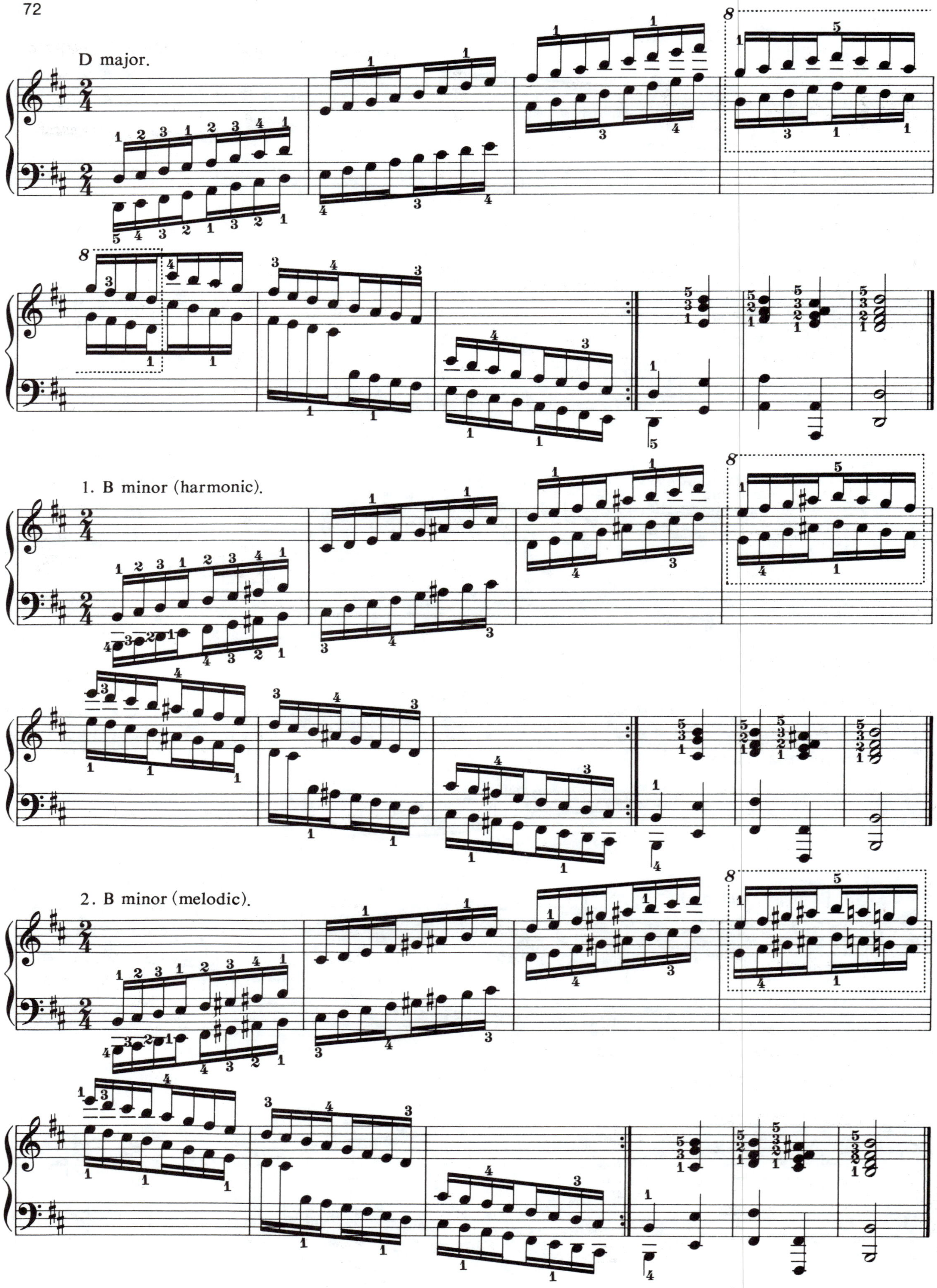
D major.
1. B minor (harmonic).
2. B minor (melodic).

G major.

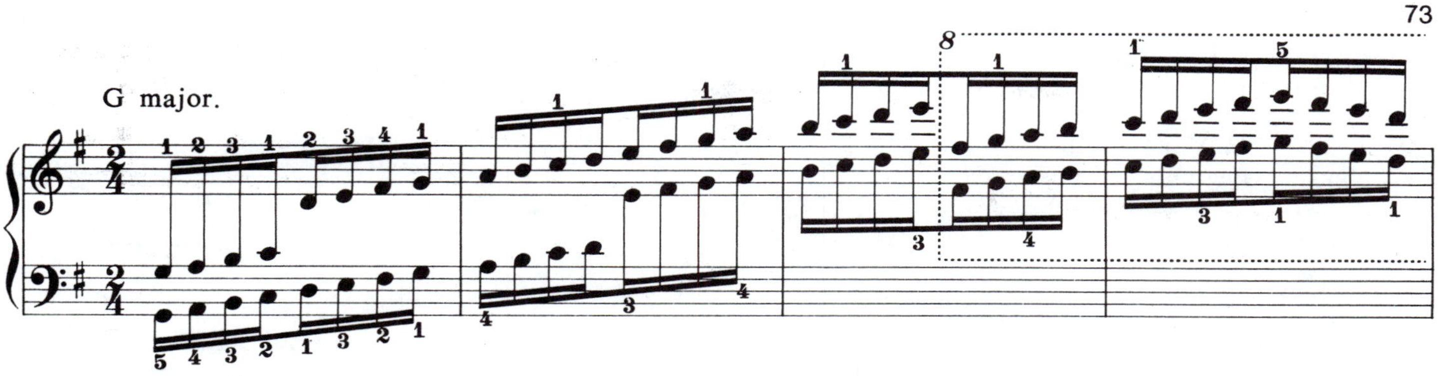

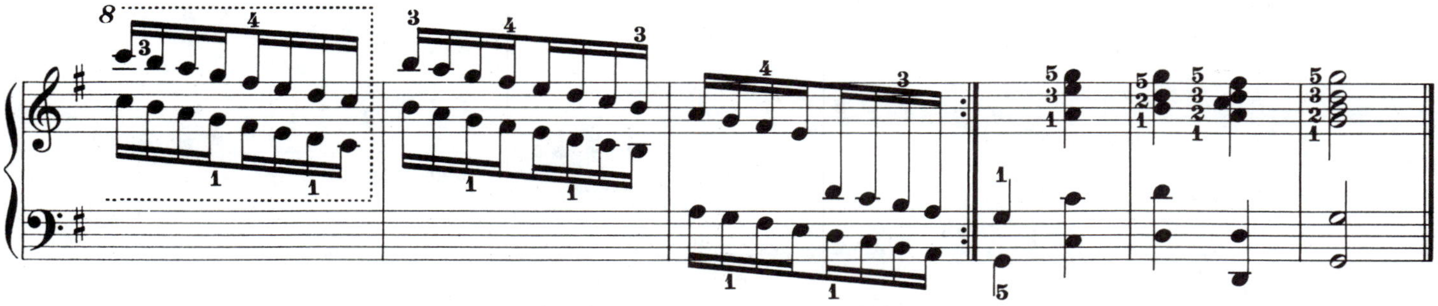

1. E minor (harmonic).

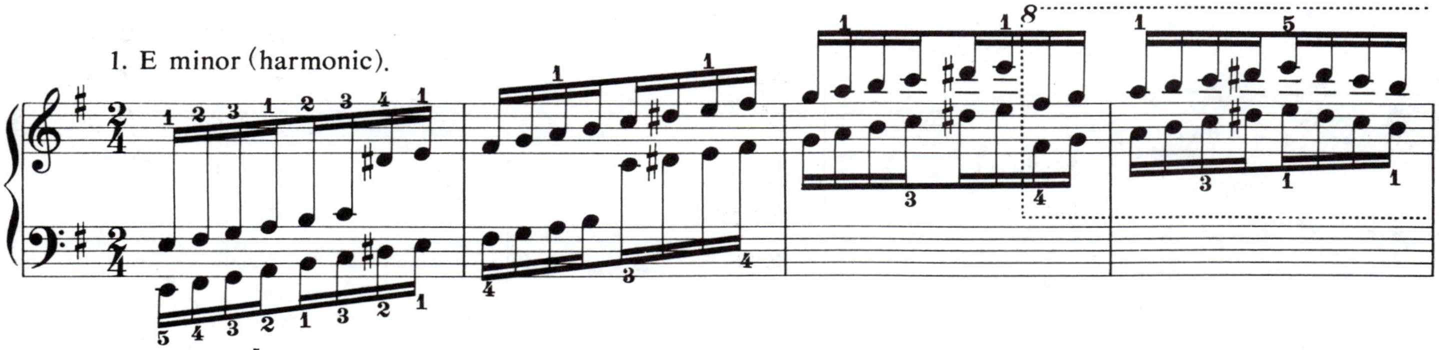

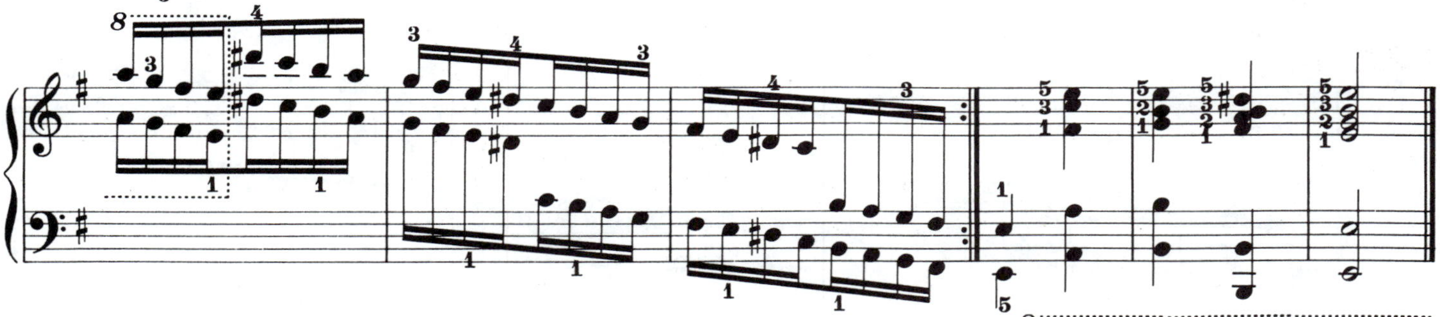

2. E minor (melodic).

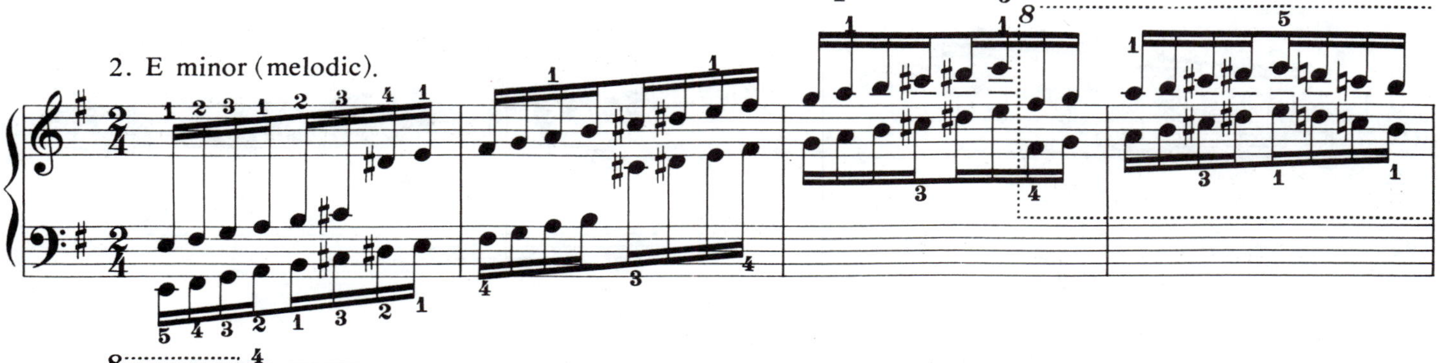

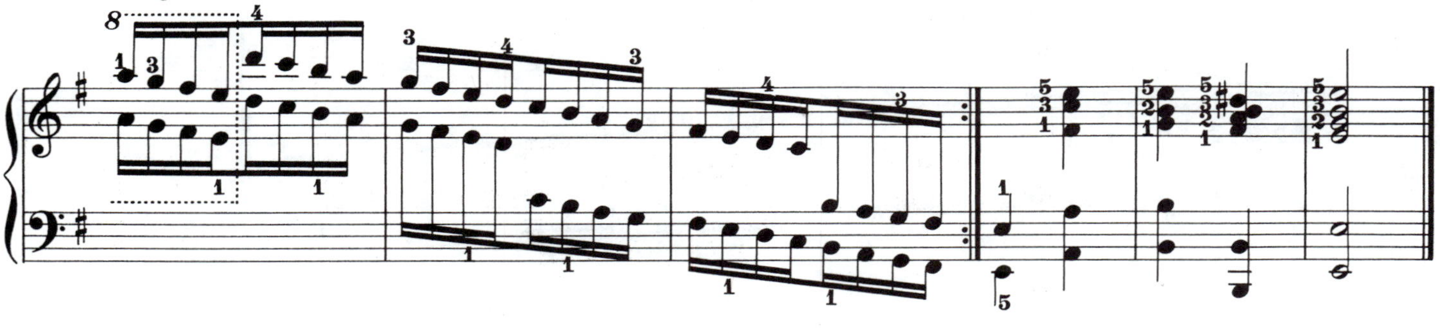

Chromatic Scales

M. M. **60** to **120**
Beginning on the octave.

40.

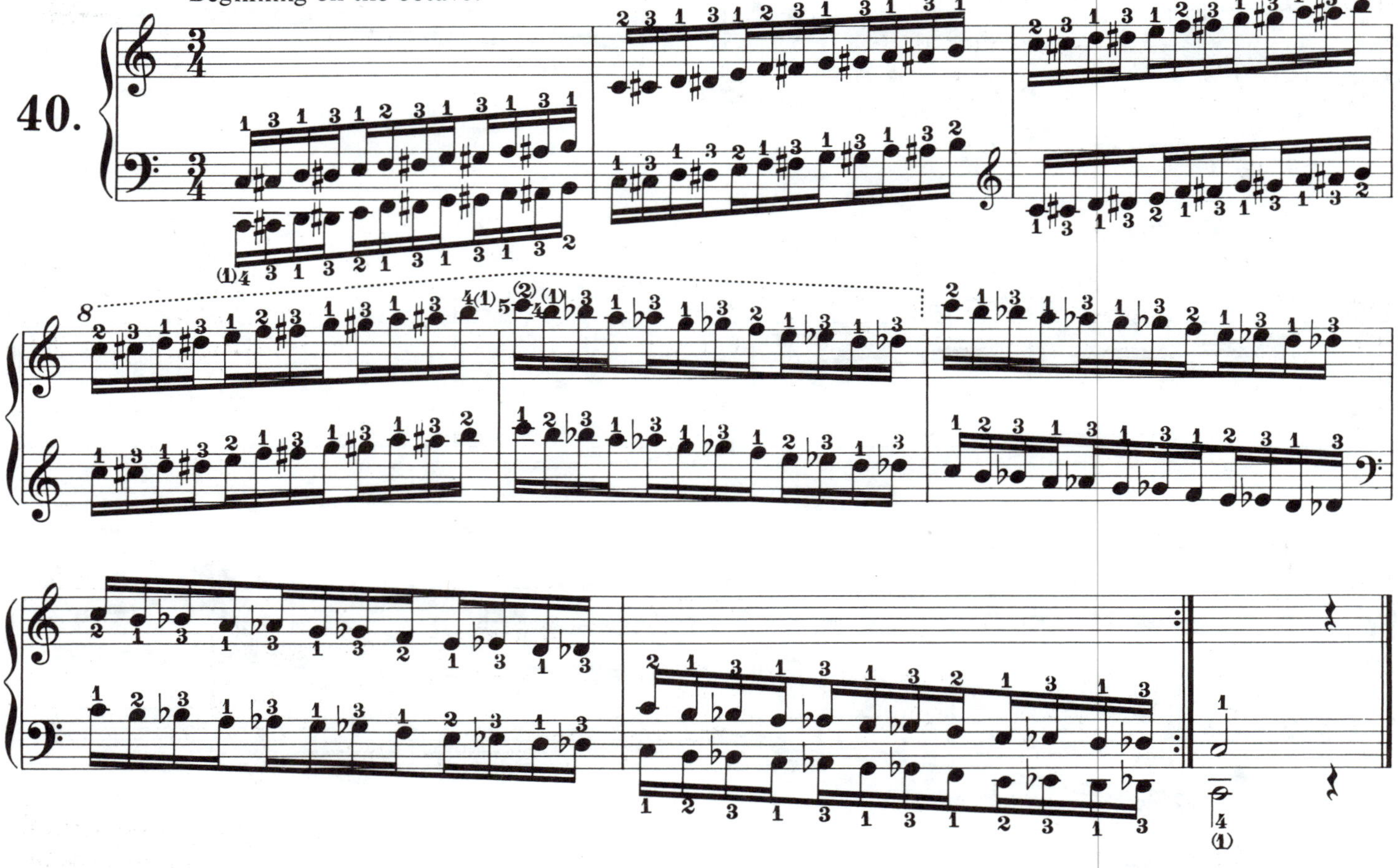

Beginning on the minor third.

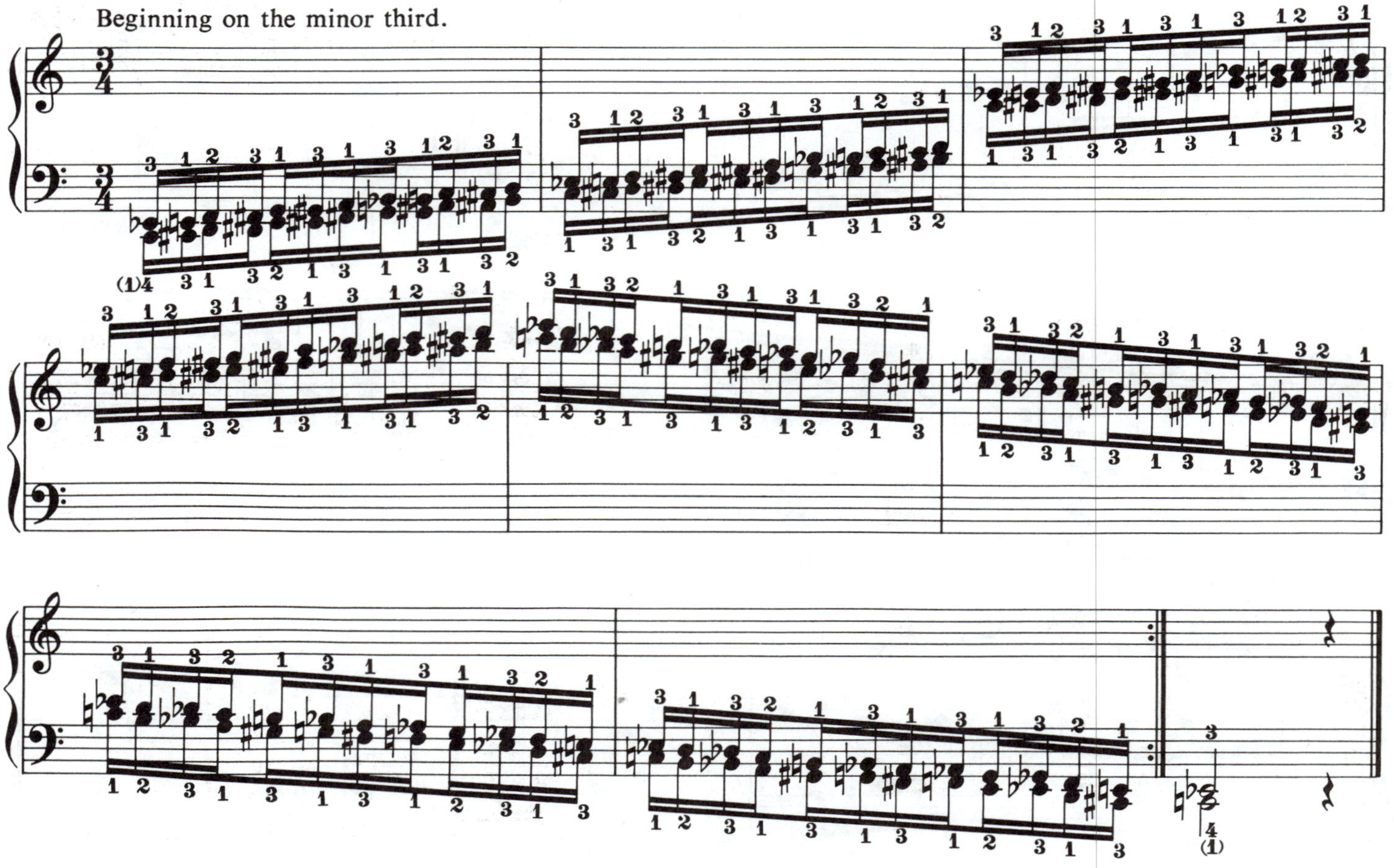

Beginning on the major sixth.

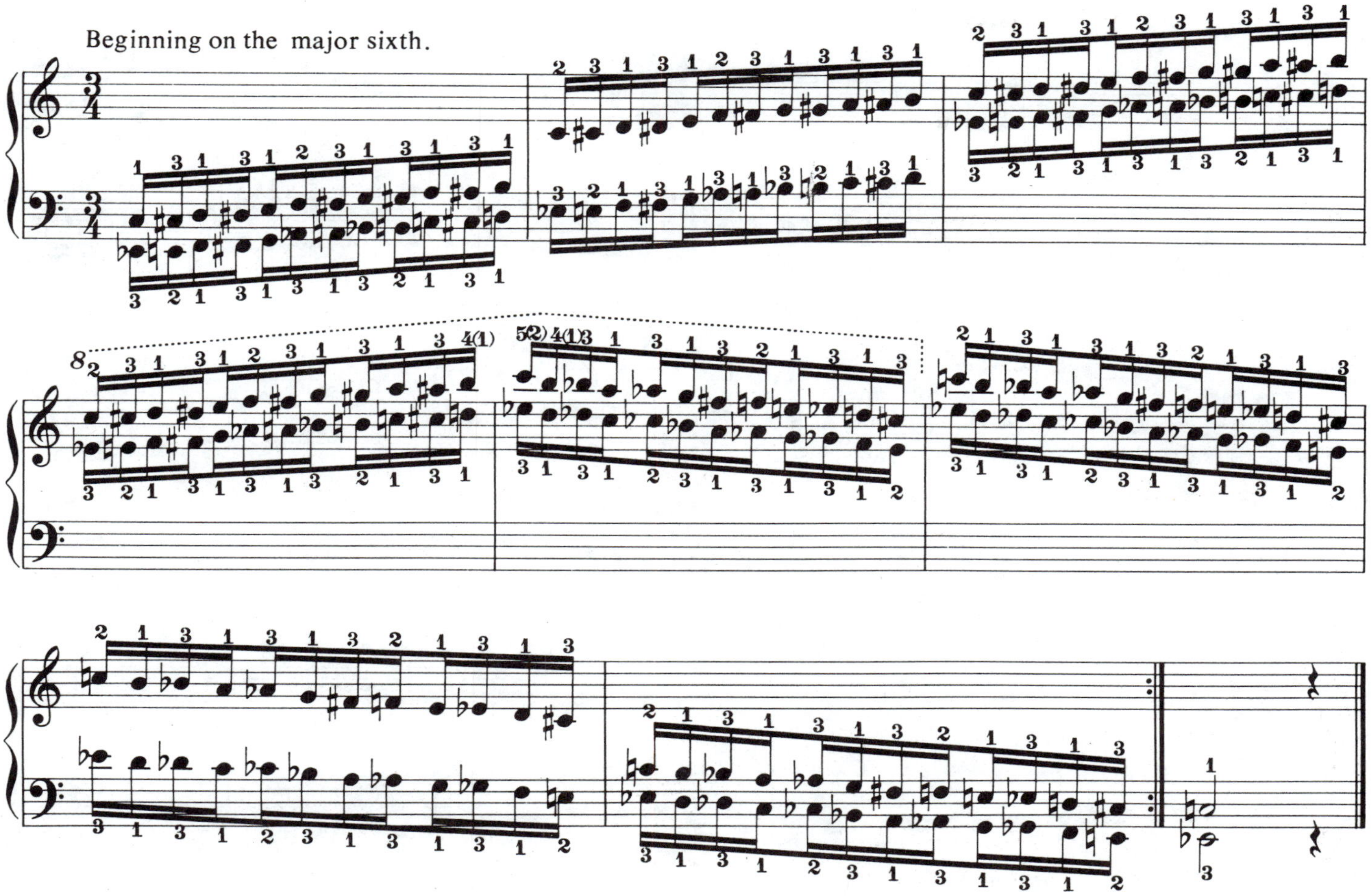

Beginning on the minor sixth.

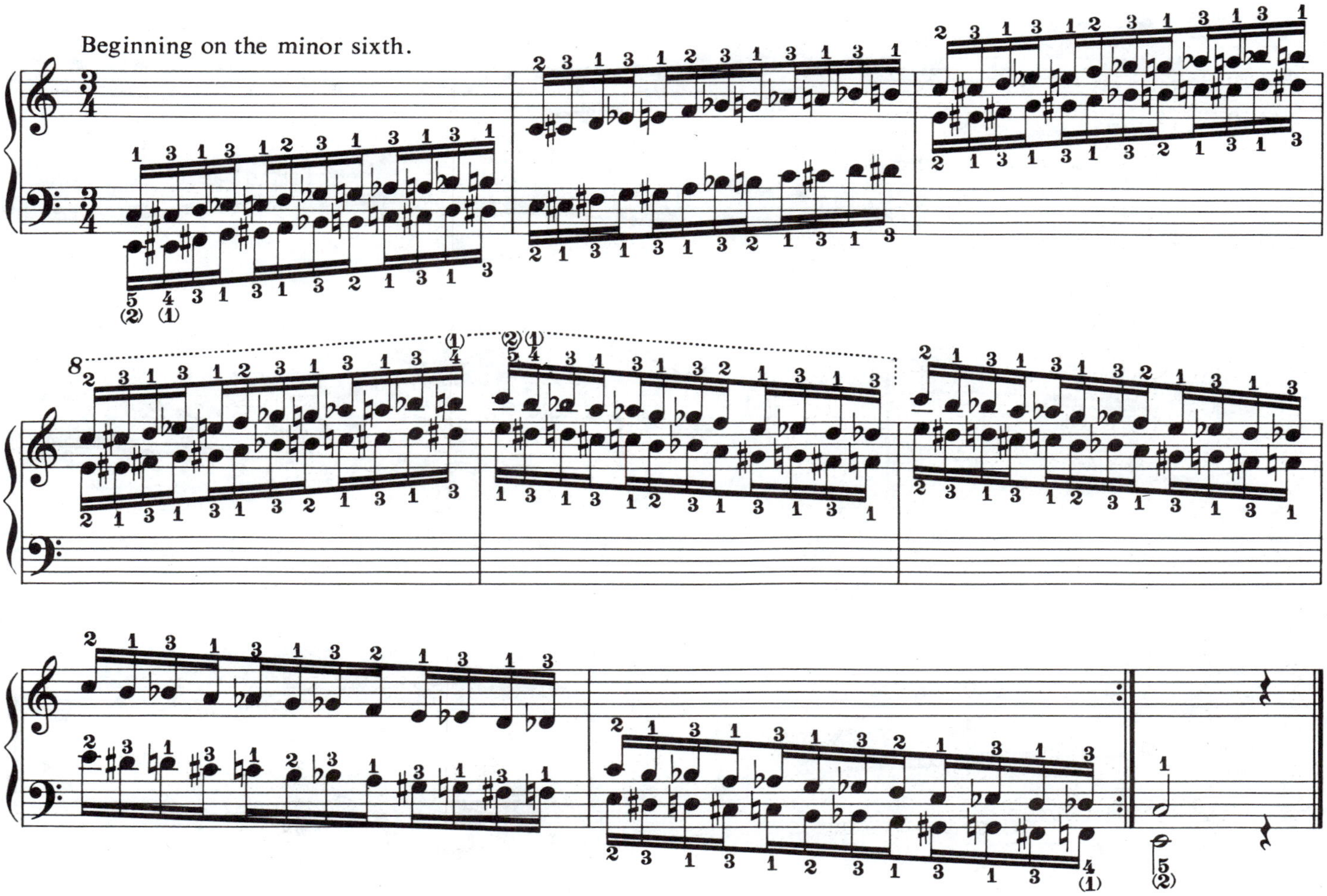

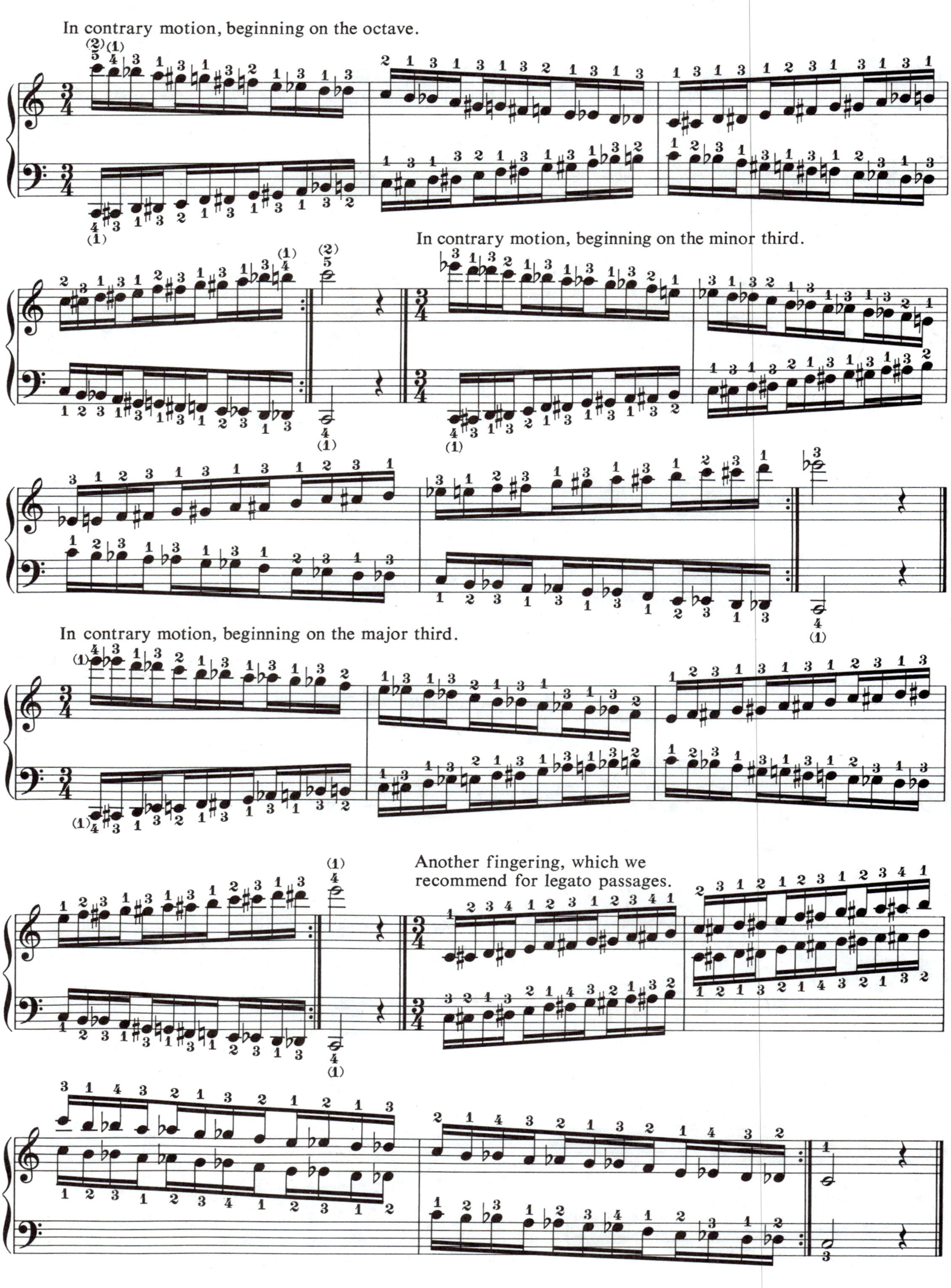
In contrary motion, beginning on the octave.
In contrary motion, beginning on the minor third.
In contrary motion, beginning on the major third.
Another fingering, which we recommend for legato passages.

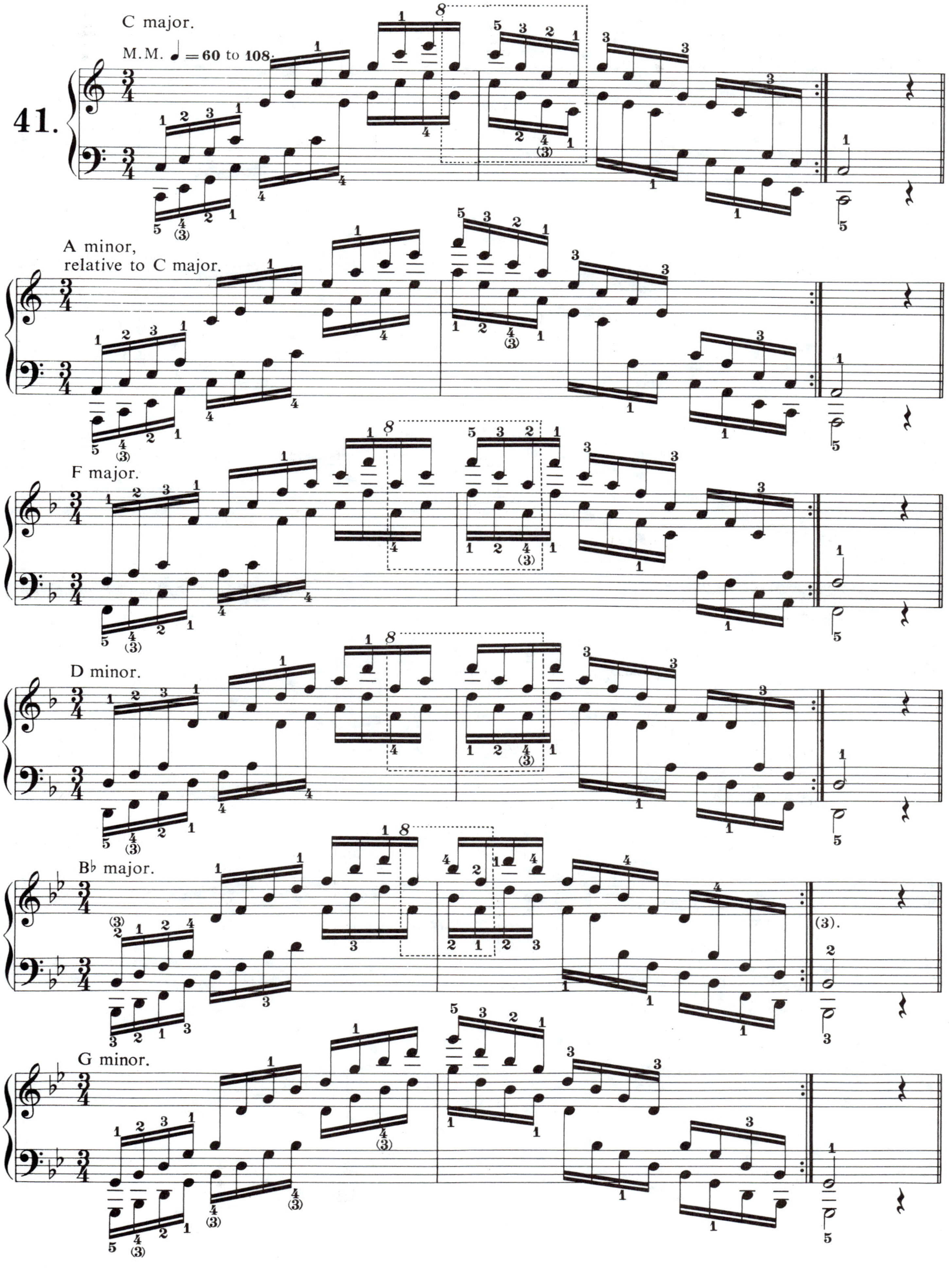
41.
C major.
M.M. ♩ = 60 to 108
A minor,
relative to C major.
F major.
D minor.
B♭ major.
G minor.

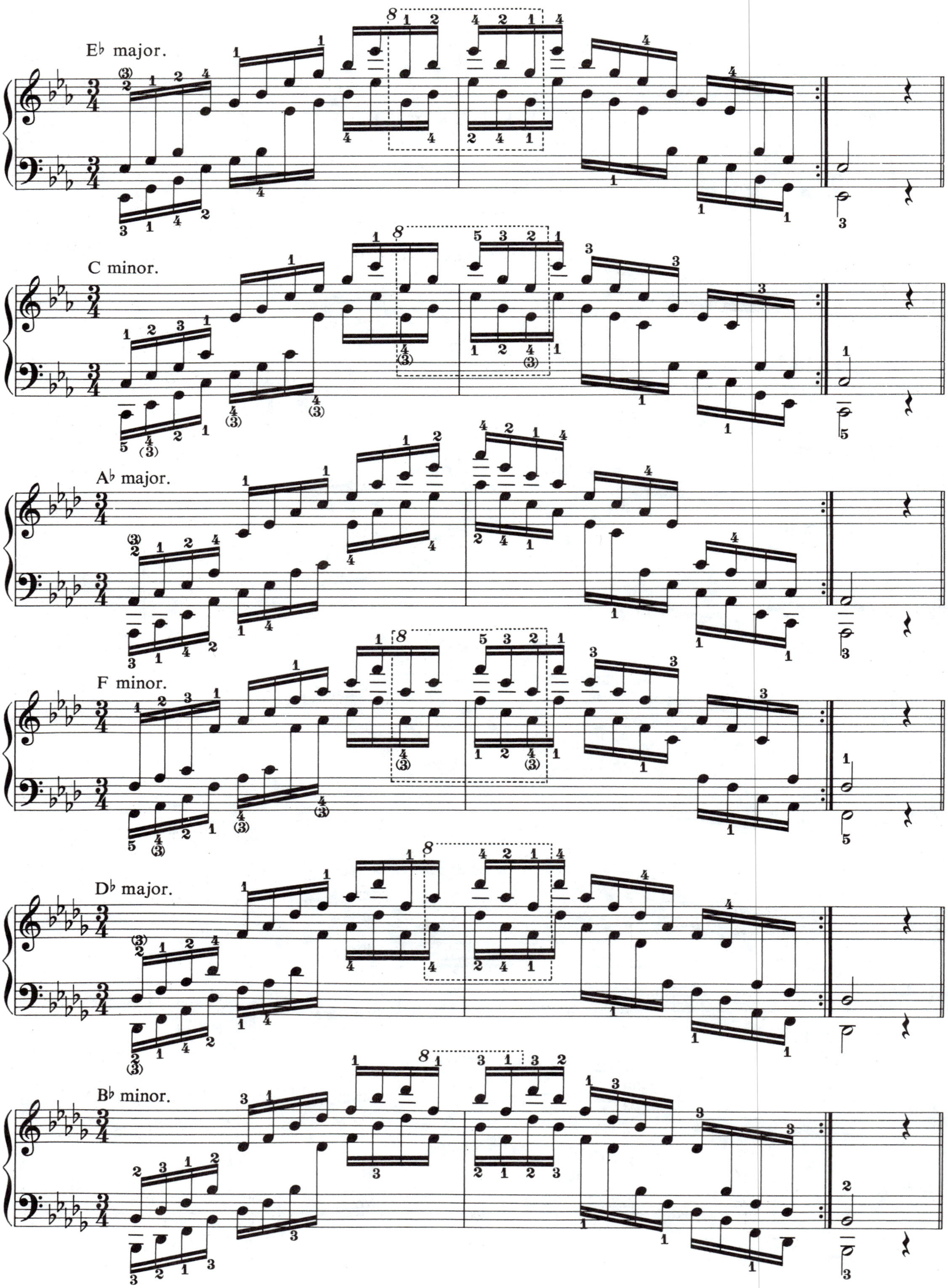
E♭ major.
C minor.
A♭ major.
F minor.
D♭ major.
B♭ minor.

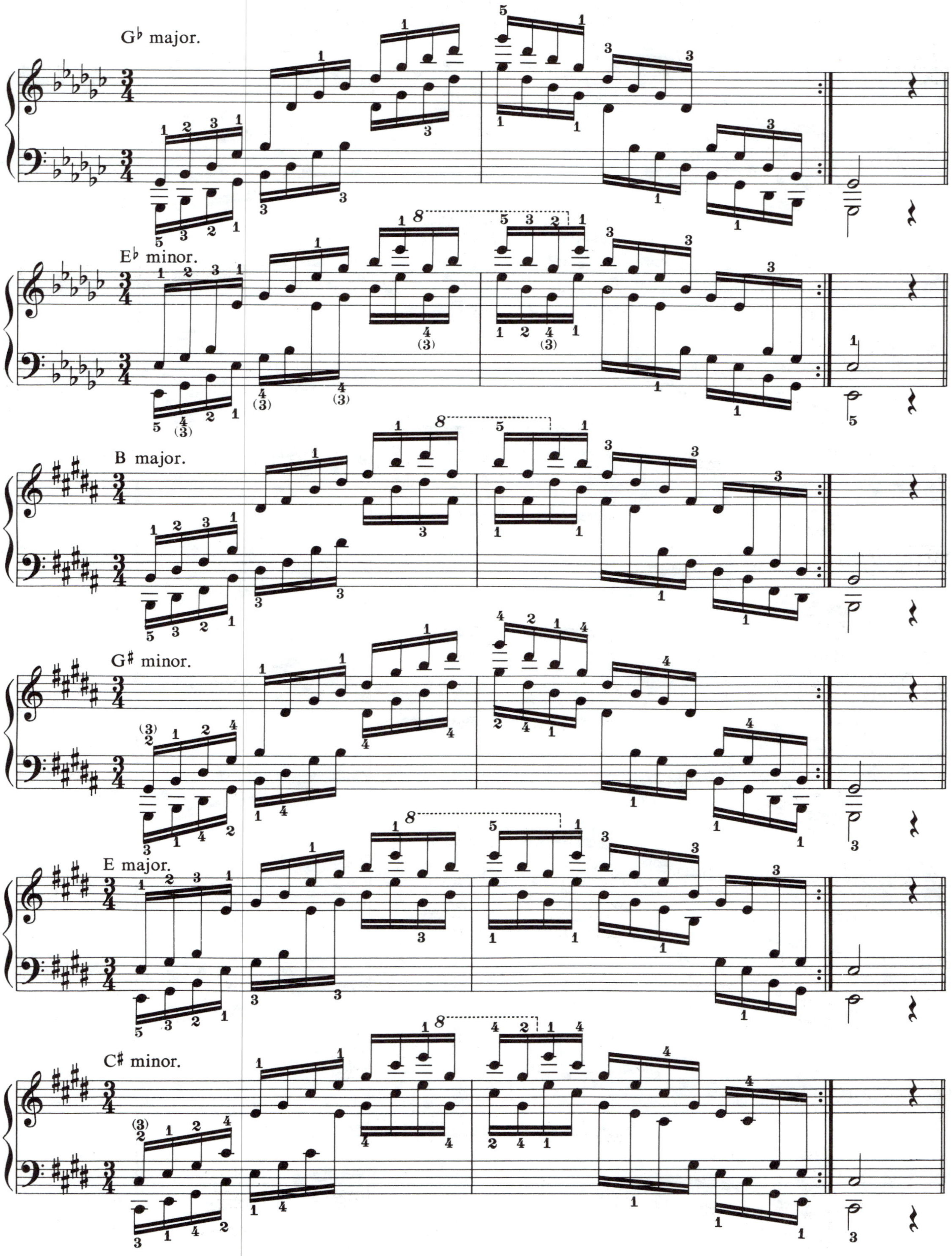

G♭ major.
E♭ minor.
B major.
G♯ minor.
E major.
C♯ minor.

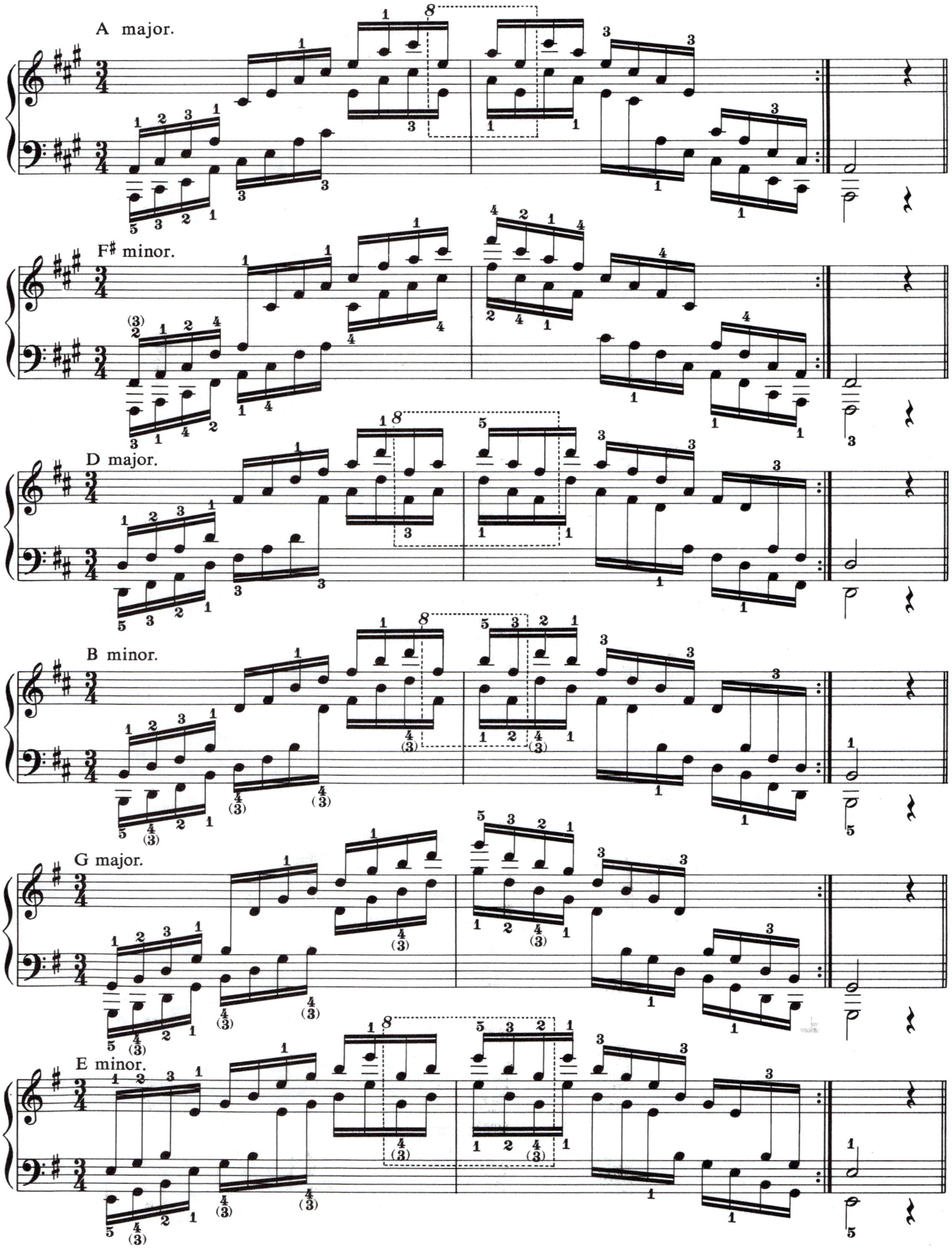
A major.
F♯ minor.
D major.
B minor.
G major.
E minor.

Arpeggios on the Diminished Seventh Chord in 7 Keys.

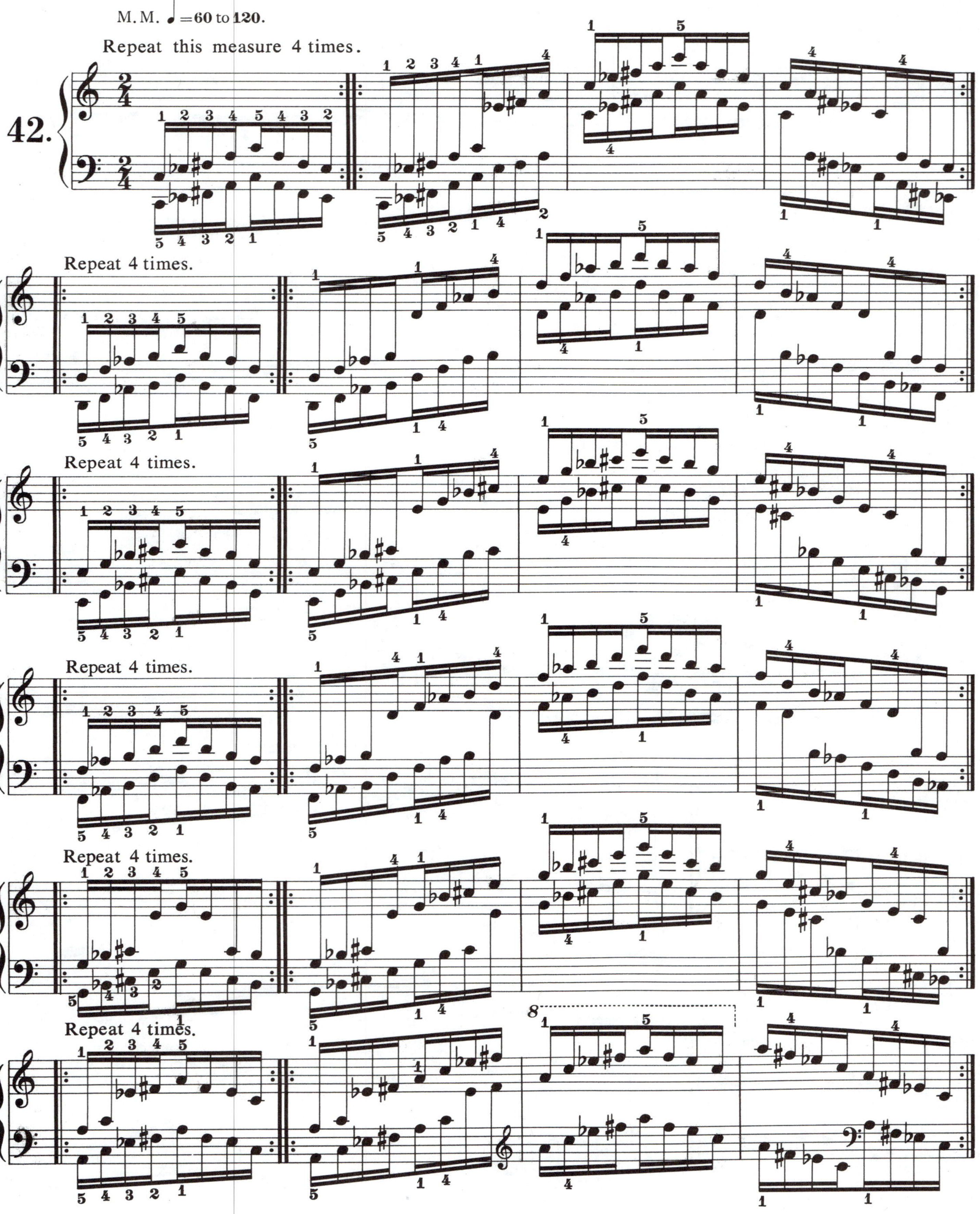

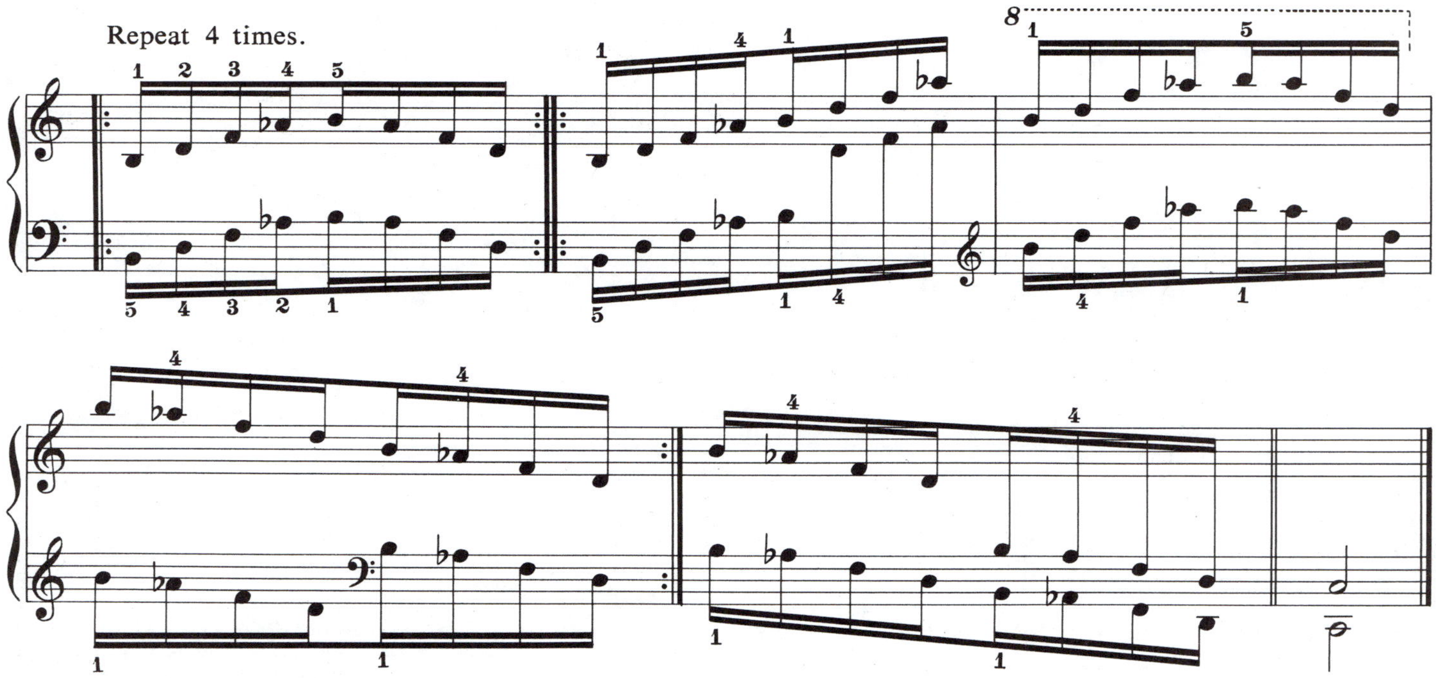

Arpeggios on the Dominant Seventh Chord in 7 Keys.

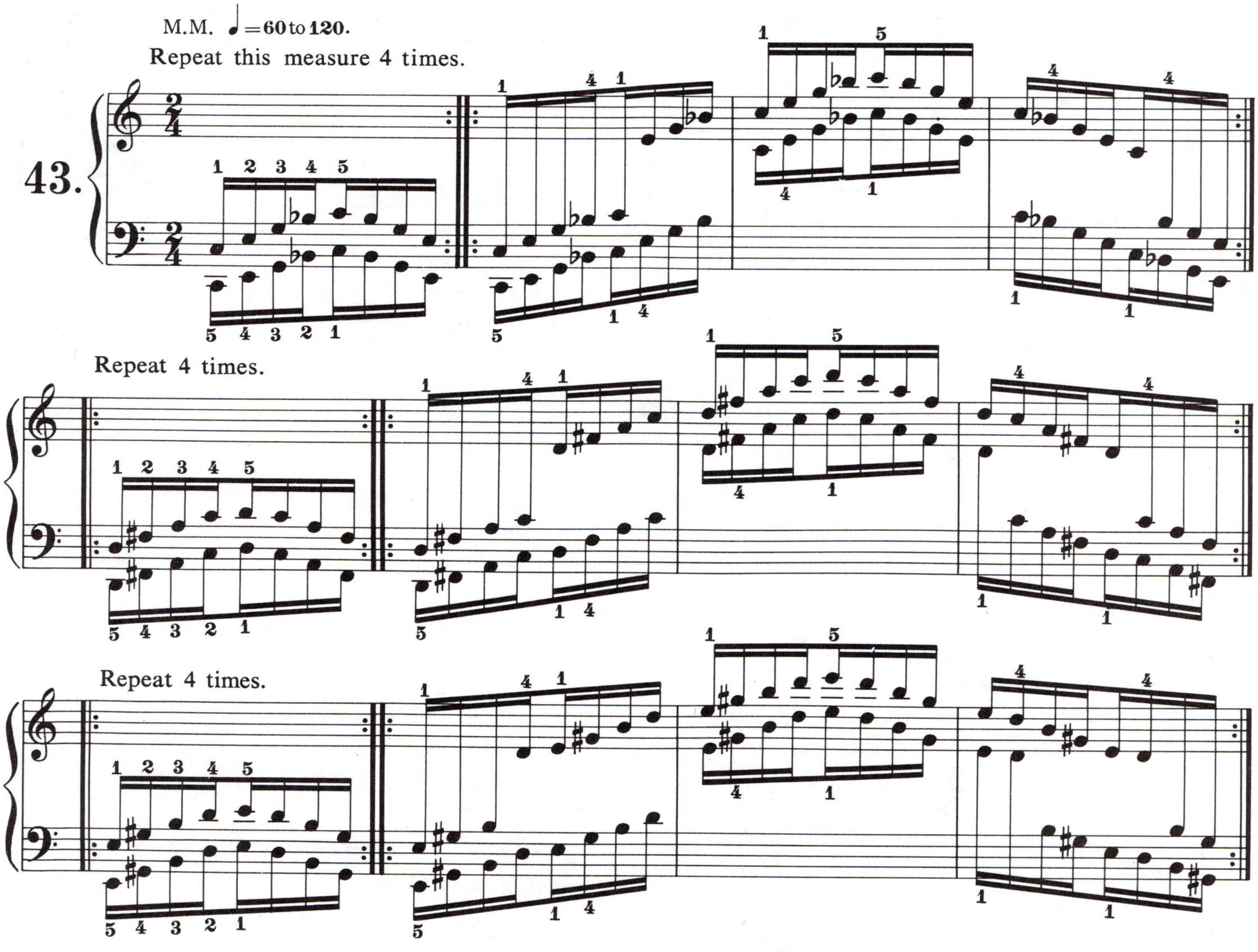

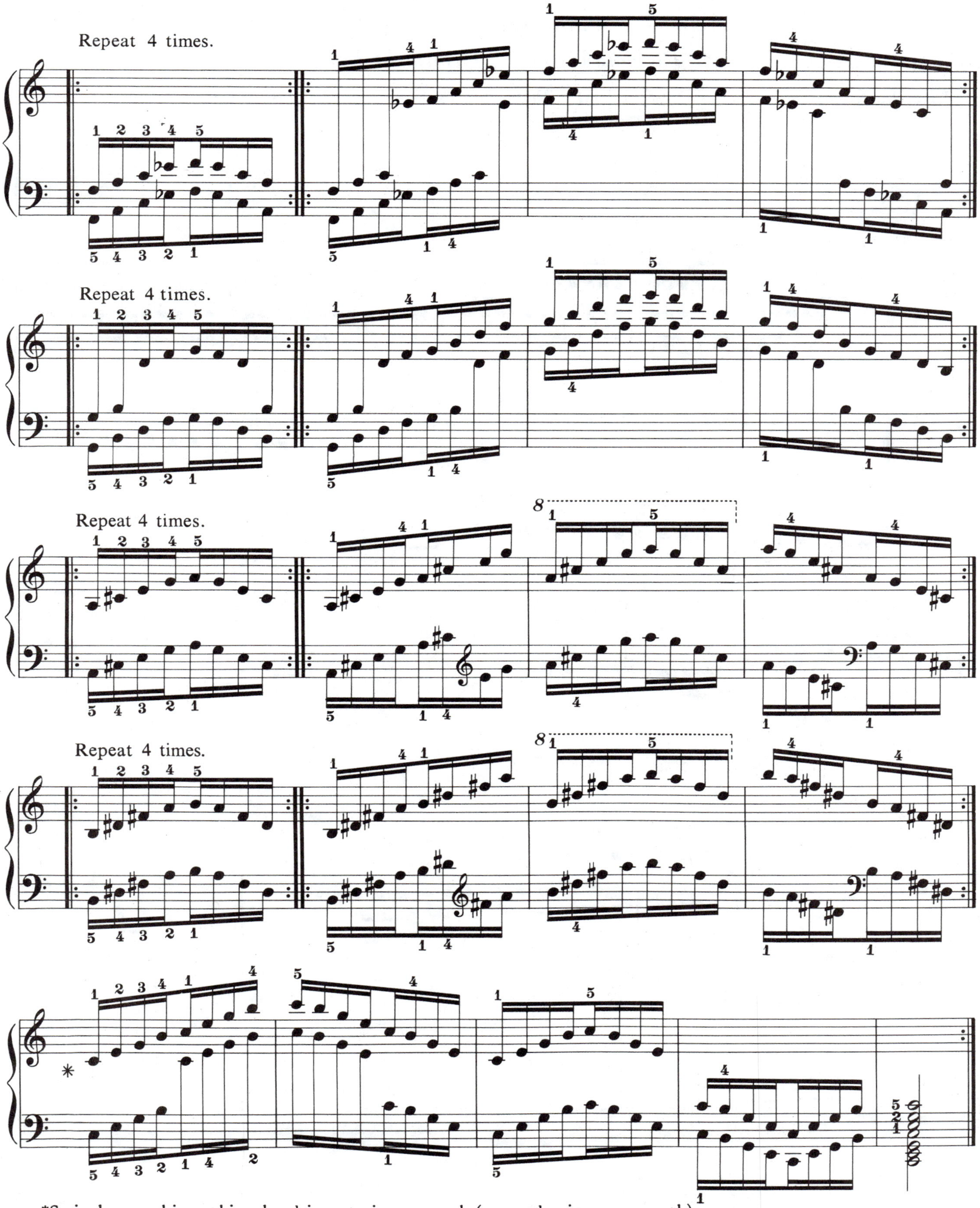

*Strictly speaking, this chord is a major seventh (not a dominant seventh).

As the difficulties in Part 3 can only be mastered with a good basic technique, it is recommended that Parts 1 and 2 be learned thoroughly before proceeding.

End of Part 2

THE VIRTUOSO PIANIST, PART 3

Virtuoso Exercises for Mastering the Greatest Technical Difficulties

Repeated Notes in Groups of Three

Lift the fingers high and with precision, without raising the hand or wrist. As soon as the first four measures are learned, practice the rest of the exercise.

M.M. ♩ = 60 to 120

C. L. HANON

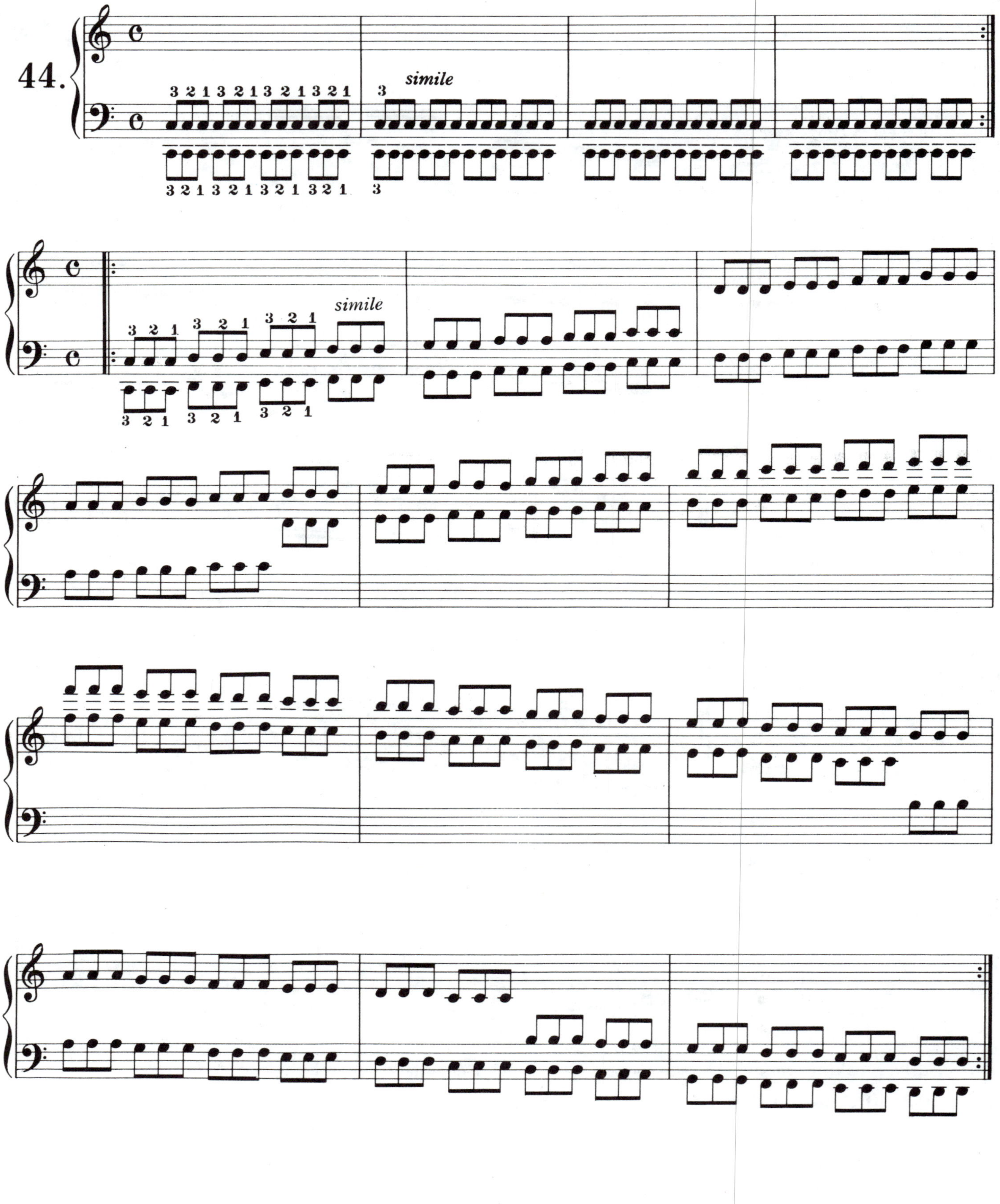

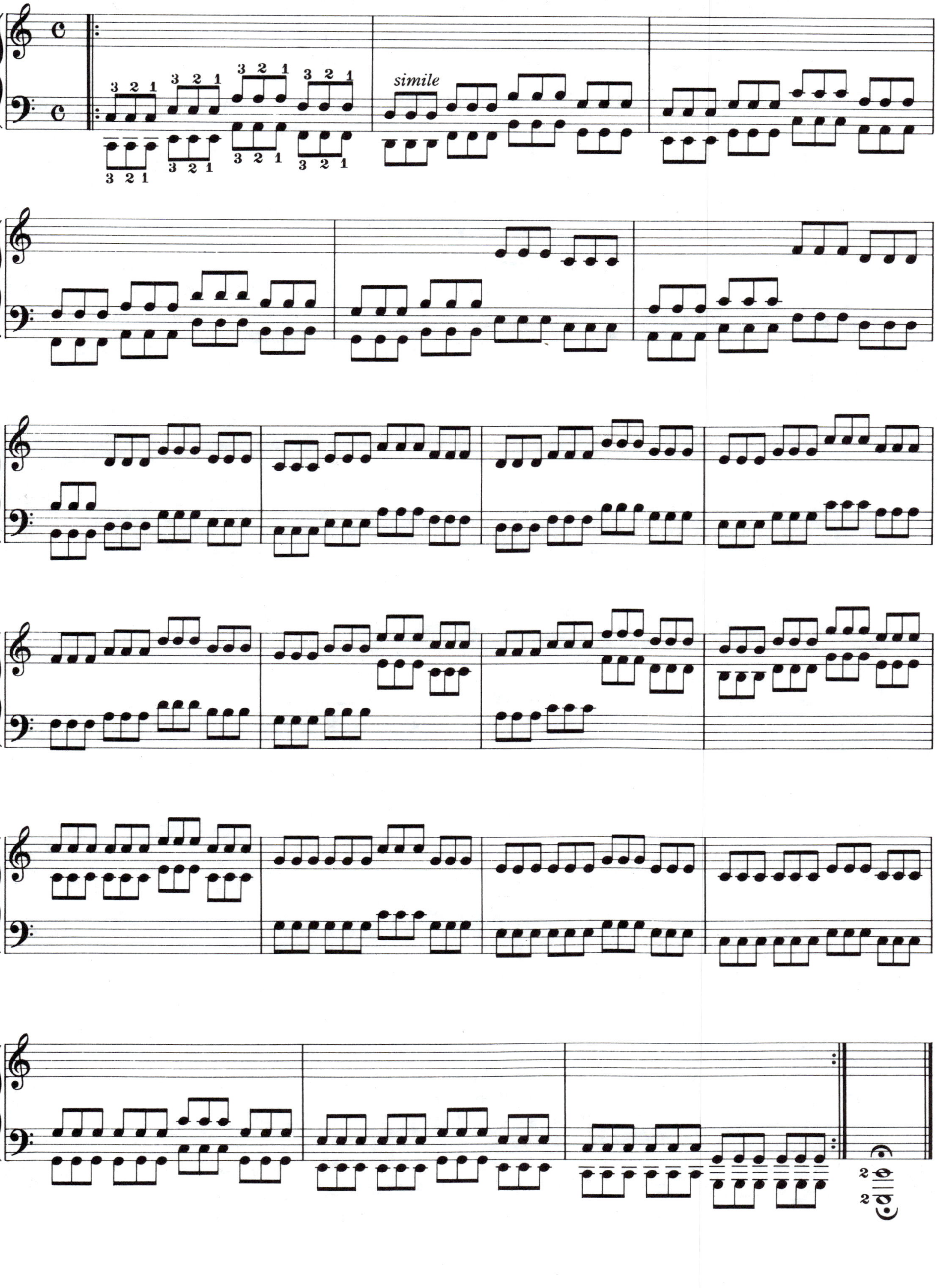
simile

Repeated Notes in Groups of Two

Study the 1st fingering until it is thoroughly mastered. Practice each of the others similarly, then play through the entire exercise without stopping.

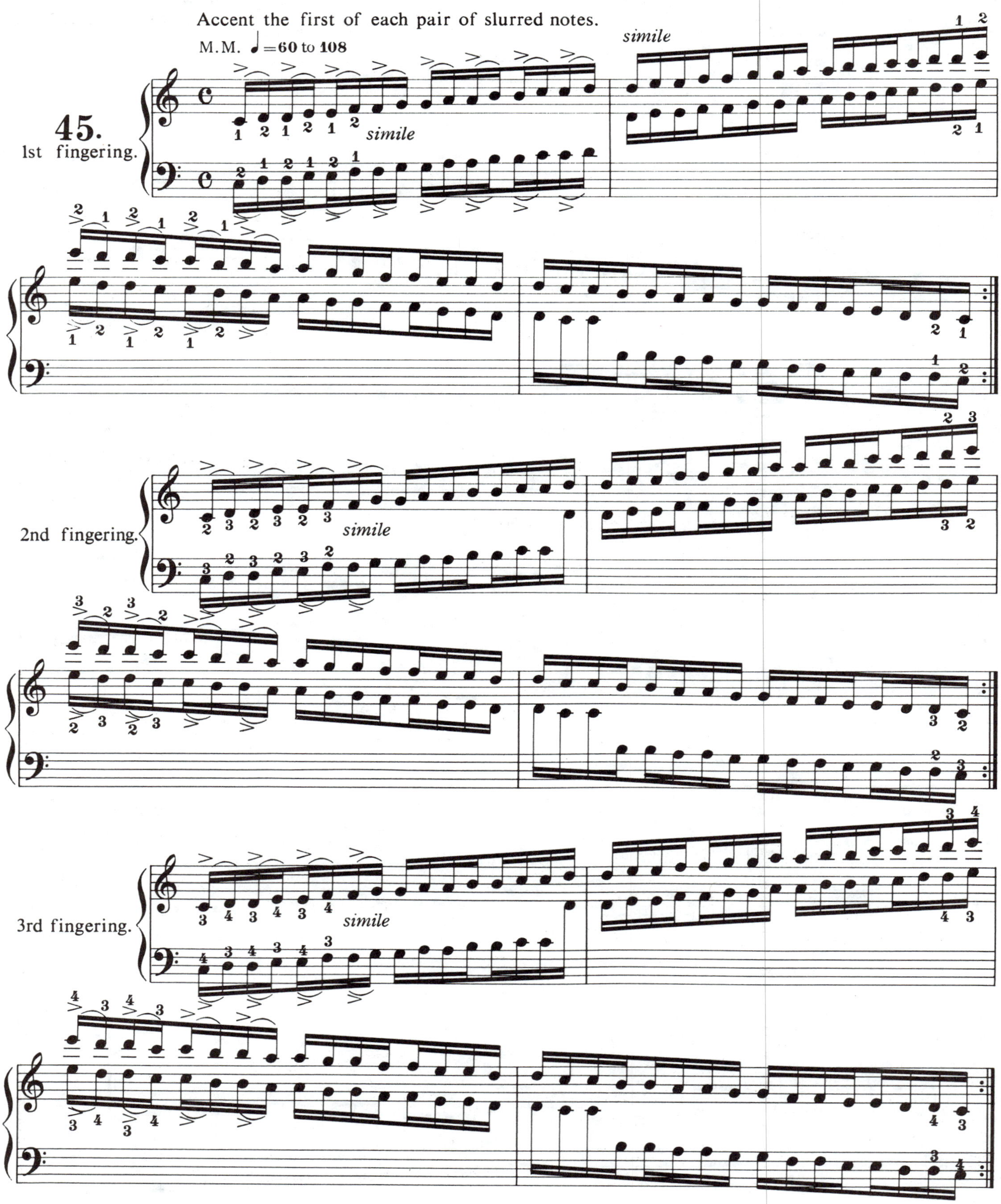

4th fingering.

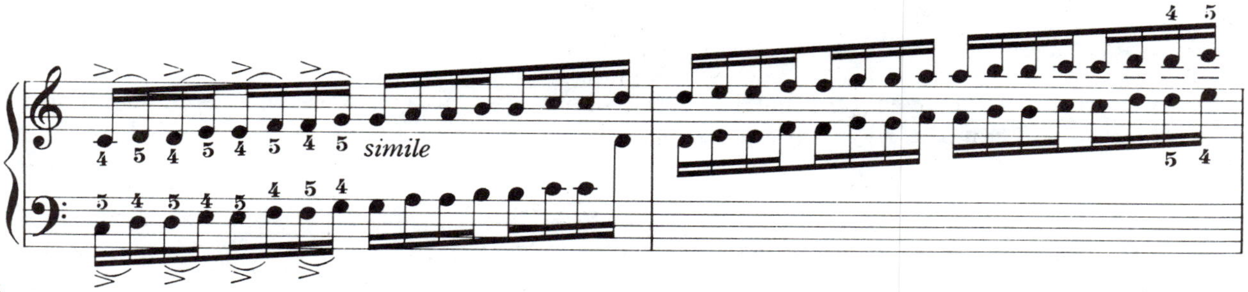

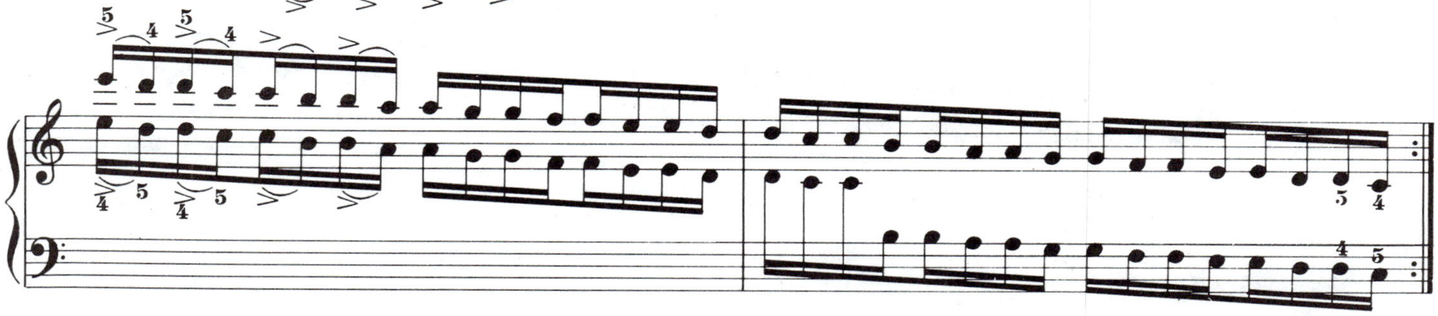

5th fingering.

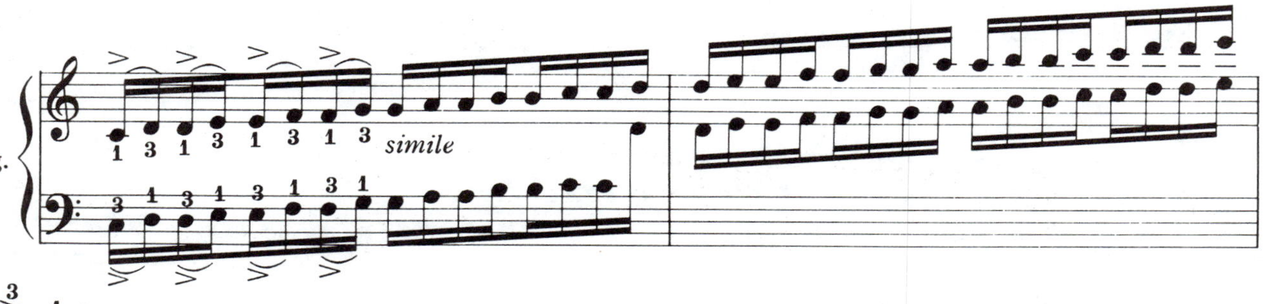

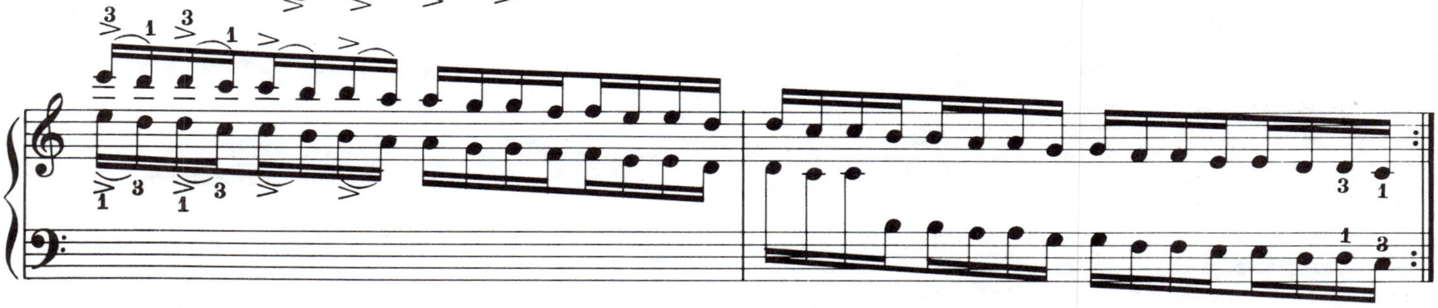

6th fingering.

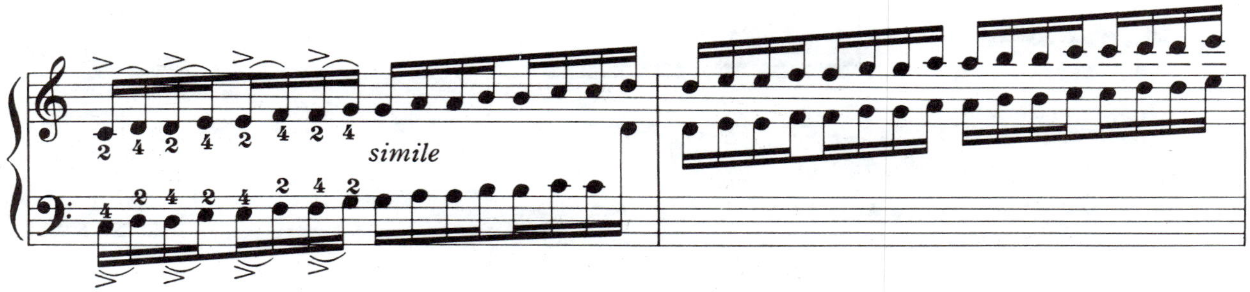

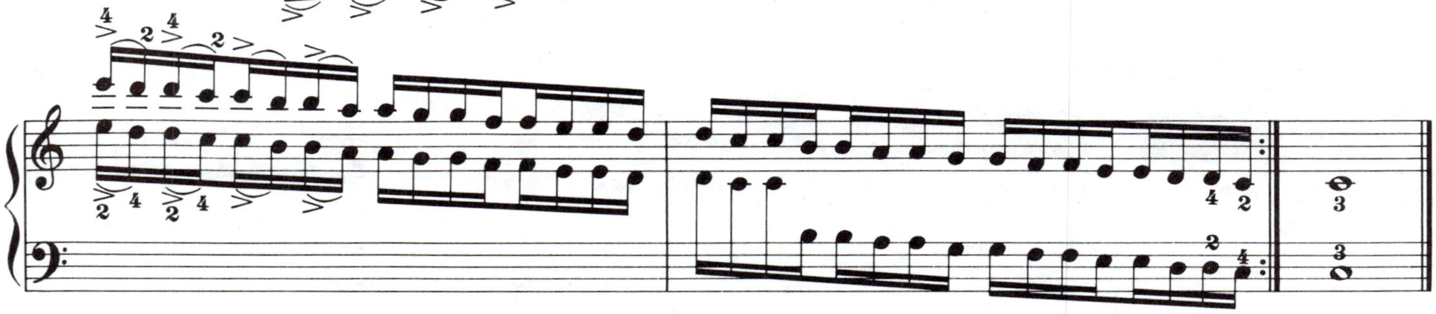

The Trill

Practice the first six measures until they can be played at a very rapid tempo, then continue through the exercise. When the fingering changes (*) in the middle of a measure, make the change smoothly.

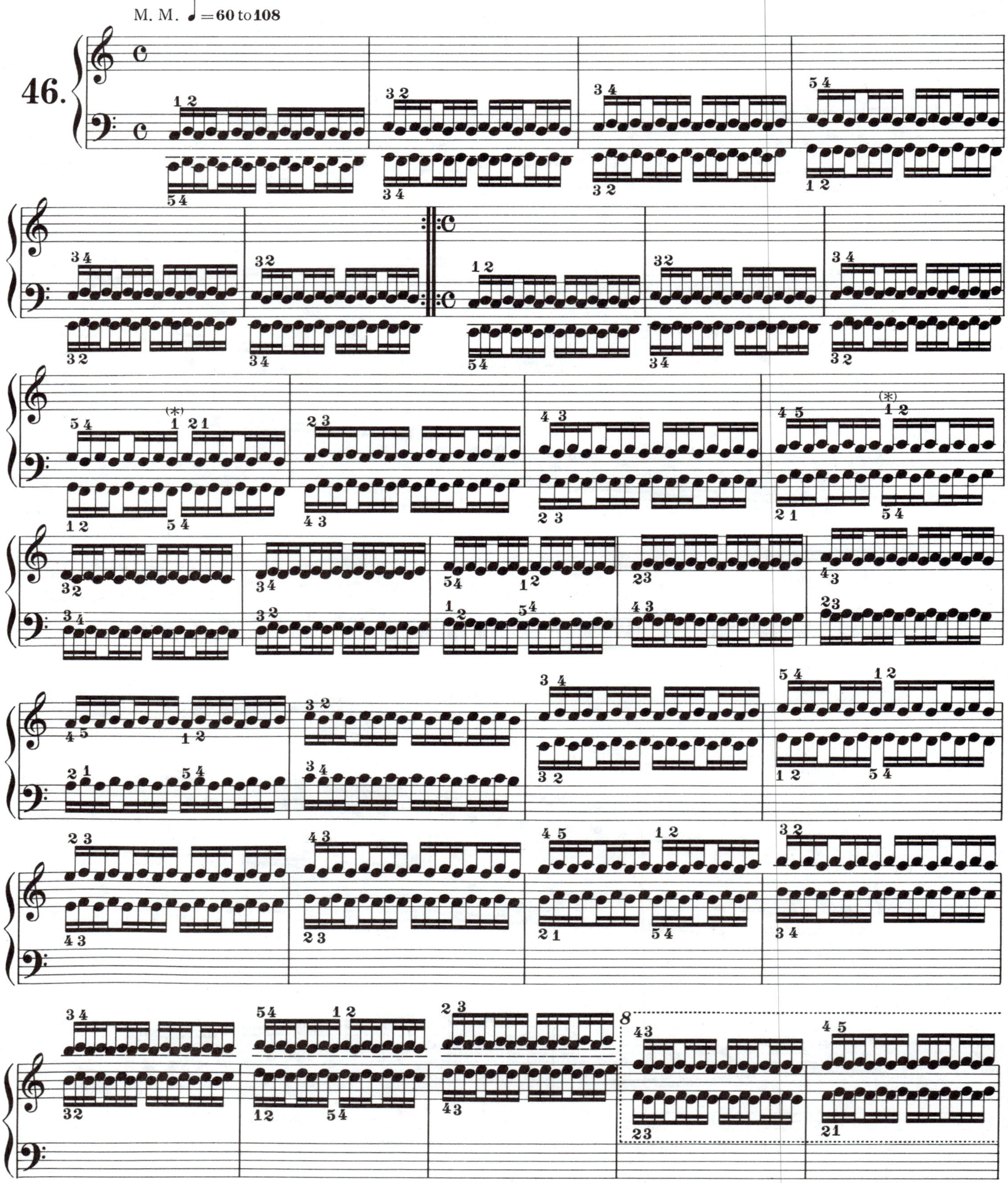

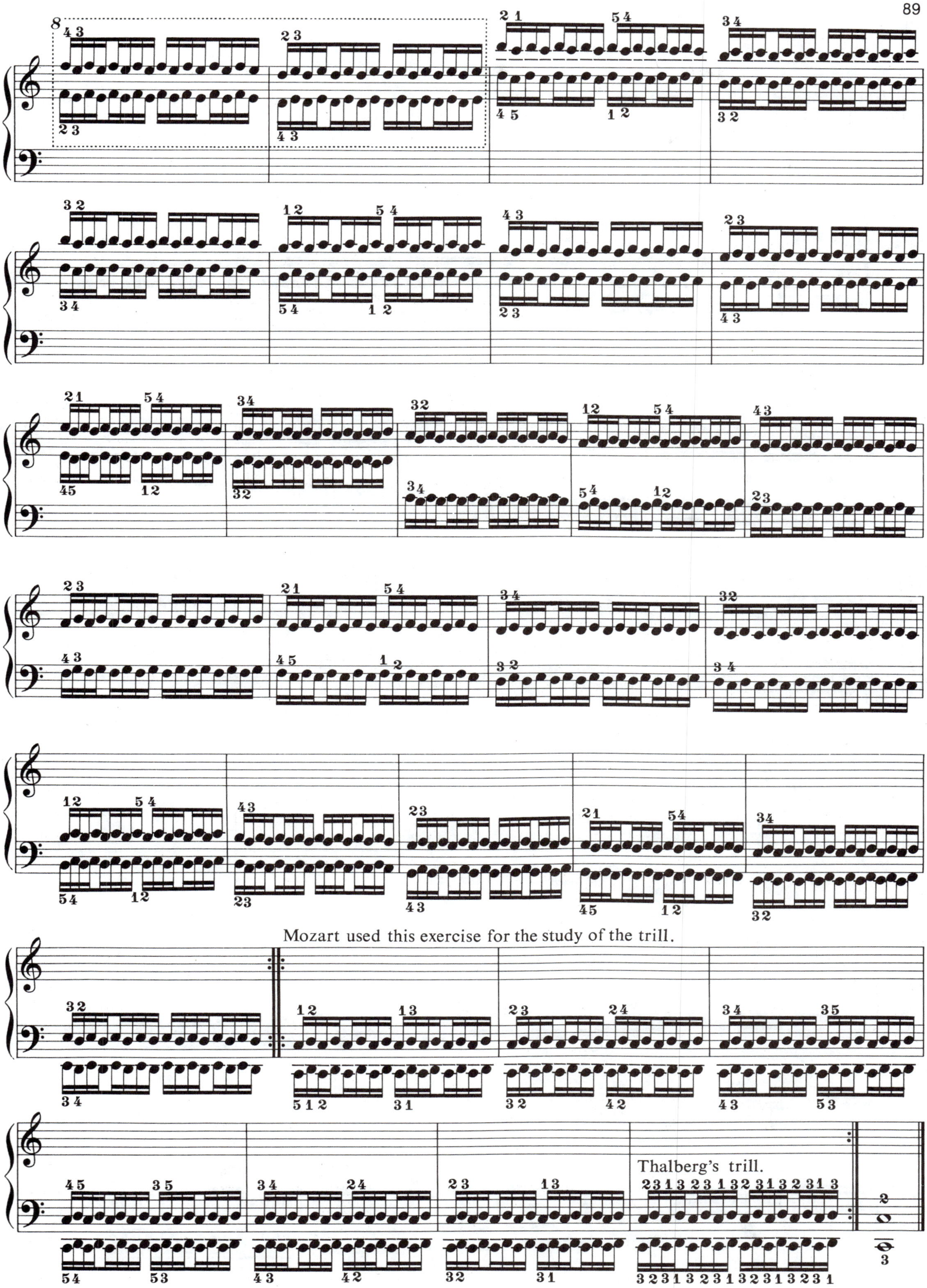
Mozart used this exercise for the study of the trill.
Thalberg's trill.

Repeated Notes in Groups of Four

Lift the fingers high and with precision throughout this exercise, without raising the hand or wrist. When the first line is mastered, practice the rest of the exercise.

47.

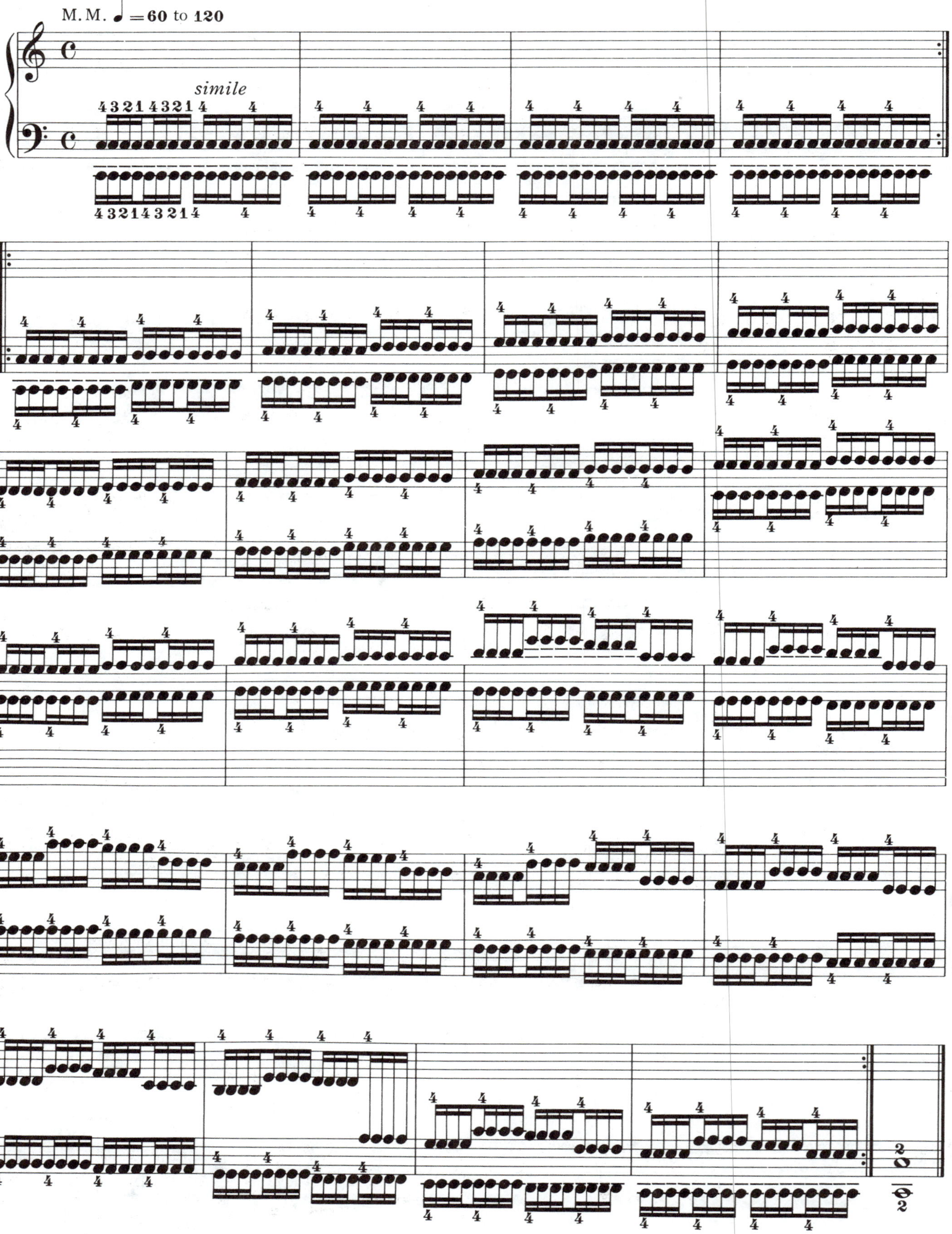

Wrist Exercise Using Detached Thirds

Lift the wrists after each stroke, holding the arms motionless. The wrists should be flexible and the fingers firm without being rigid. Practice the first four measures until an easy wrist movement is achieved, then play the rest of the exercise.

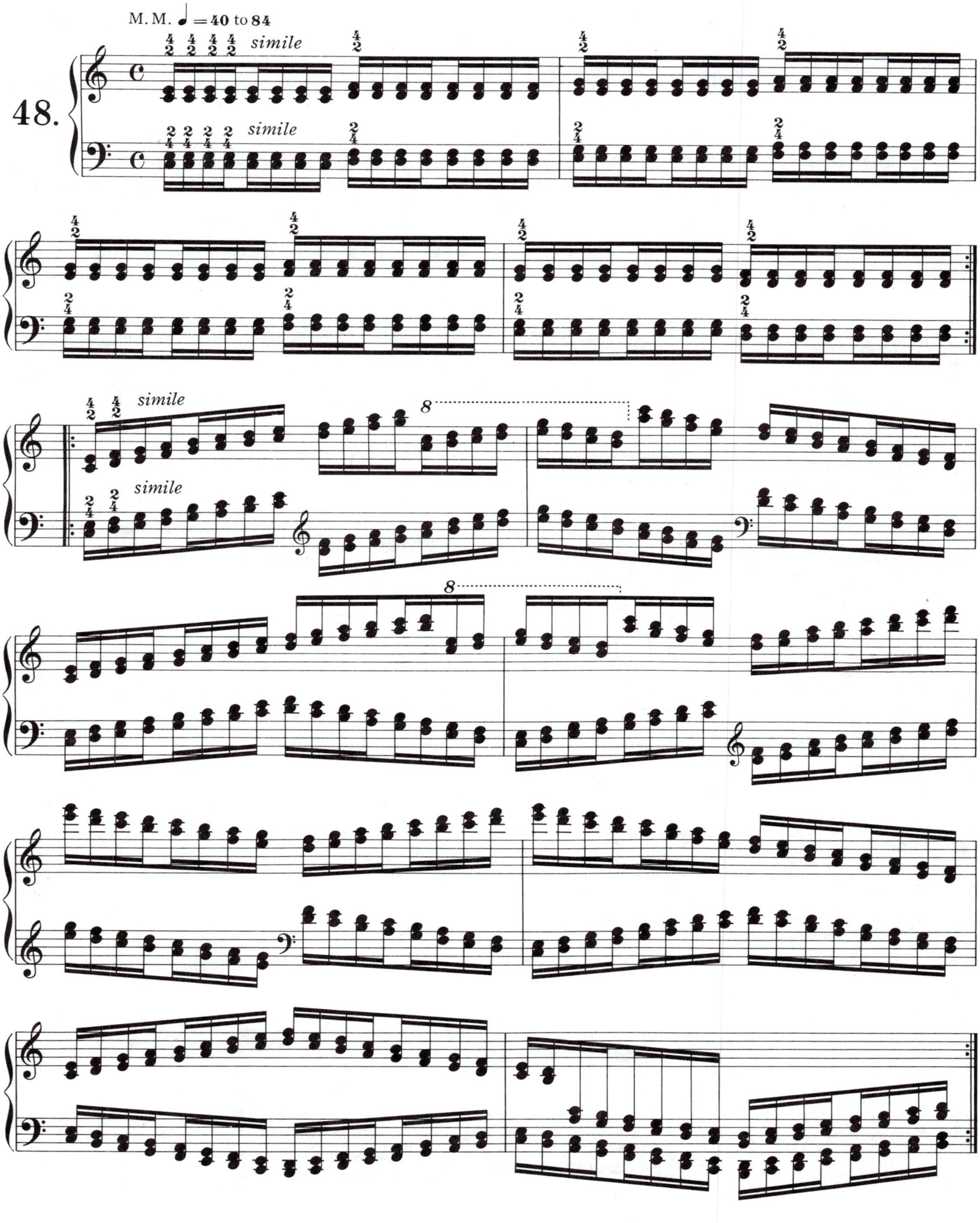

Wrist Exercise Using Detached Sixths

Same comments as for the thirds.

M. M. ♩ = 40 to 84

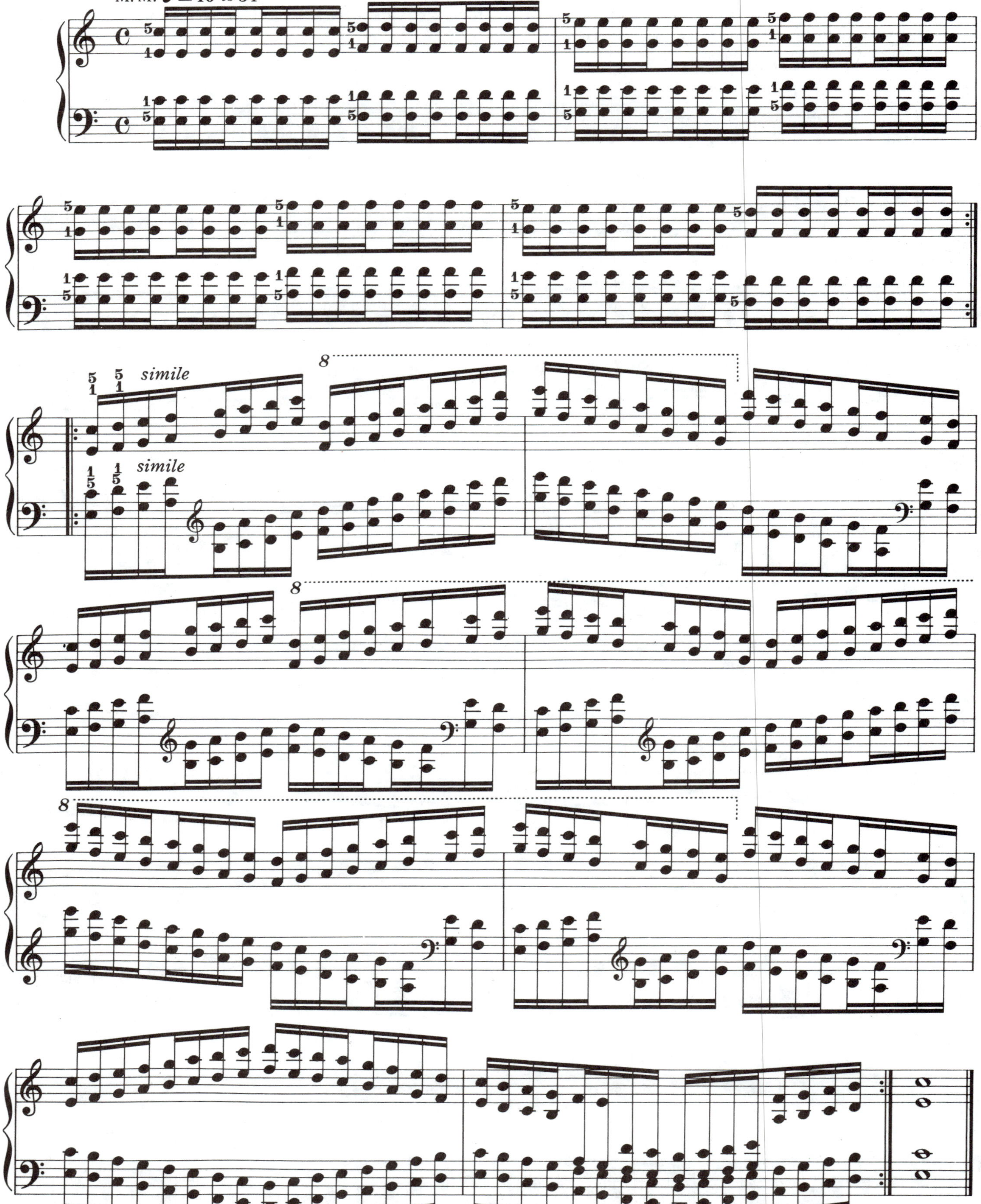

Stretches from the 1st to the 4th fingers, and from the 2nd to the 5th, in each hand.

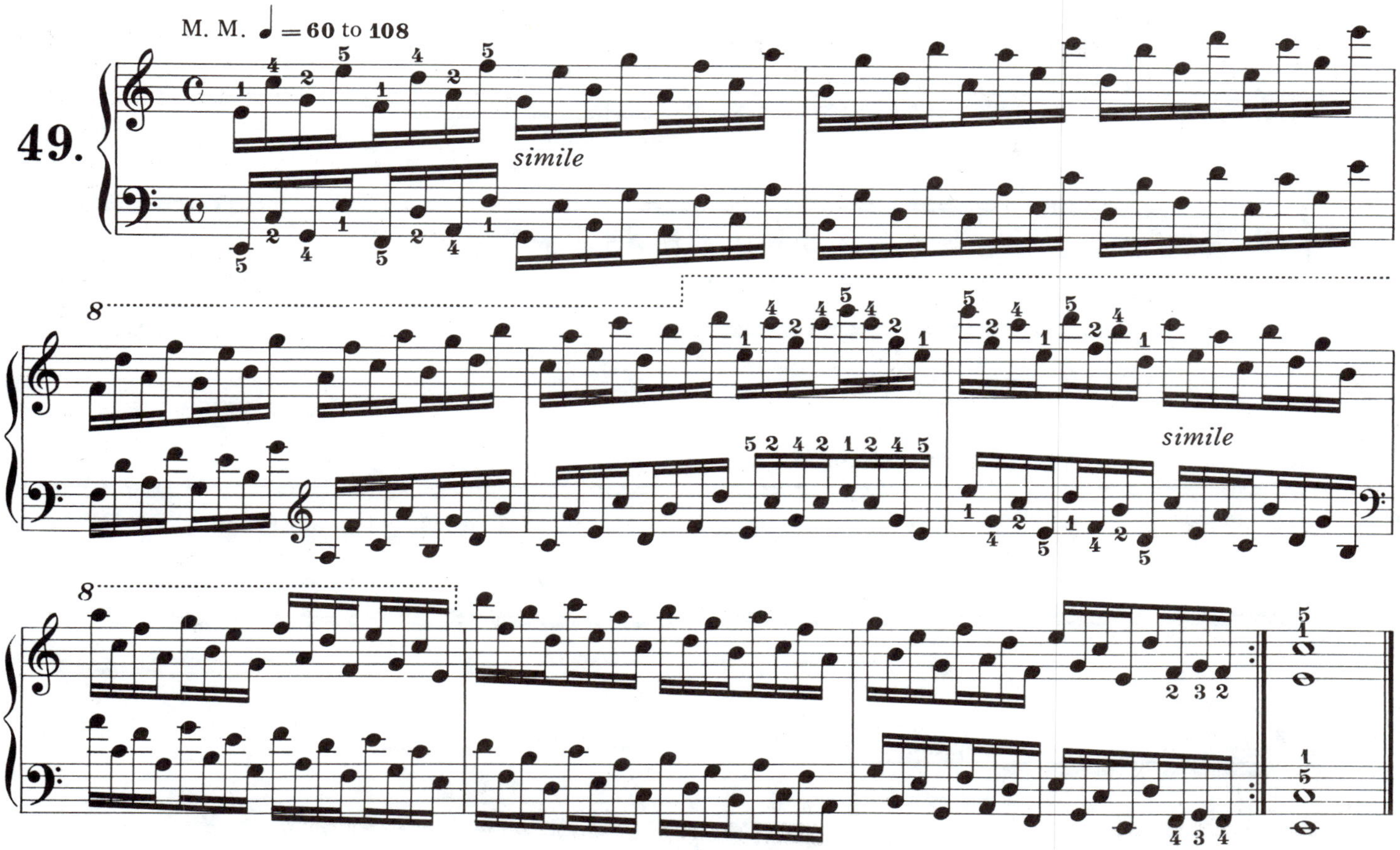

Continuation of the preceding exercise.

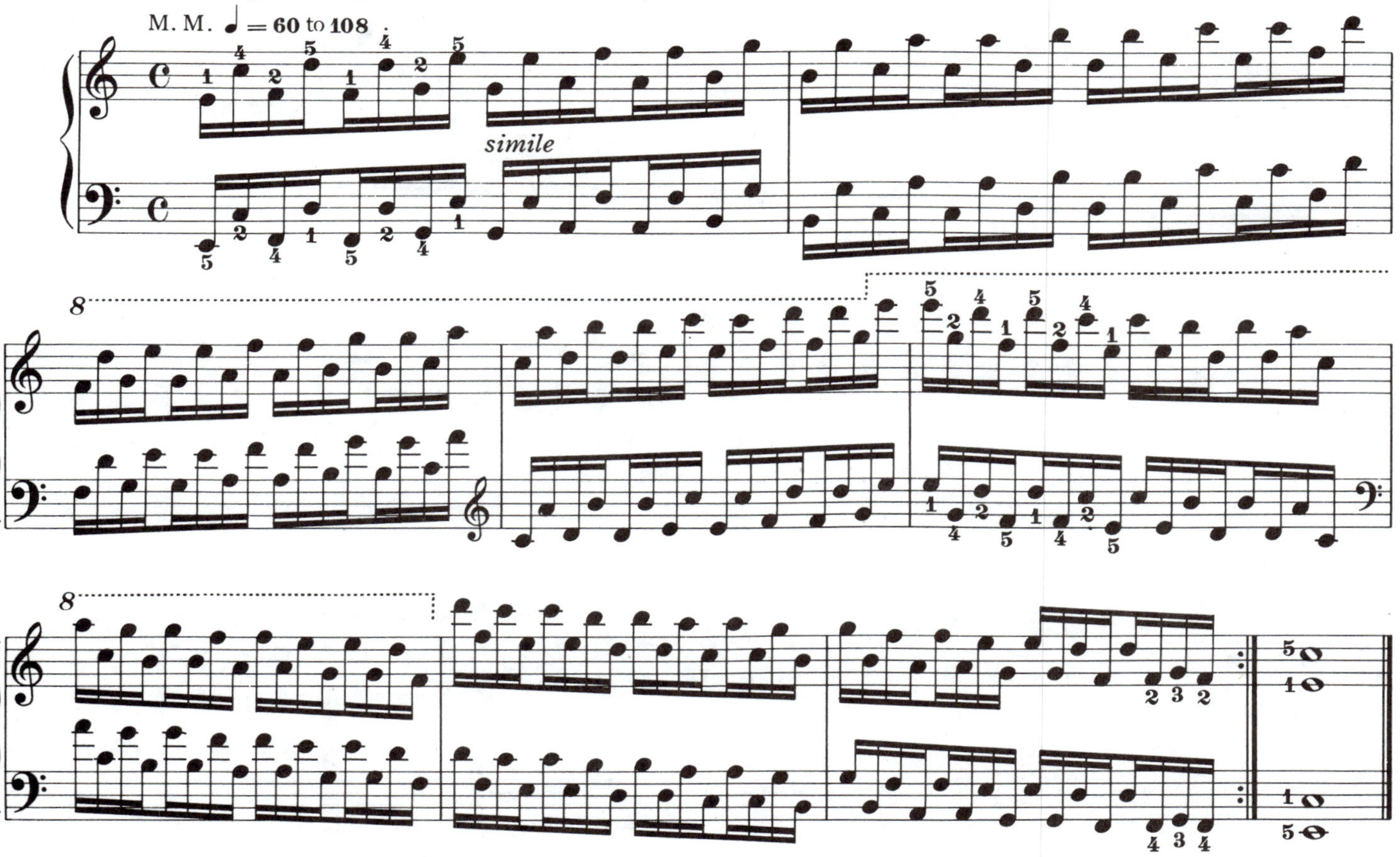

Legato Thirds

We recommend careful study of this exercise, as thirds are used extensively in difficult music. All notes must be struck evenly and distinctly.

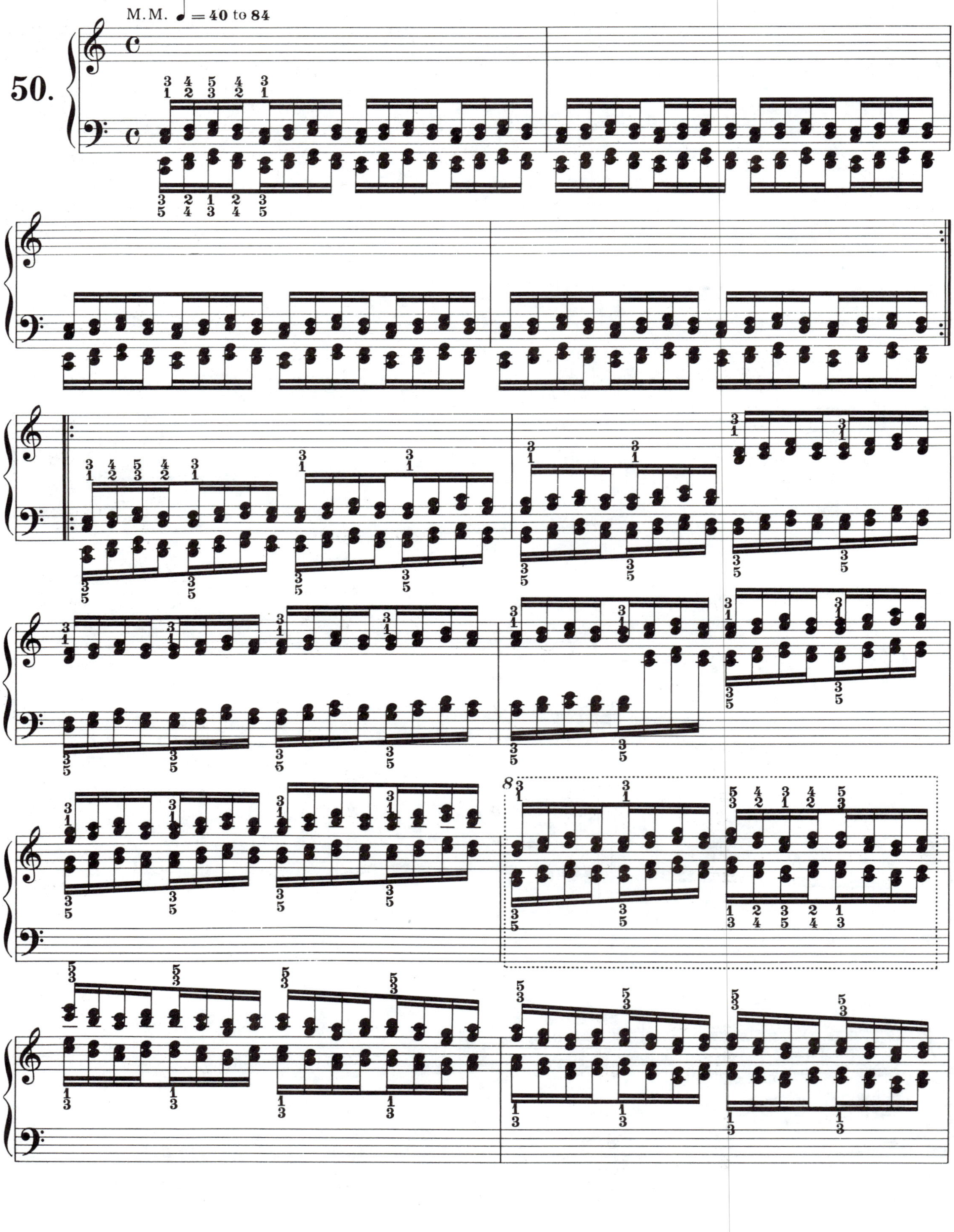

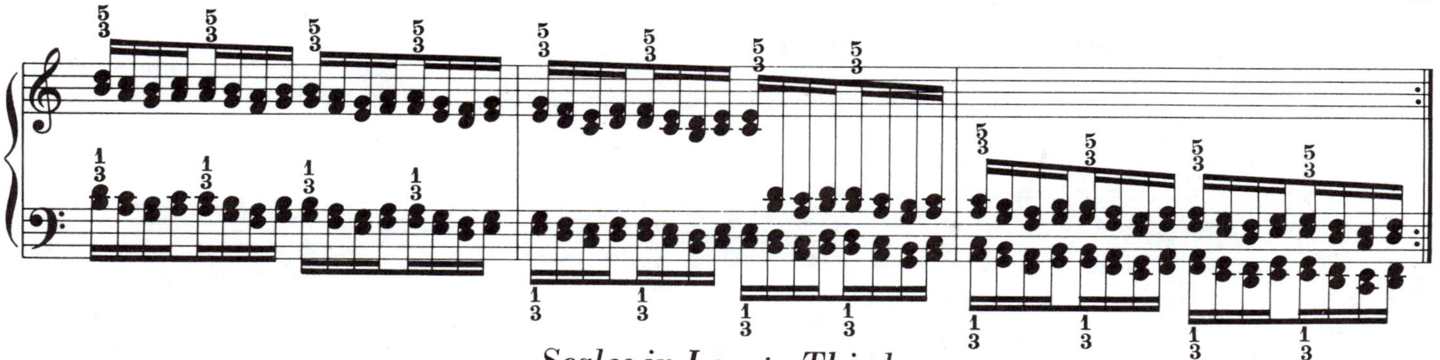

Scales in Legato Thirds

To achieve a smooth legato, keep the 5th finger of the right hand on its note for an instant while the thumb and 3rd finger are passing over to the next third. In the left hand, the thumb is similarly held for an instant. Notes to be held are indicated by half notes (*). Proceed similarly in the chromatic scale further on, and in all scales in thirds.

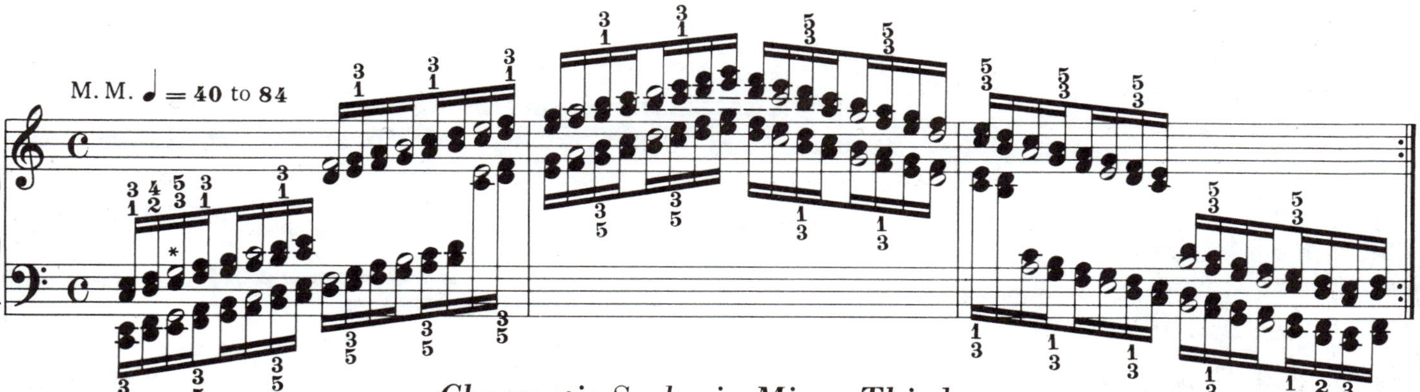

Chromatic Scales in Minor Thirds

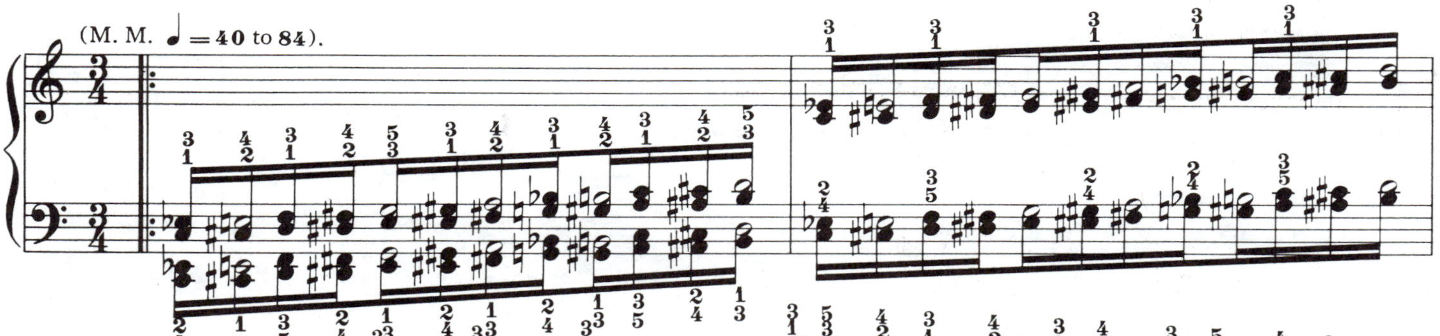

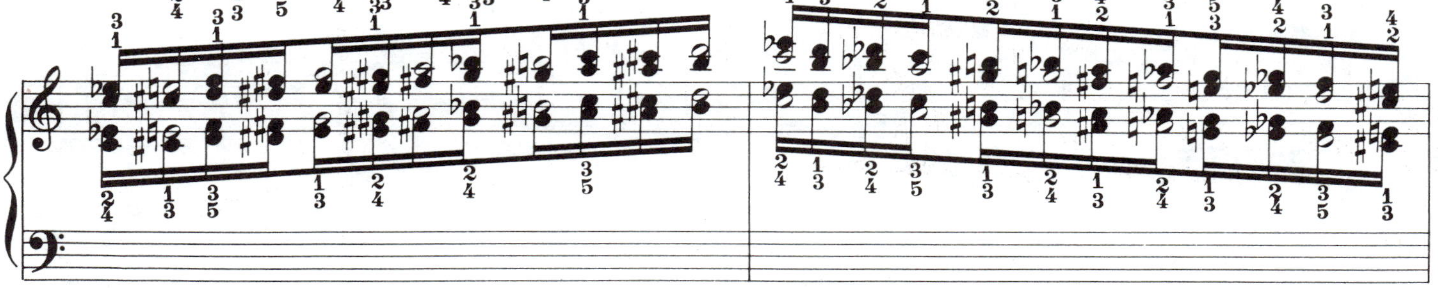

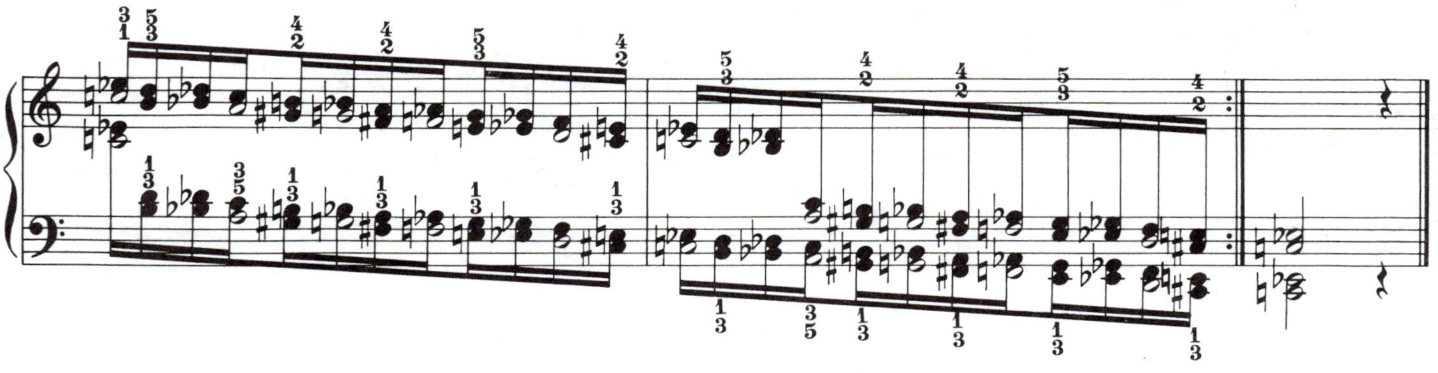

Preparatory Exercise for Scales in Octaves

The wrists should be very flexible. The fingers playing the octaves should be held firmly but not rigid, while the other fingers remain in a slightly rounded position.
Repeat the first three lines slowly until a good wrist movement is achieved. Then accelerate the tempo and continue the exercise without stopping. If the wrists become tired, play slowly for a while, then gradually increase the tempo again.

51.

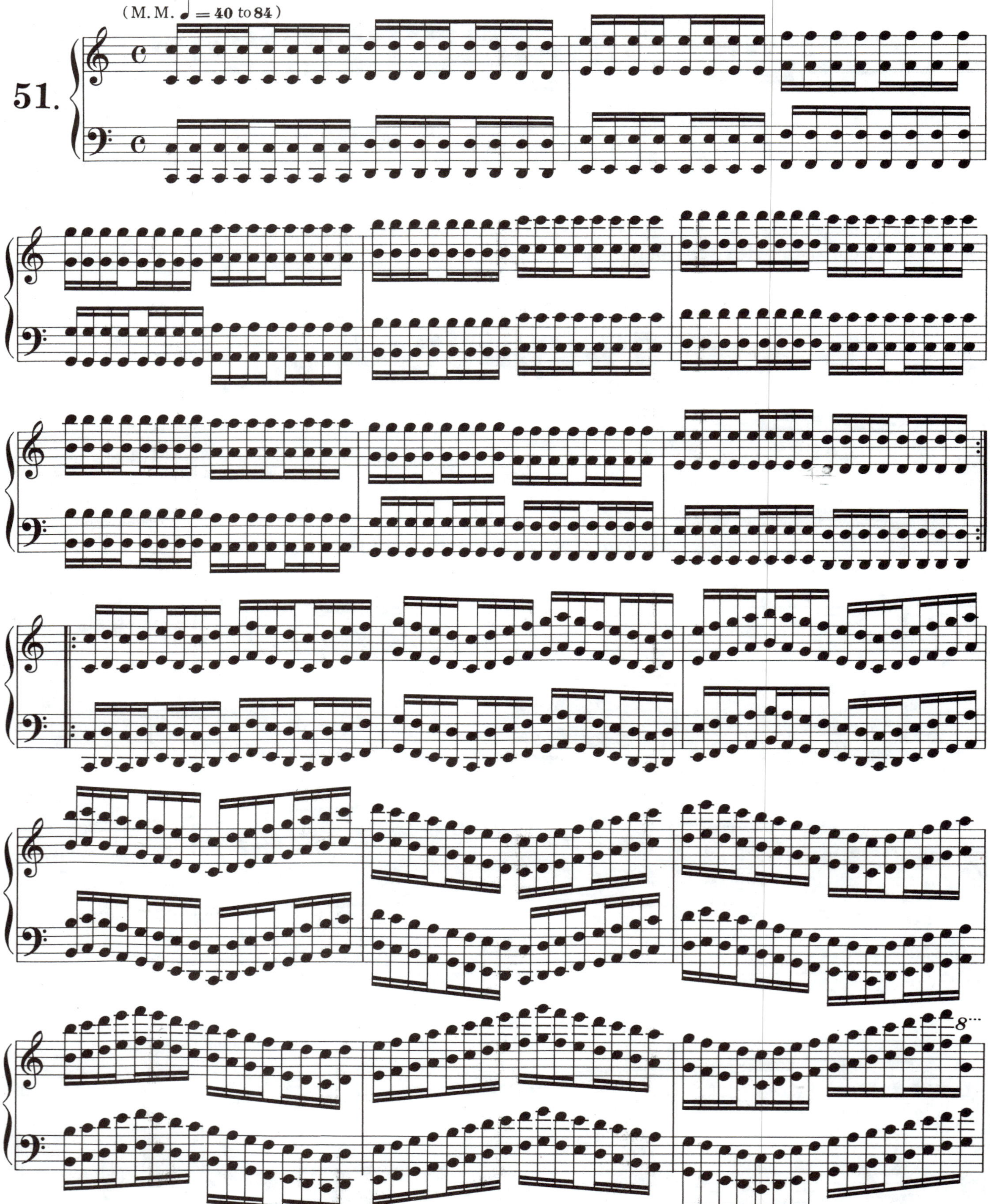

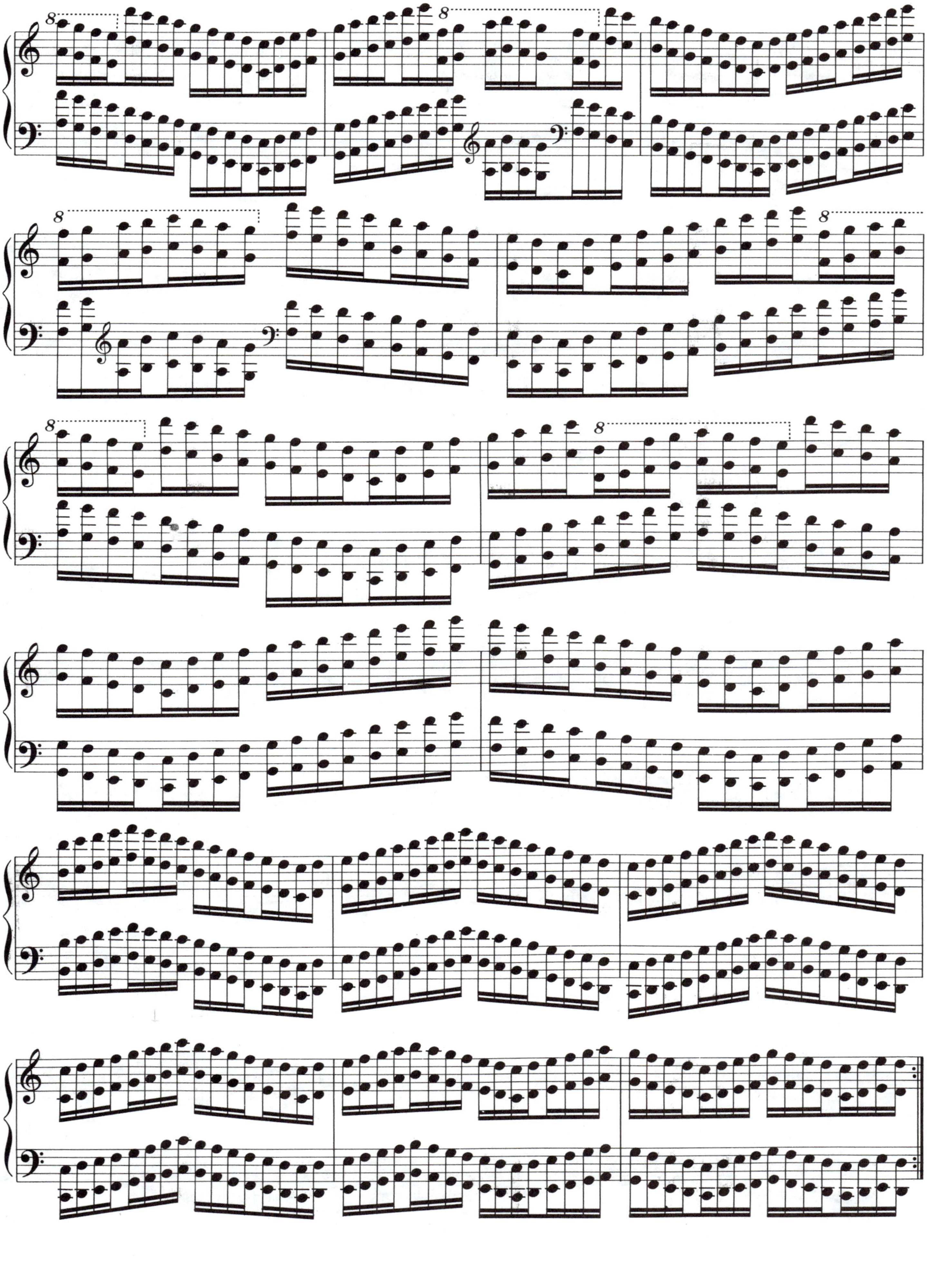

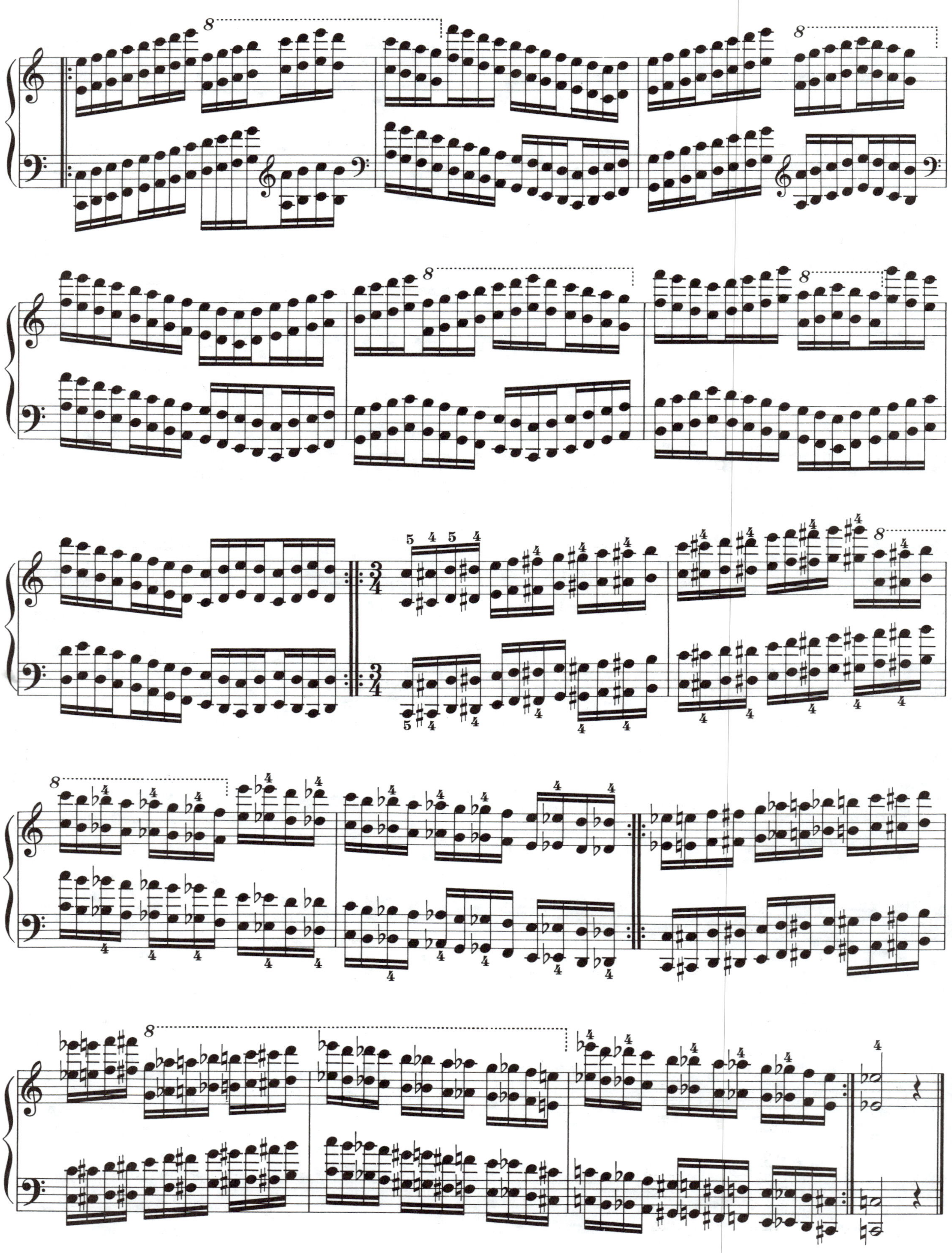

Scales in Thirds, in the Most Used Keys

Play these scales legato and very evenly. It is important to master them thoroughly. See comments to No. 50.

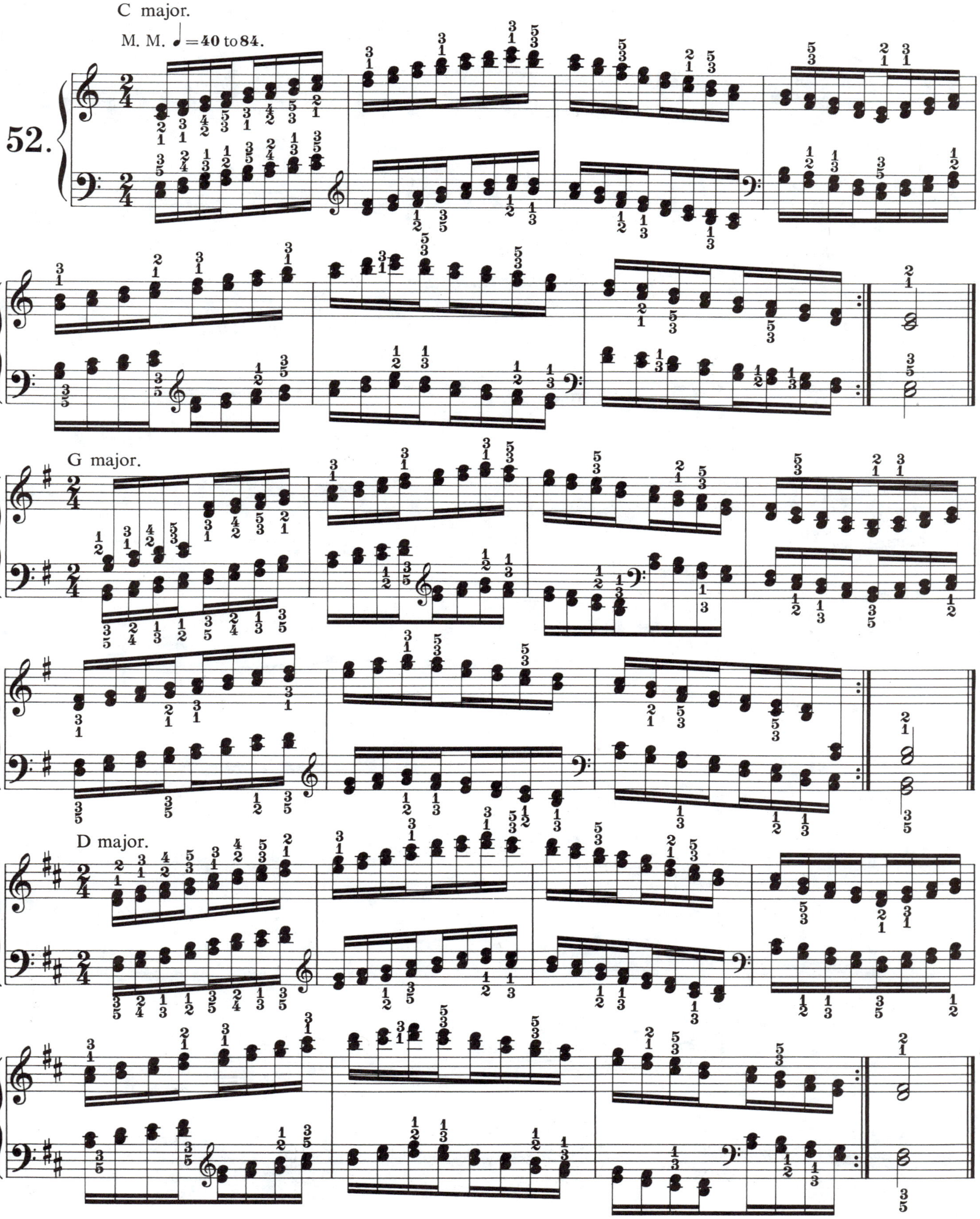

A major.

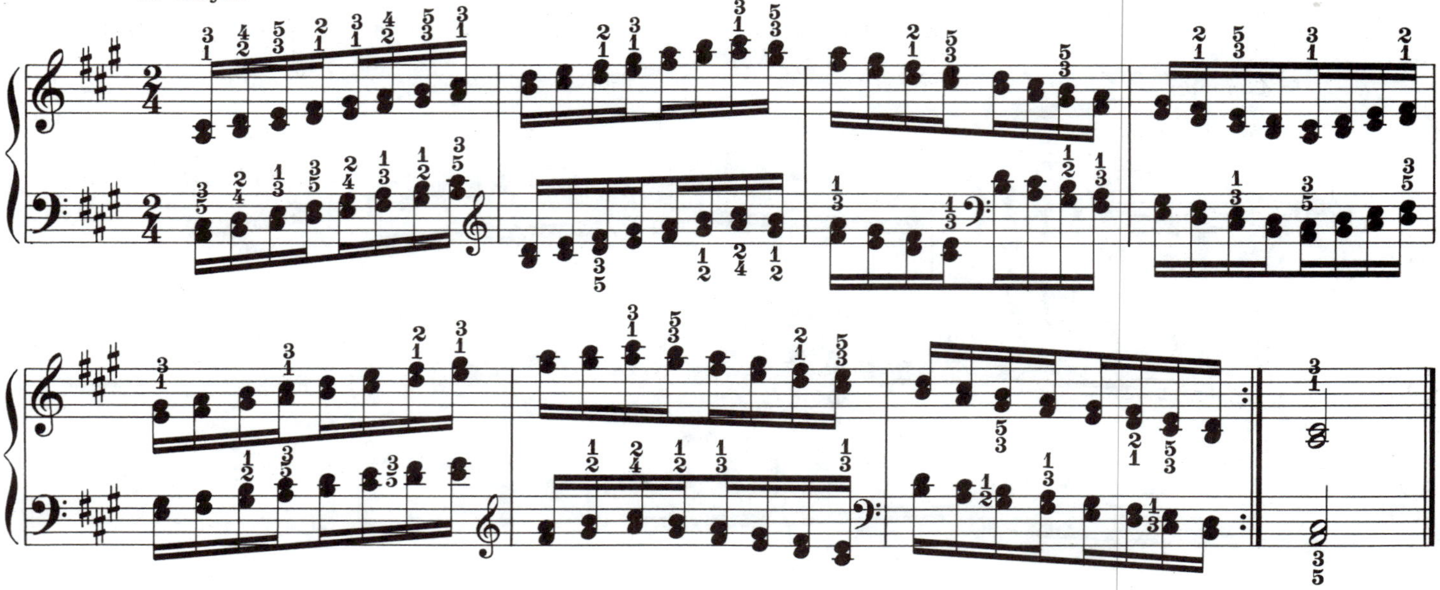

E major.

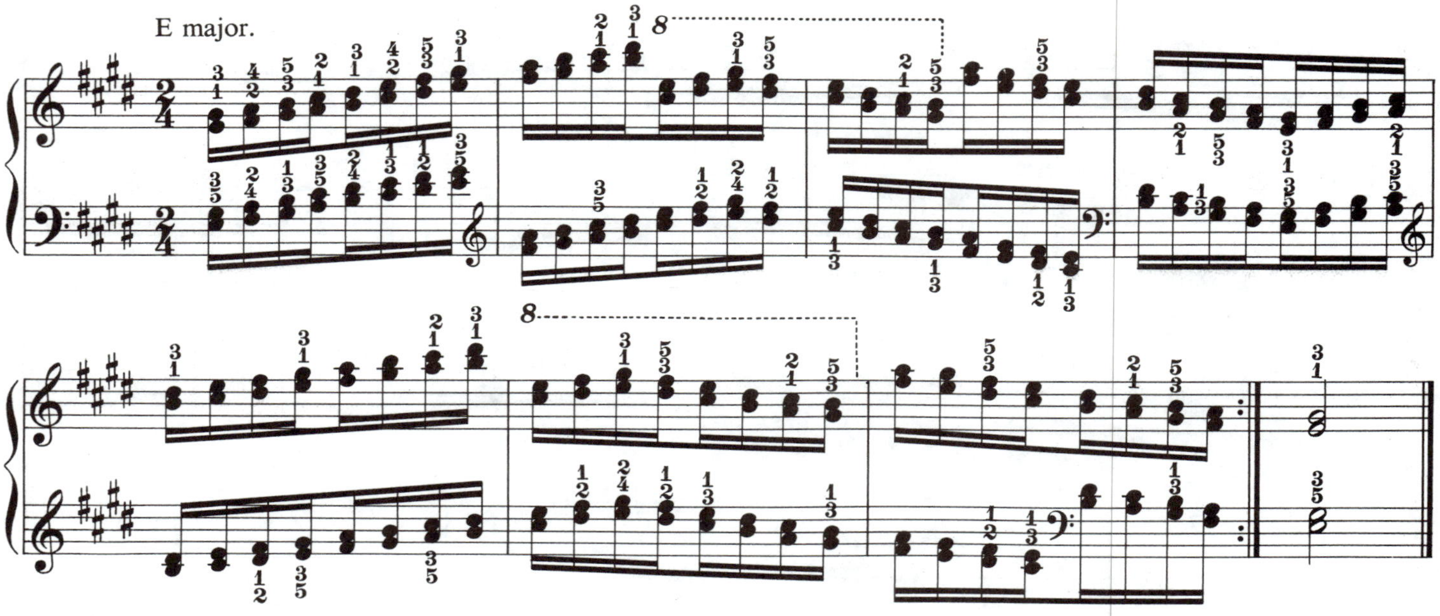

F major.

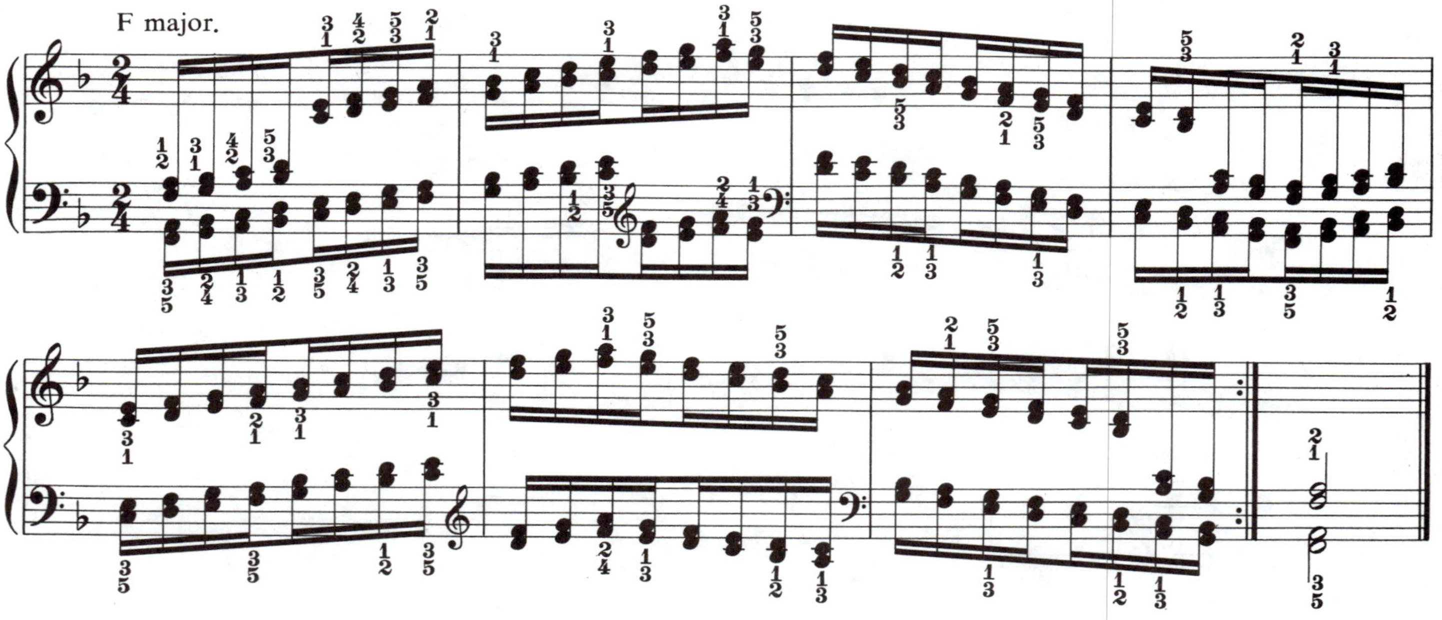

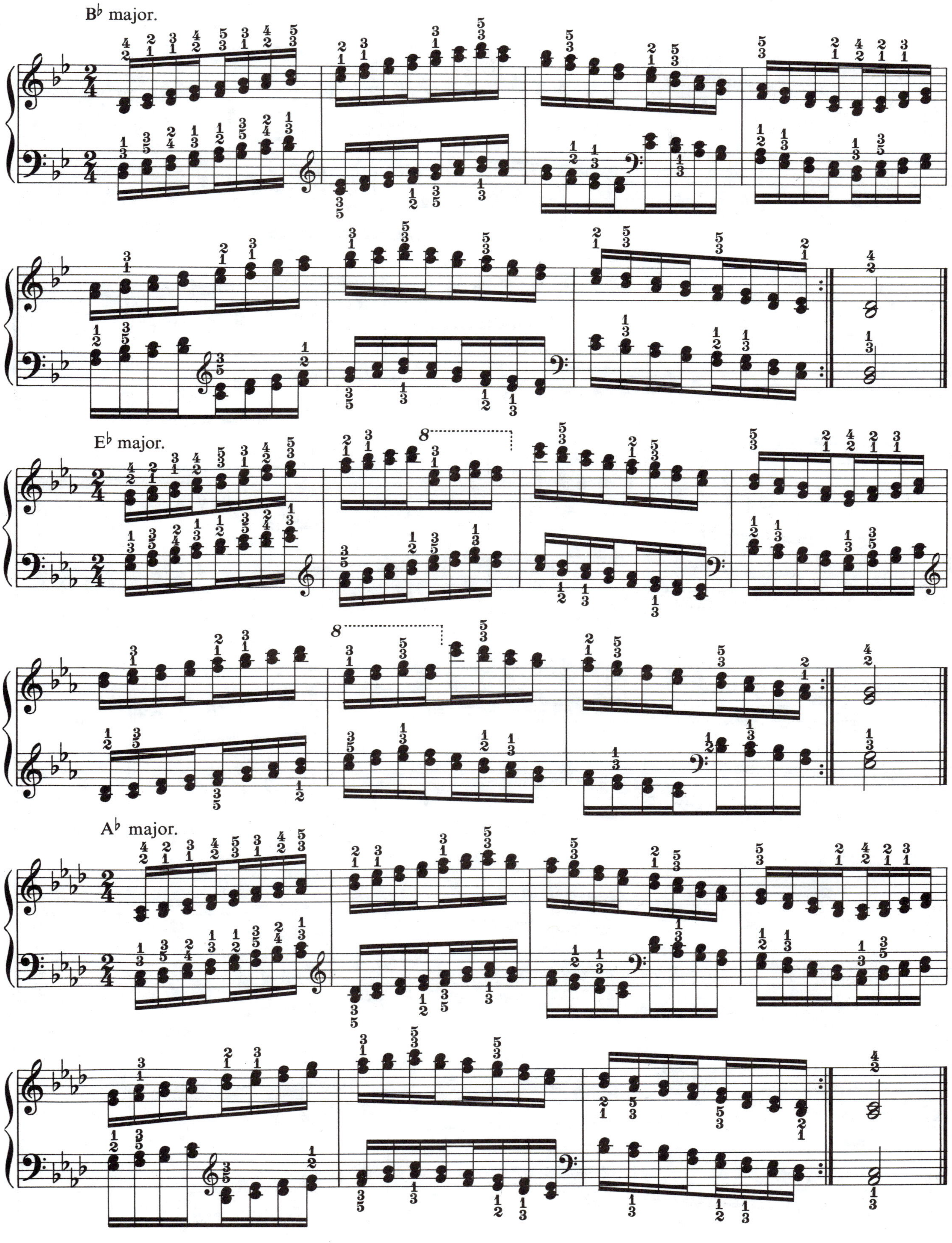
B♭ major.
E♭ major.
A♭ major.

A minor.

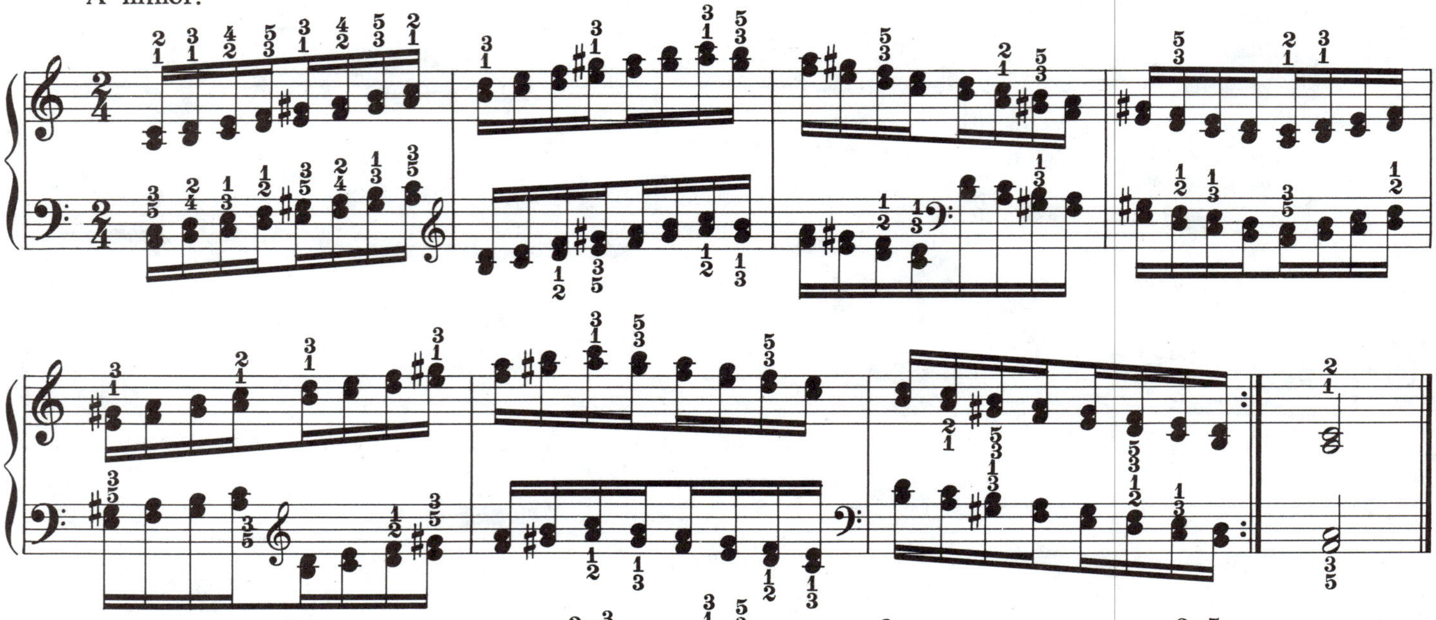

D minor.

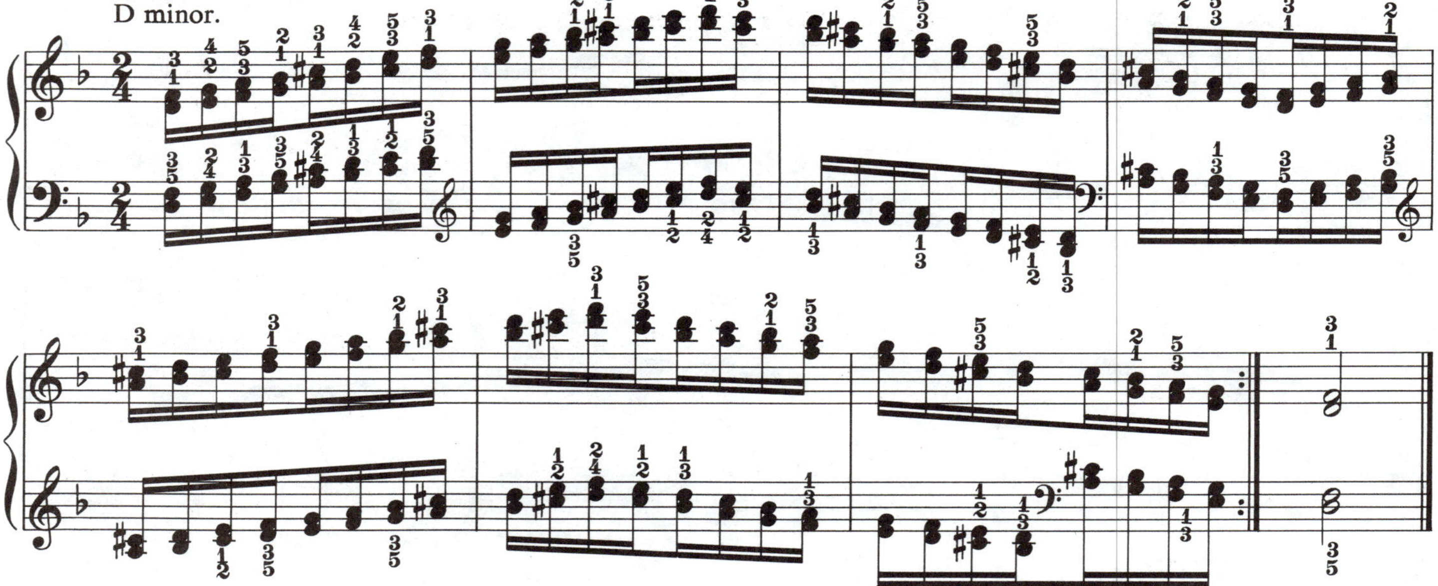

G minor.

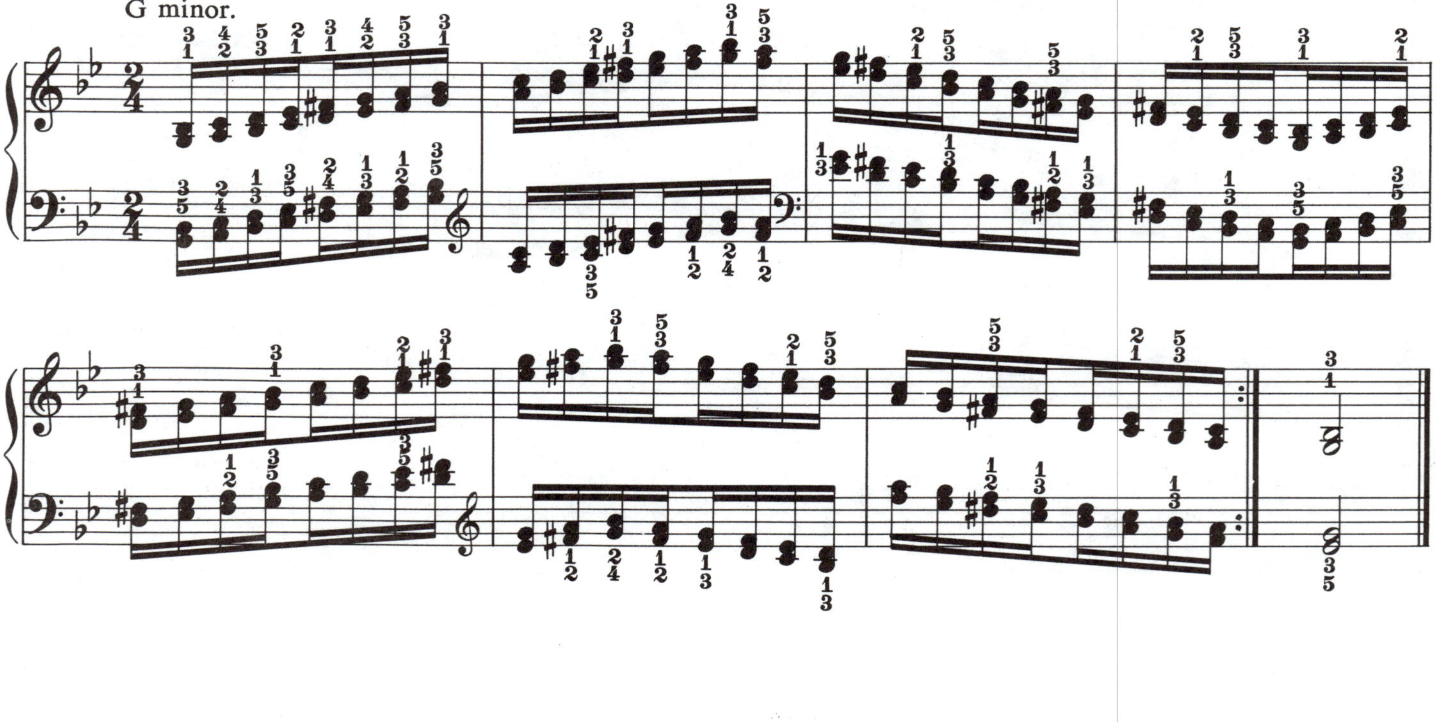

Scales in Octaves in the 24 Keys

Practice each of the scales until they can be played easily, then play through all 24 without stopping. To play octaves rapidly and with vigor, proper wrist movement is essential. The wrist must be flexible and not rigid.

In playing octave scales, the black keys may be played with the 4th finger. See comment to Nos. 48 and 51.

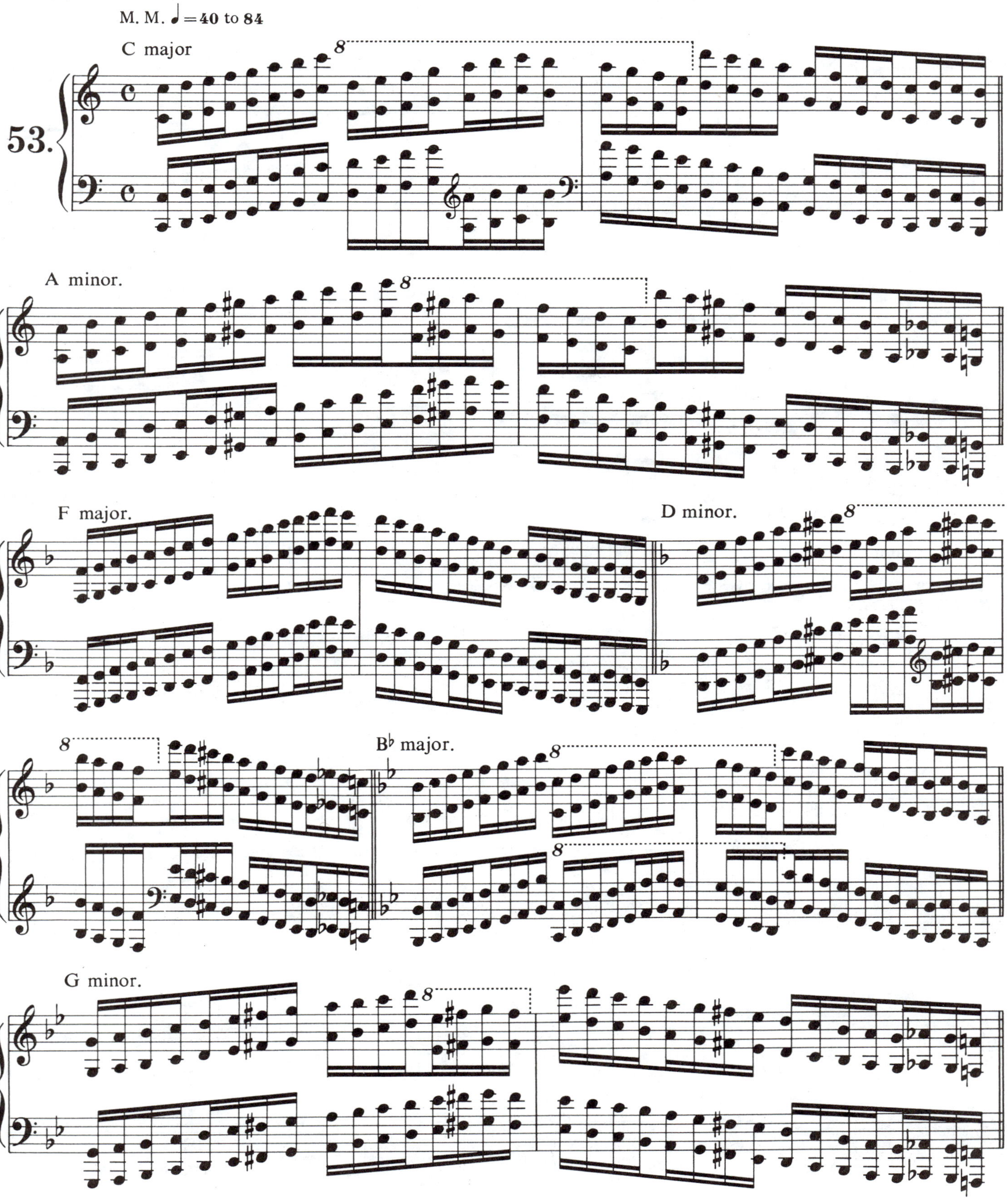

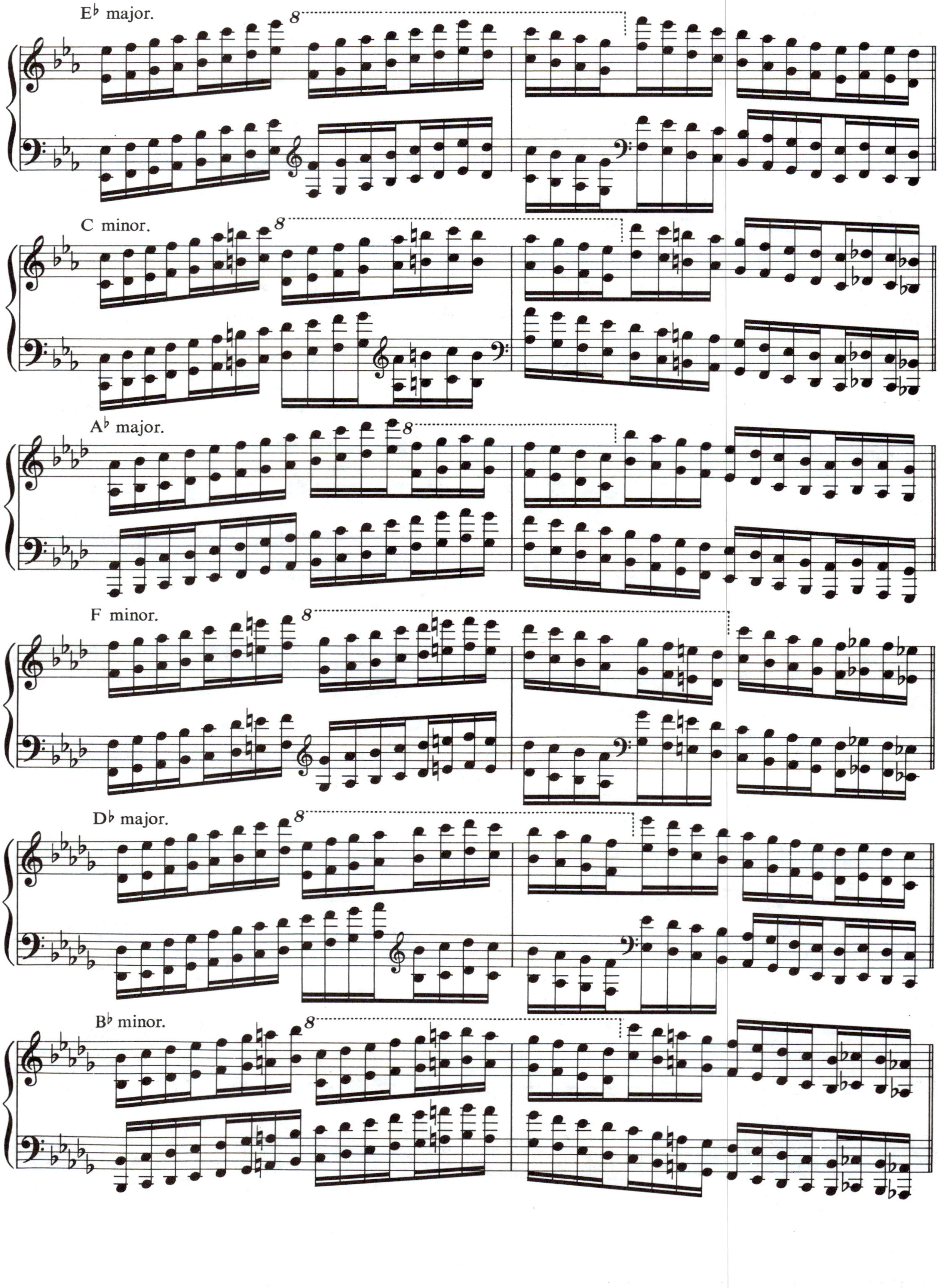
E♭ major.
8
C minor.
8
A♭ major.
8
F minor.
8
D♭ major.
8
B♭ minor.
8

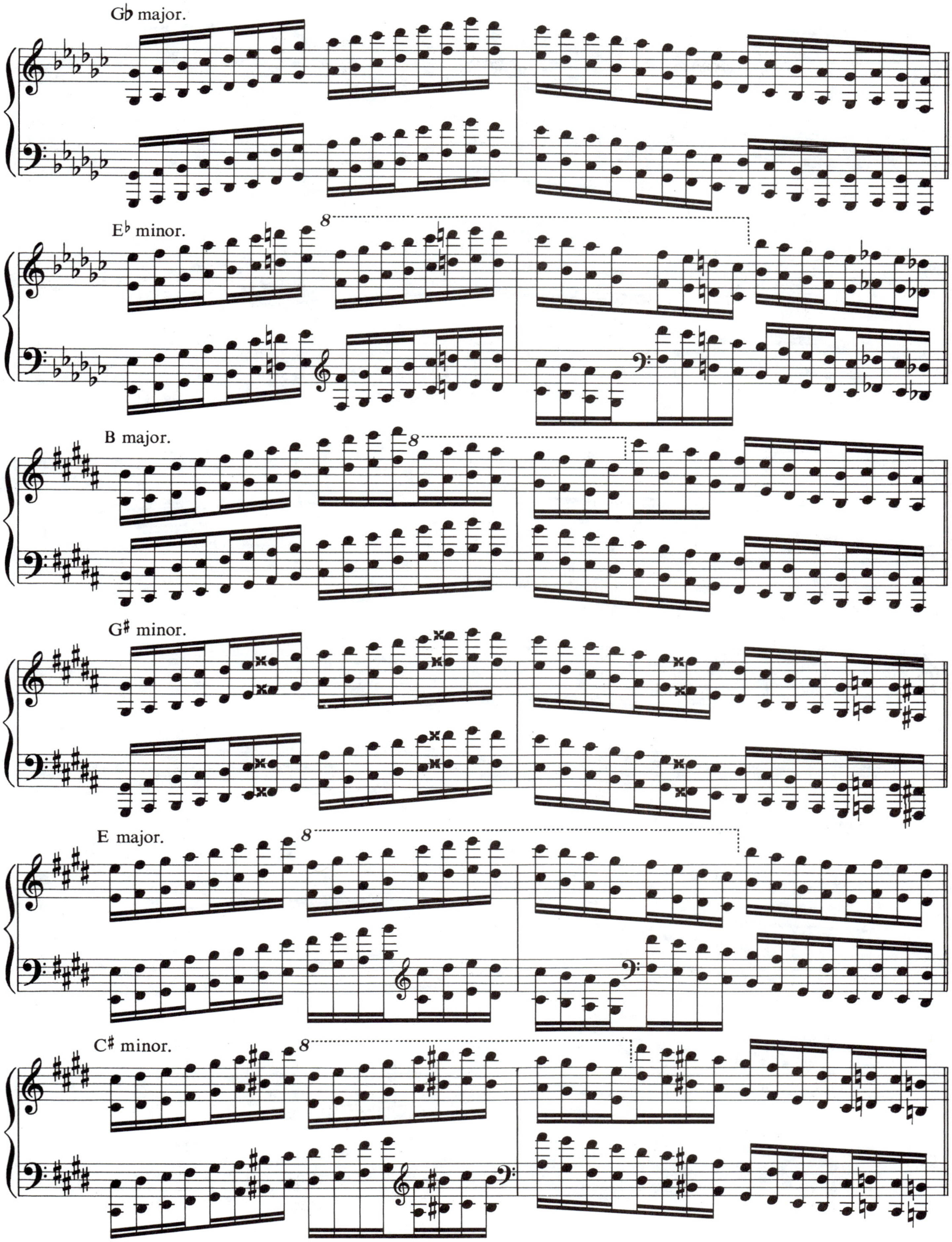
G♭ major.
E♭ minor.
B major.
G♯ minor.
E major.
C♯ minor.

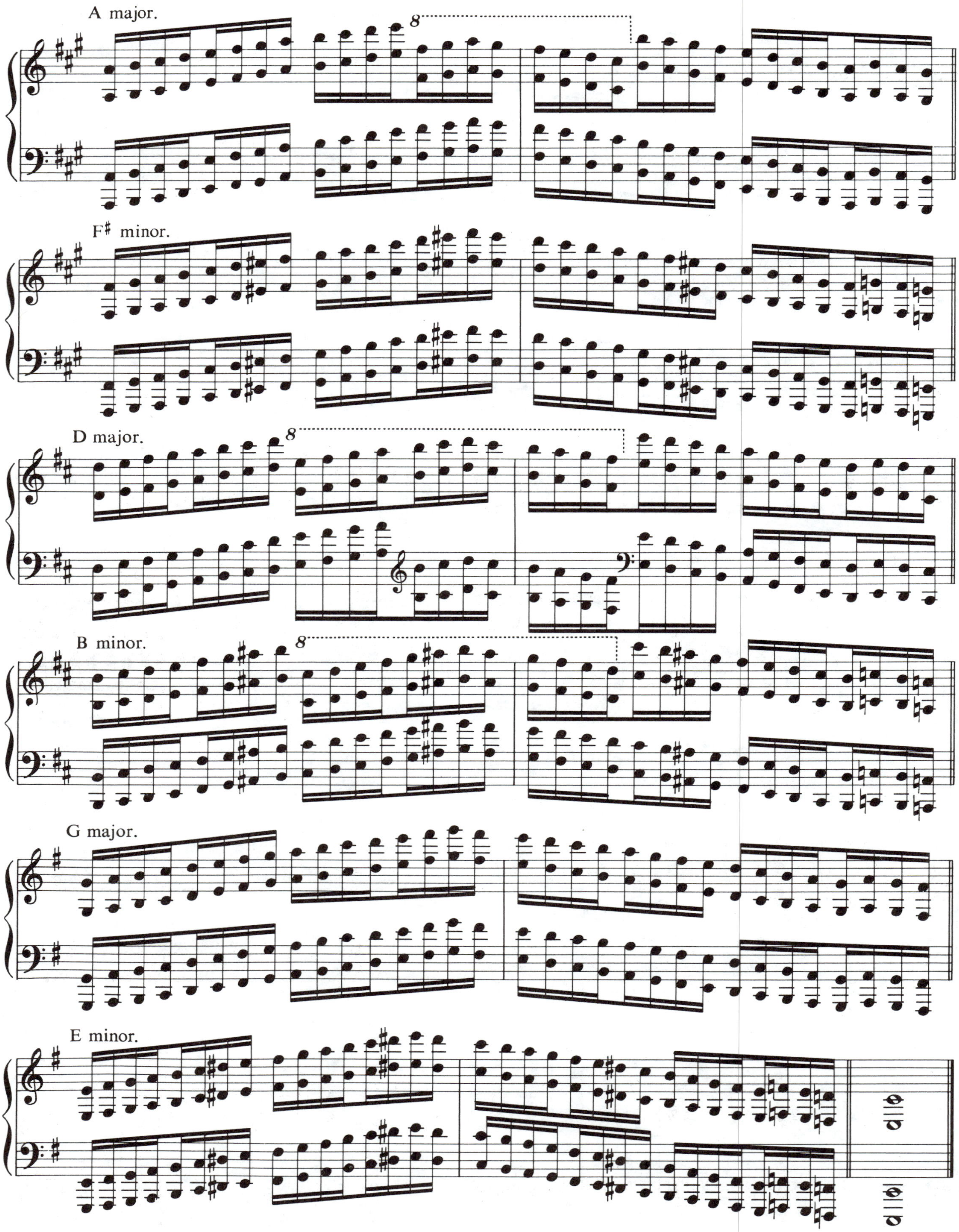
A major.
8
F♯ minor.
D major.
8
B minor.
8
G major.
E minor.

The Four-Note Trill in Thirds

Practice this exercise very smoothly and evenly, striking each third very clearly.

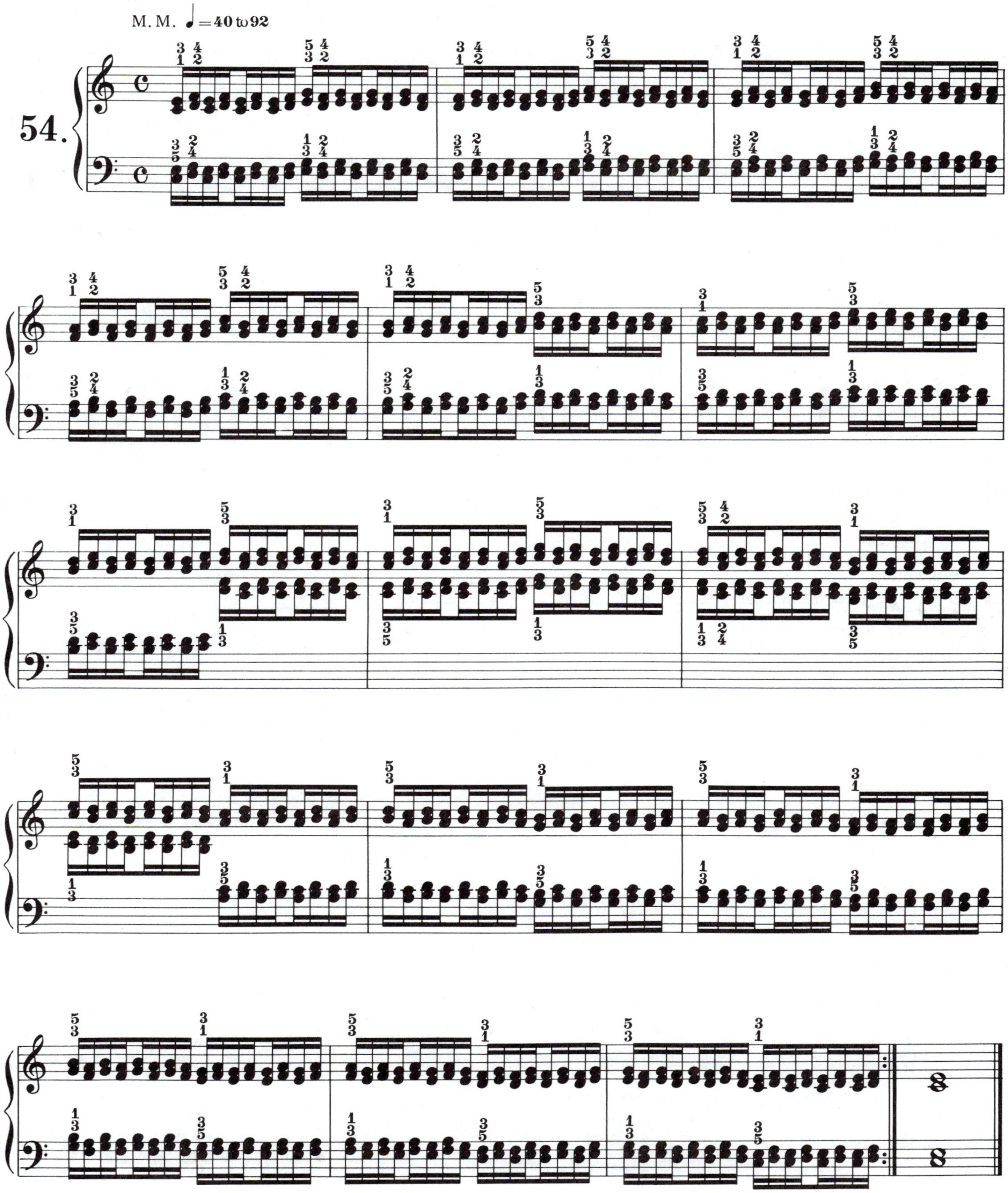

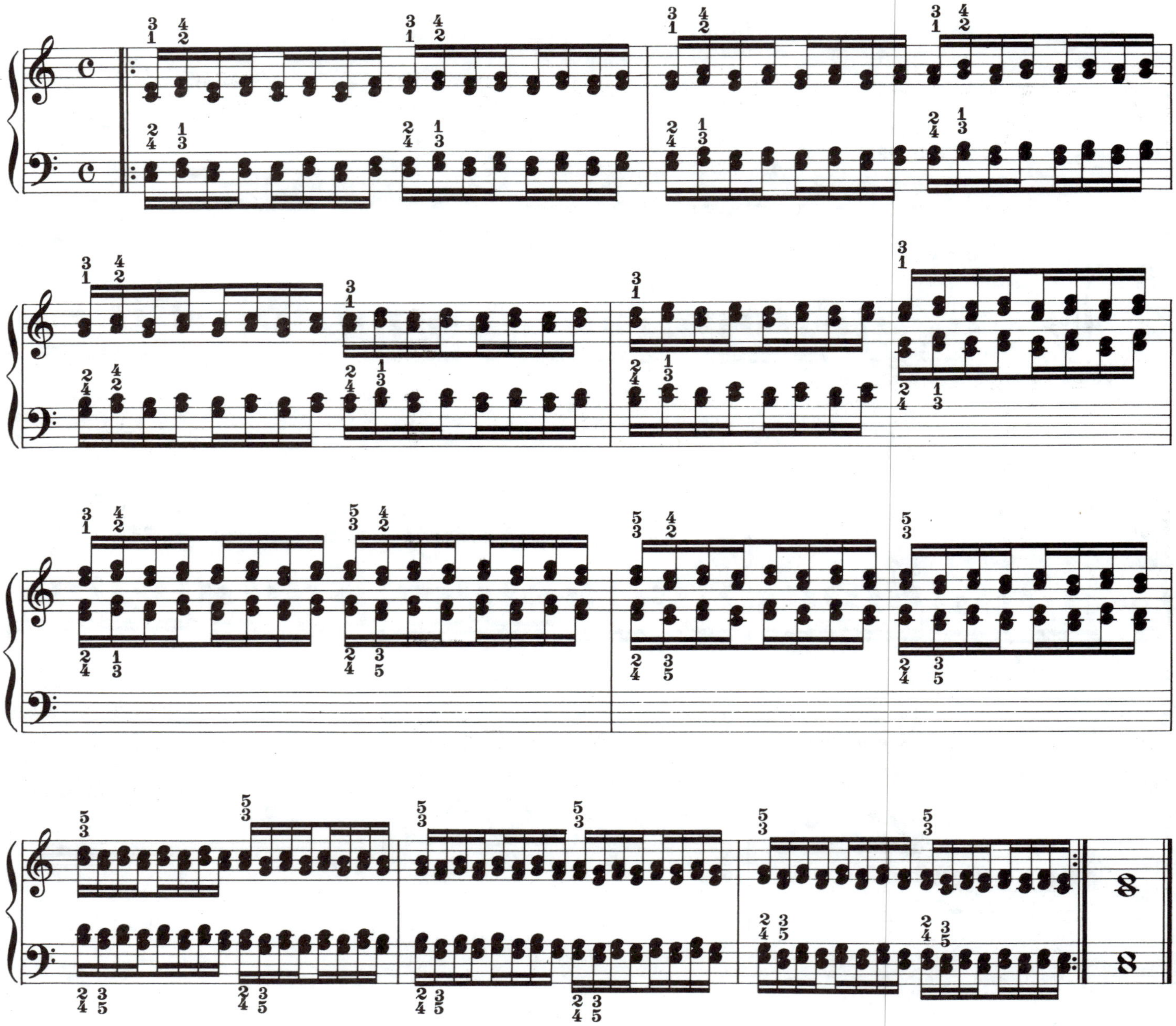

The Three-Note Trill

Same comment as for No.54.

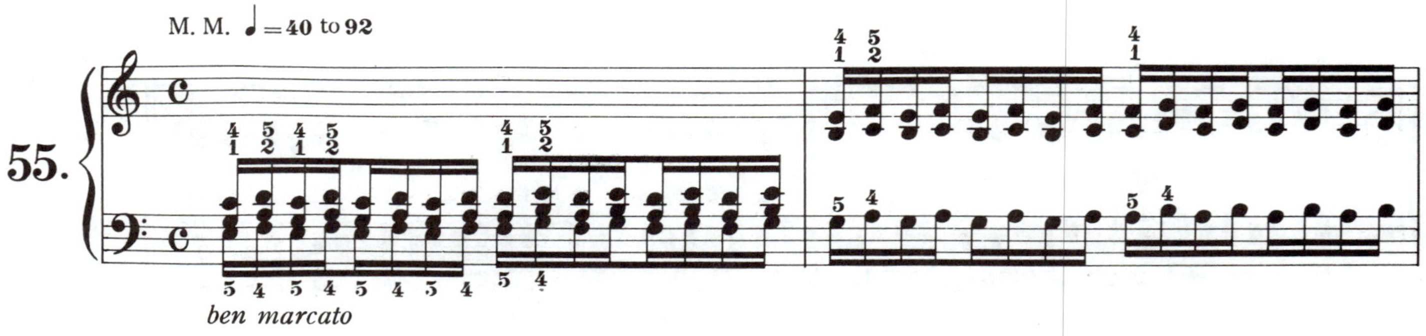

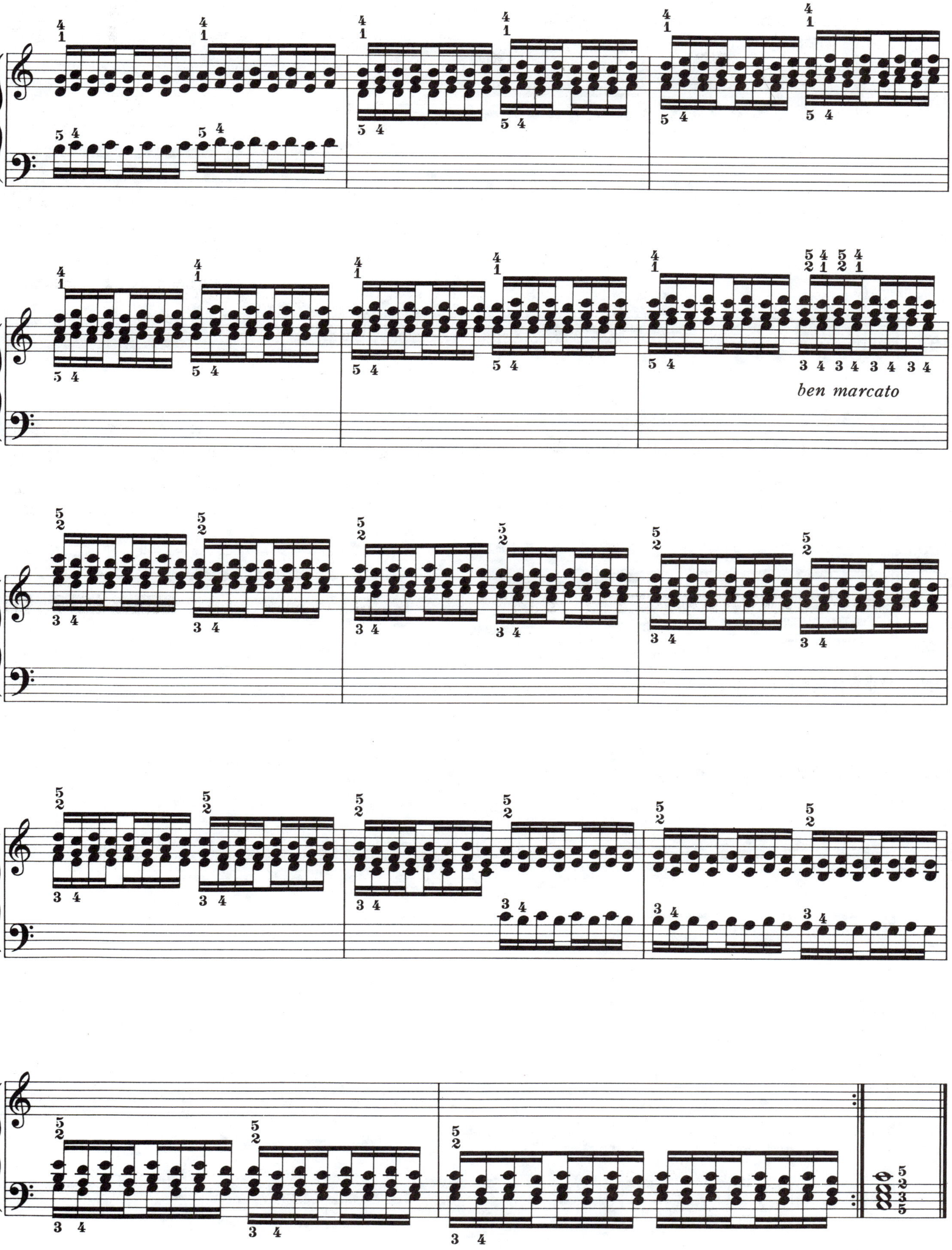
ben marcato

Special Fingerings for the Four-Note Trill

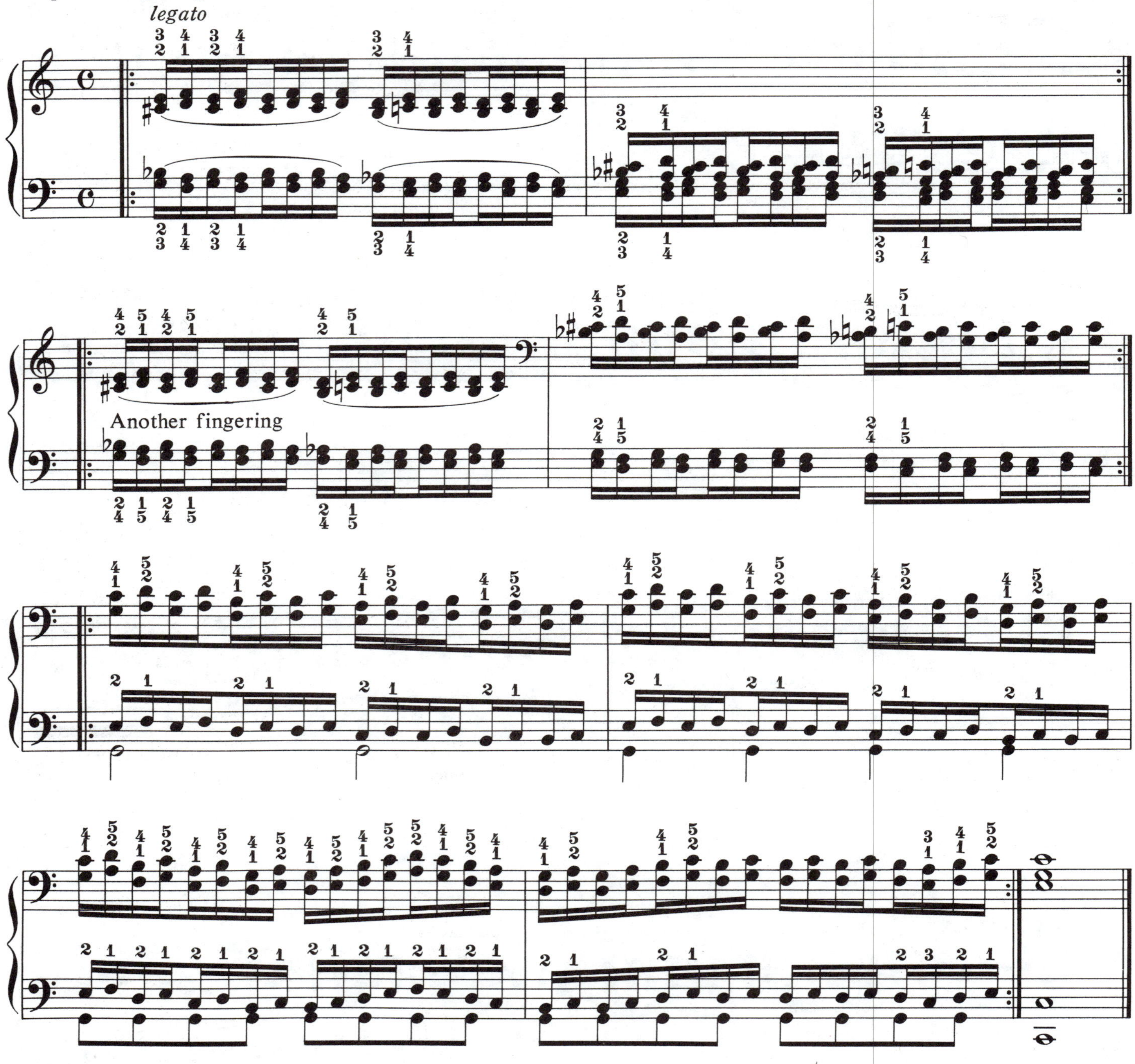

Scales in Broken Octaves in the 24 Keys

Play them through without stopping. This important exercise also prepares the wrists for the study of the tremolo.

56.

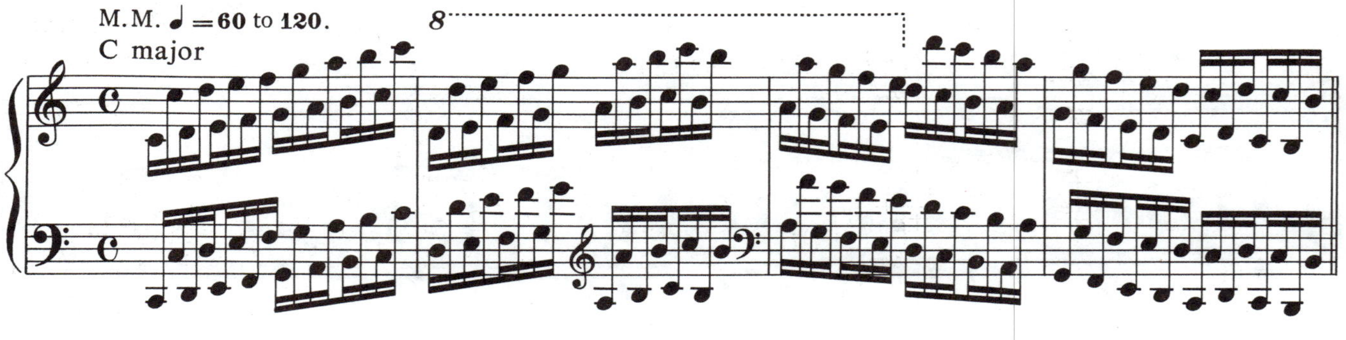

The black keys may be played with the 4th finger.

A minor.

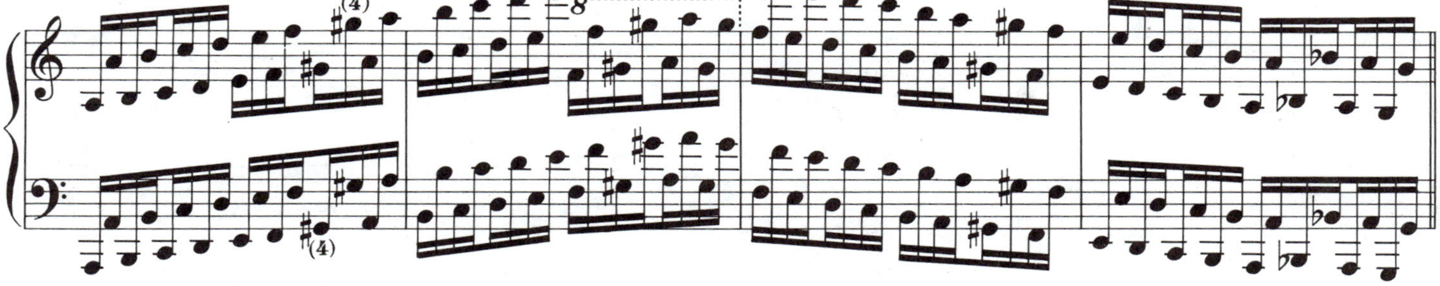

F major.

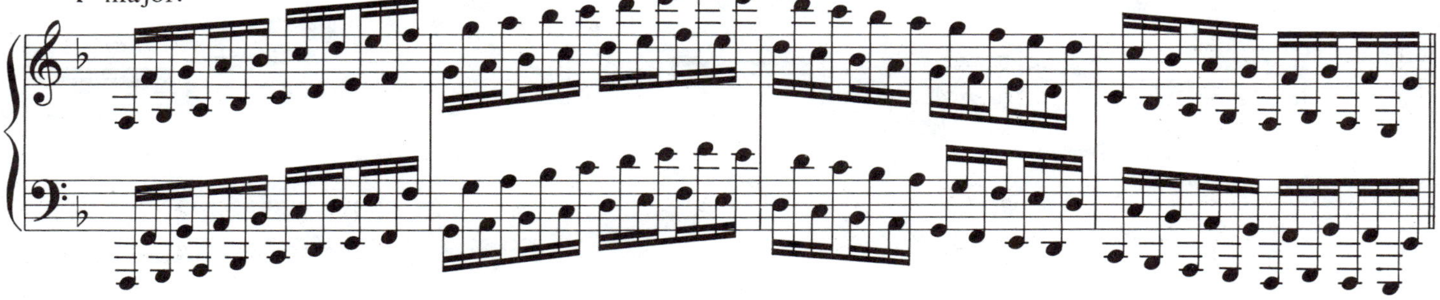

D minor.

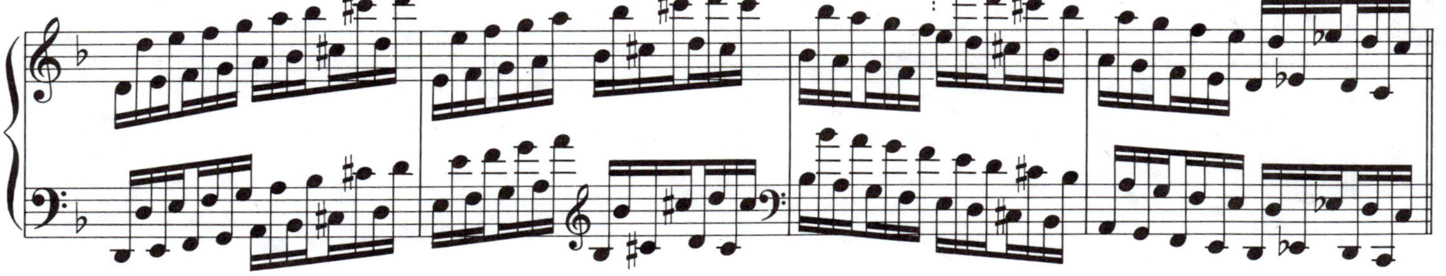

B♭ major.

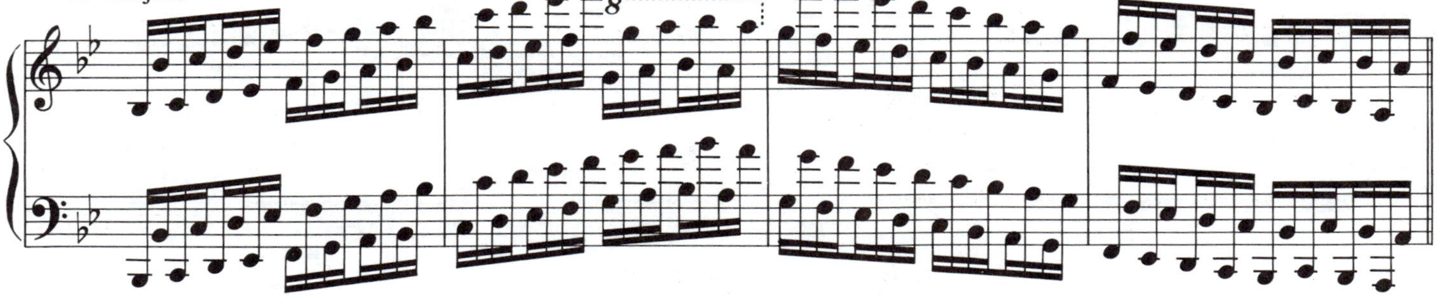

G minor.

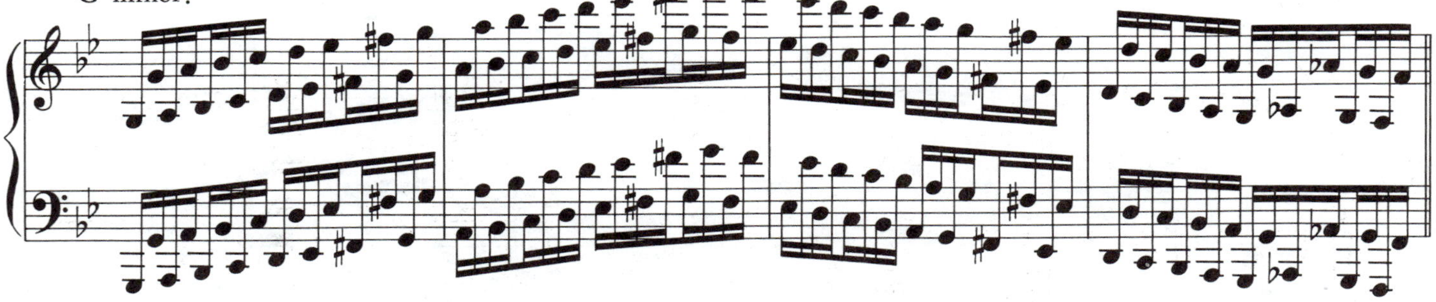

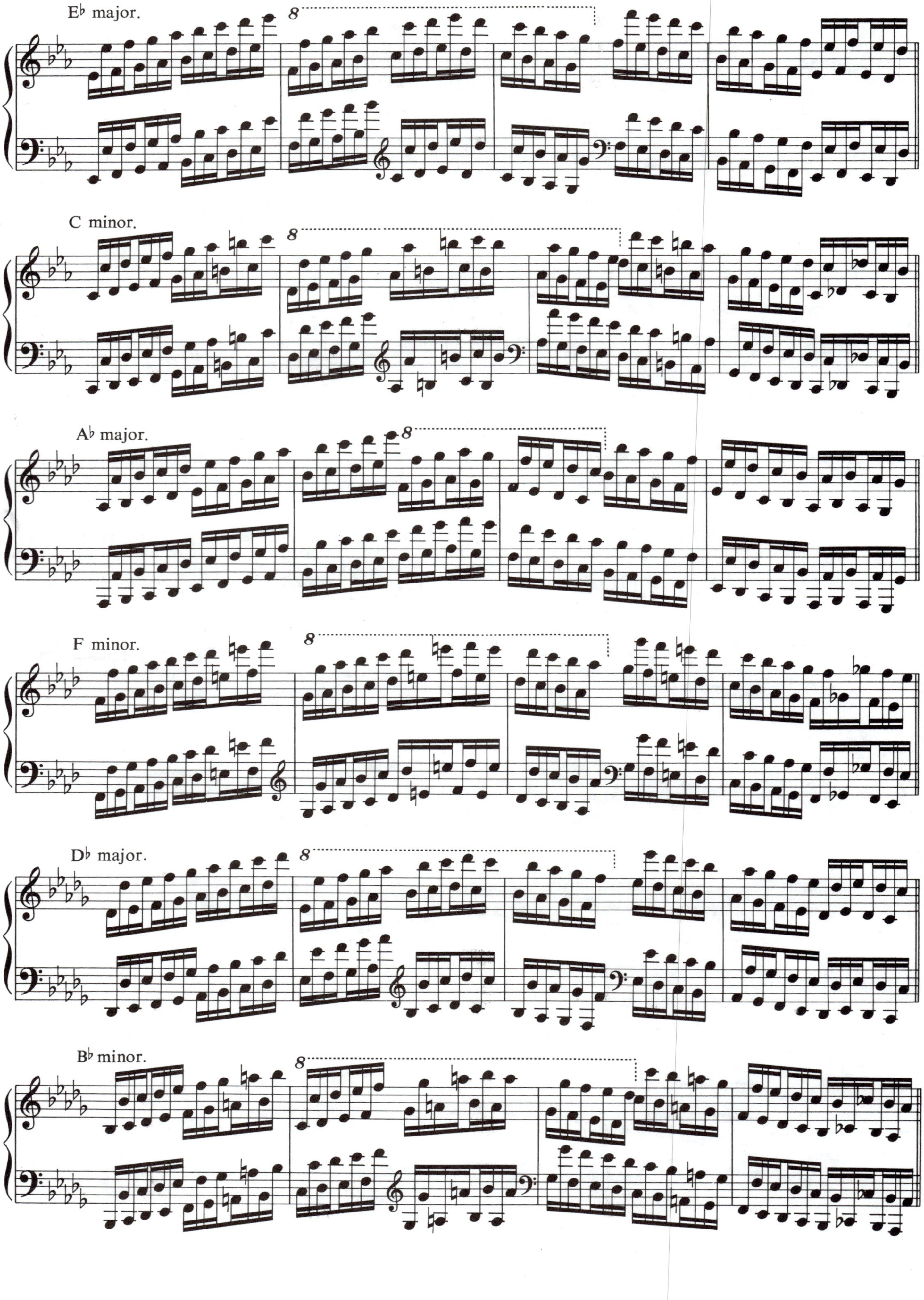
E♭ major.
8
C minor.
8
A♭ major.
8
F minor.
8
D♭ major.
8
B♭ minor.
8

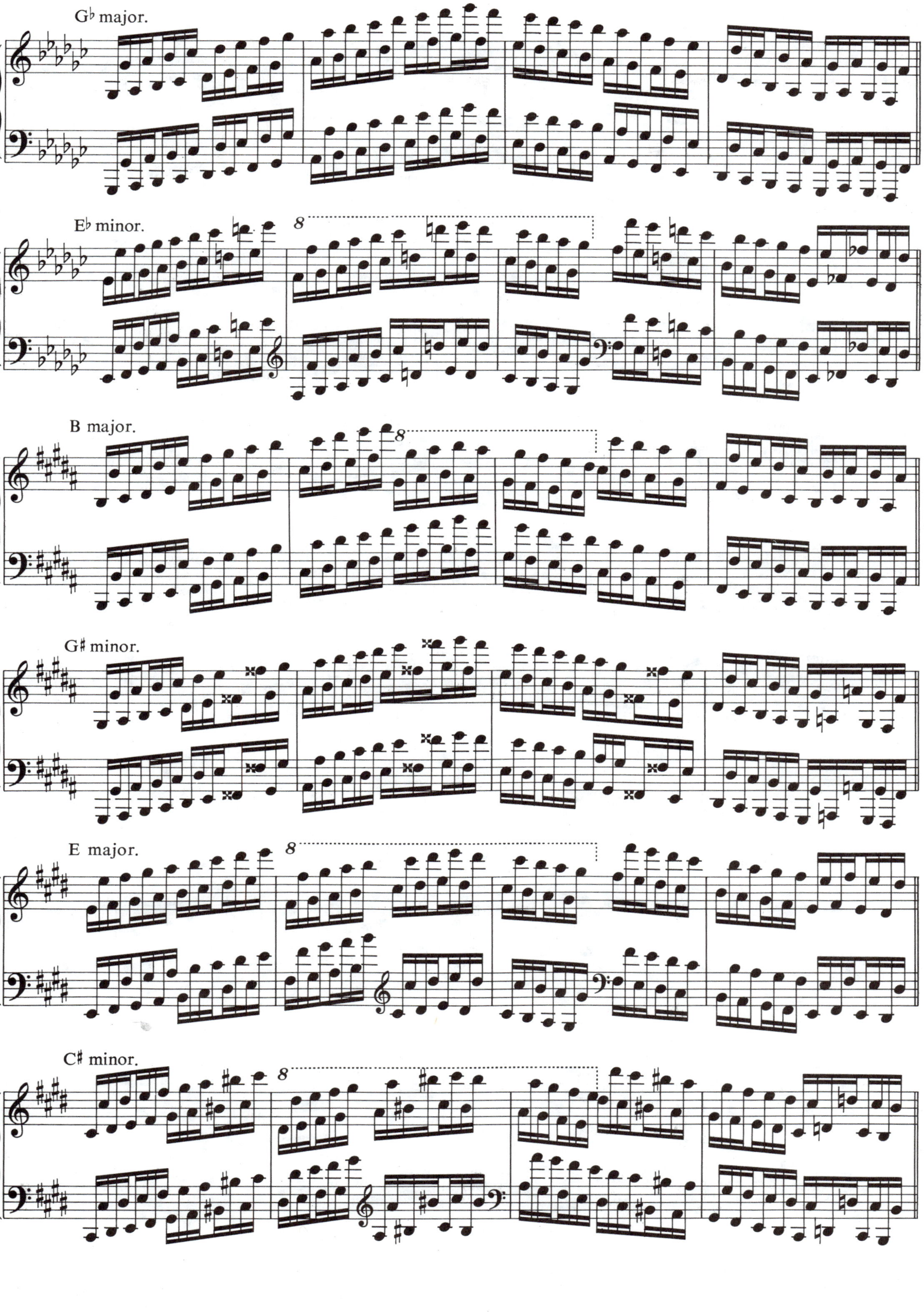
G♭ major.
E♭ minor.
B major.
G♯ minor.
E major.
C♯ minor.

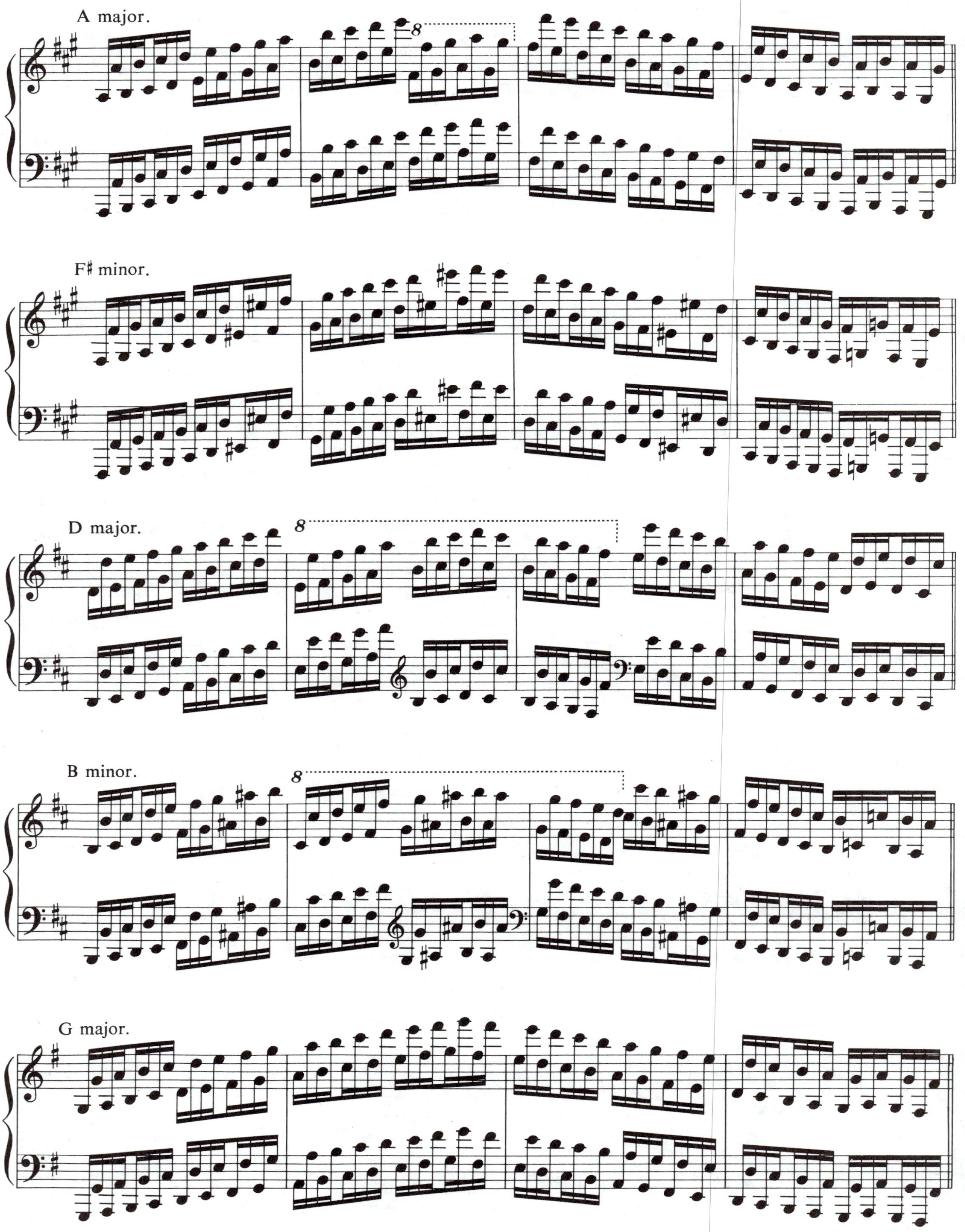
A major.
8
F♯ minor.
D major.
8
B minor.
8
G major.

E minor.

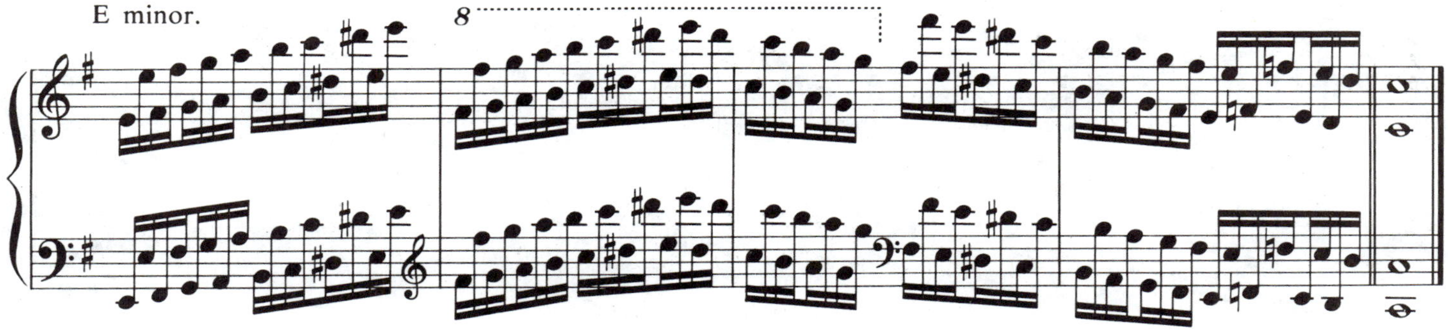

Broken Arpeggios in Octaves in the 24 Keys

Repeat the first arpeggio in C until it can be played cleanly with good wrist movement, before beginning the next in A minor.

Practice each of the arpeggios until they can be played very easily, then play through all 24 without stopping. The black keys may be played with the 4th finger.

M. M. ♩ = 40 to 72.

C major. A minor.

57.

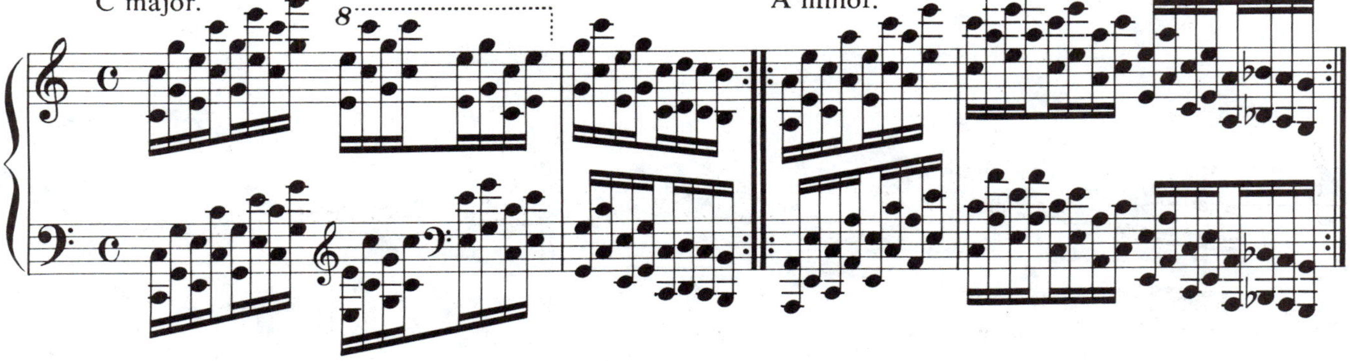

F major. D minor.

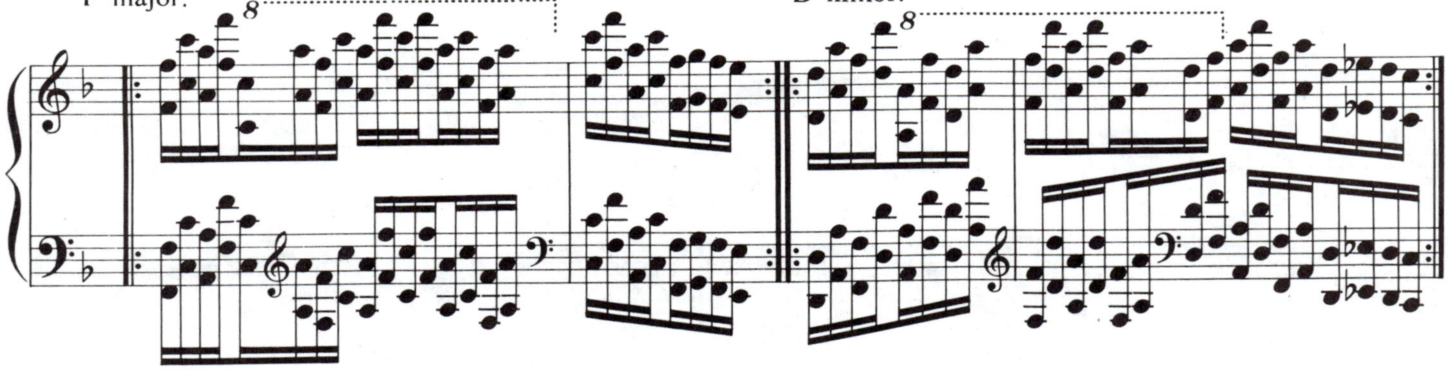

B♭ major. G minor.

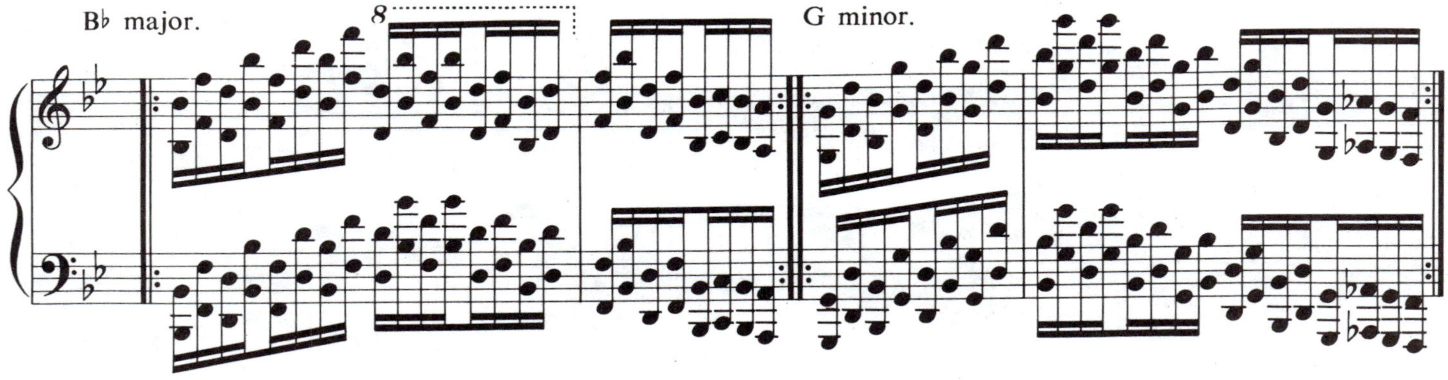

E♭ major. C minor.

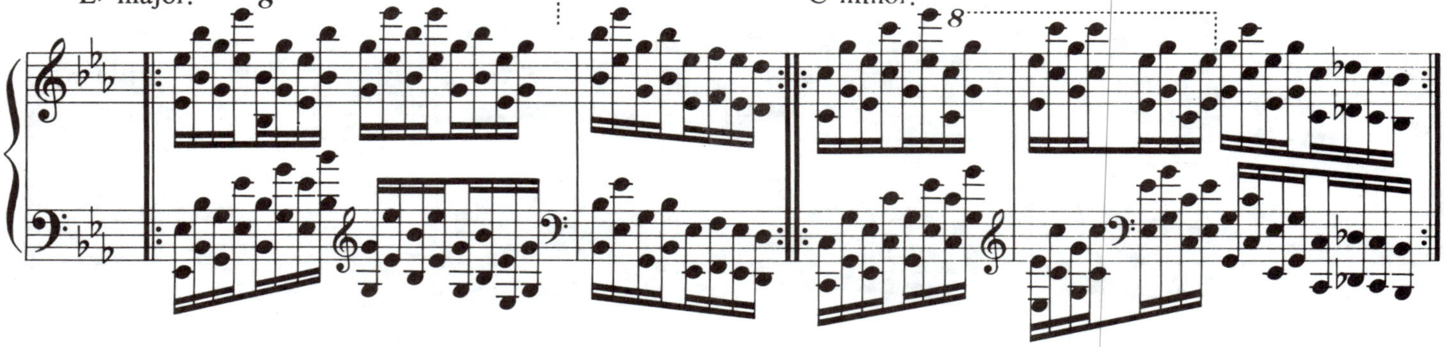

A♭ major. F minor.

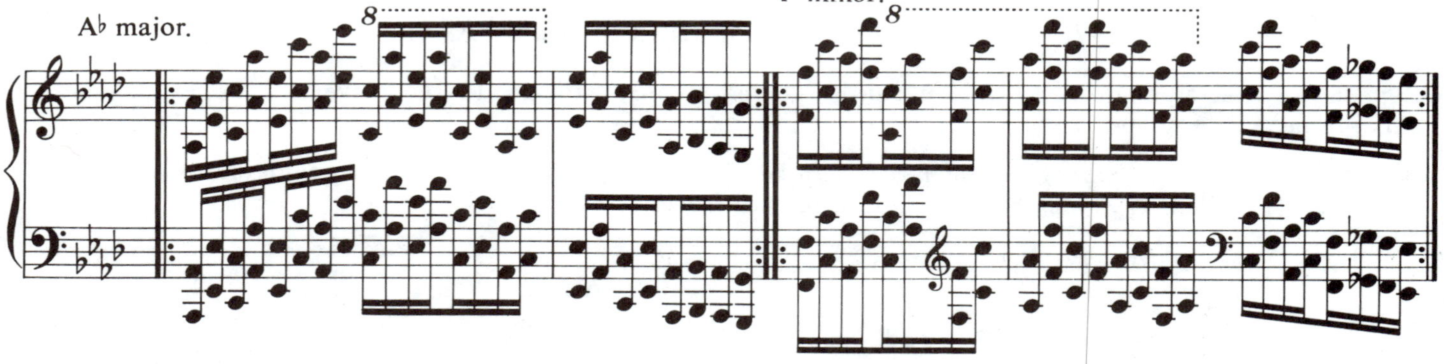

D♭ major. B♭ minor.

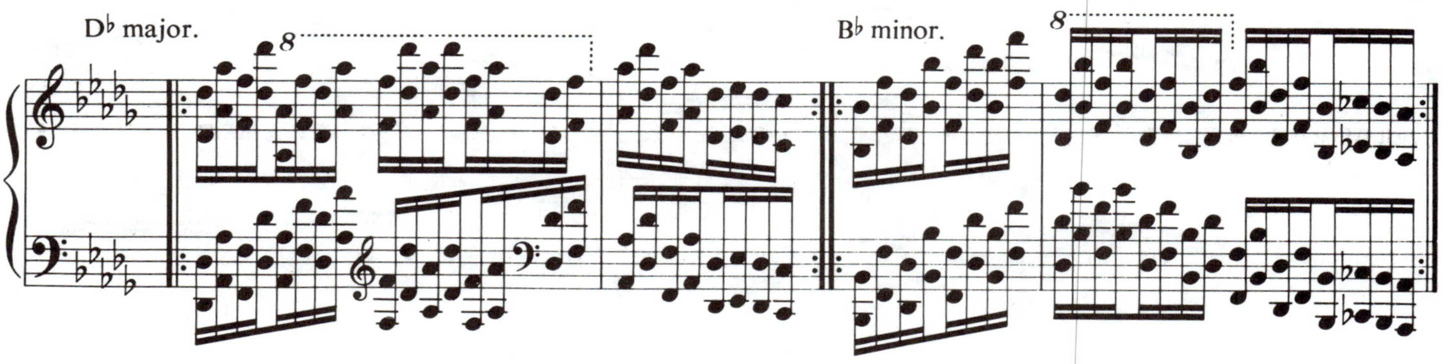

G♭ major.* E♭ minor.*

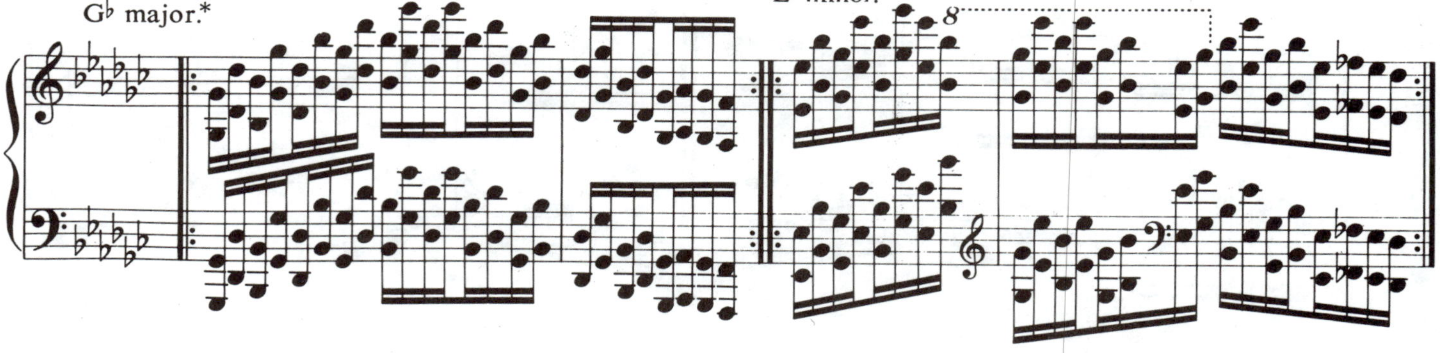

B major. G♯ minor.

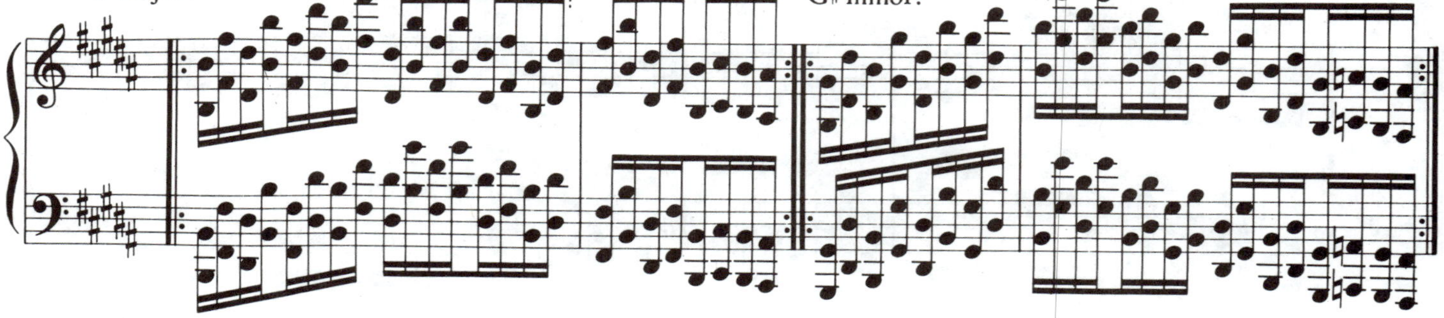

*As all notes are played on the black keys, either the 4th or 5th finger may be used.

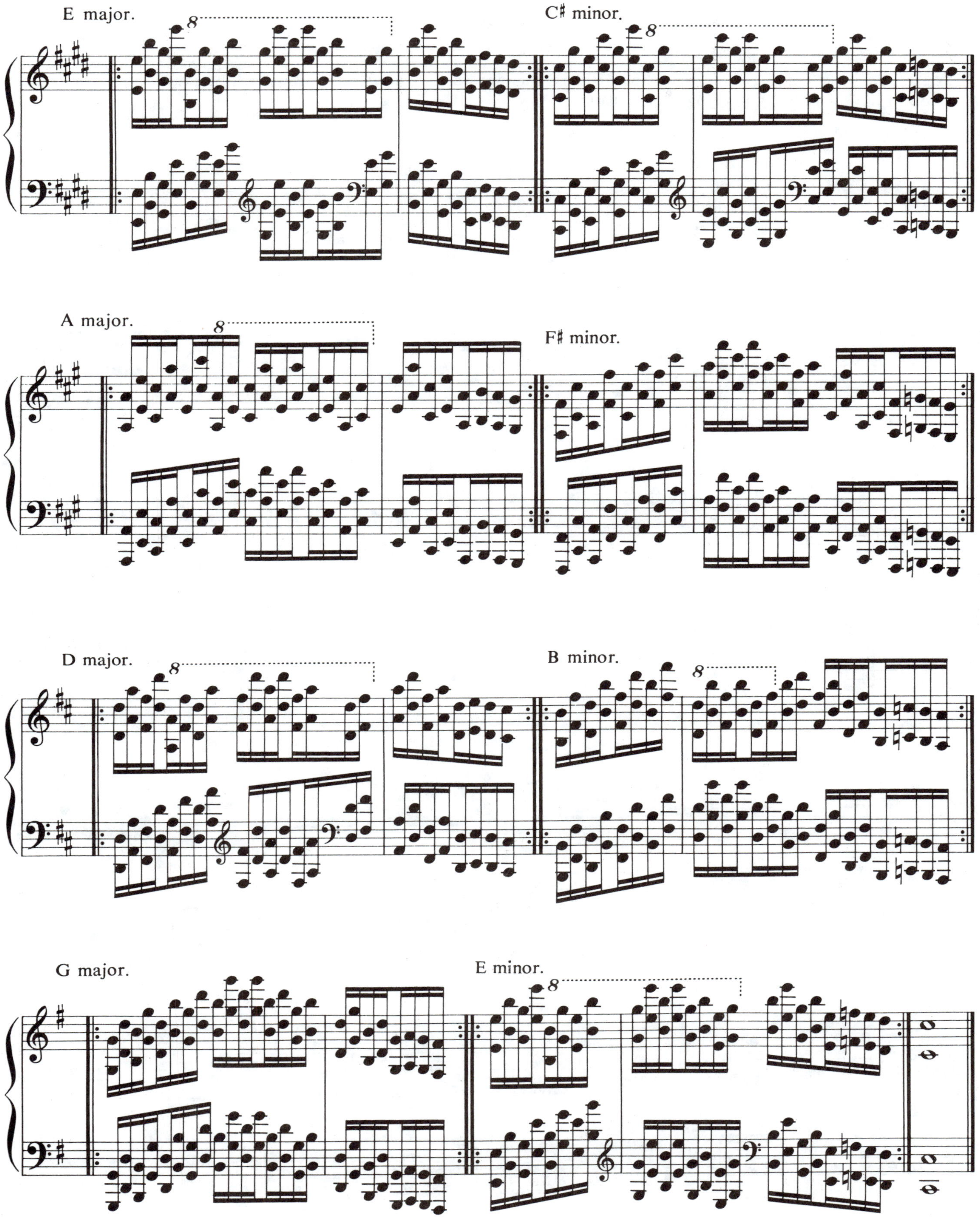
E major.
C♯ minor.
A major.
F♯ minor.
D major.
B minor.
G major.
E minor.

Sustained Octaves with Detached Notes

Strike the octaves vigorously without lifting the wrists and hold them down while playing the intermediate notes with a good finger movement.

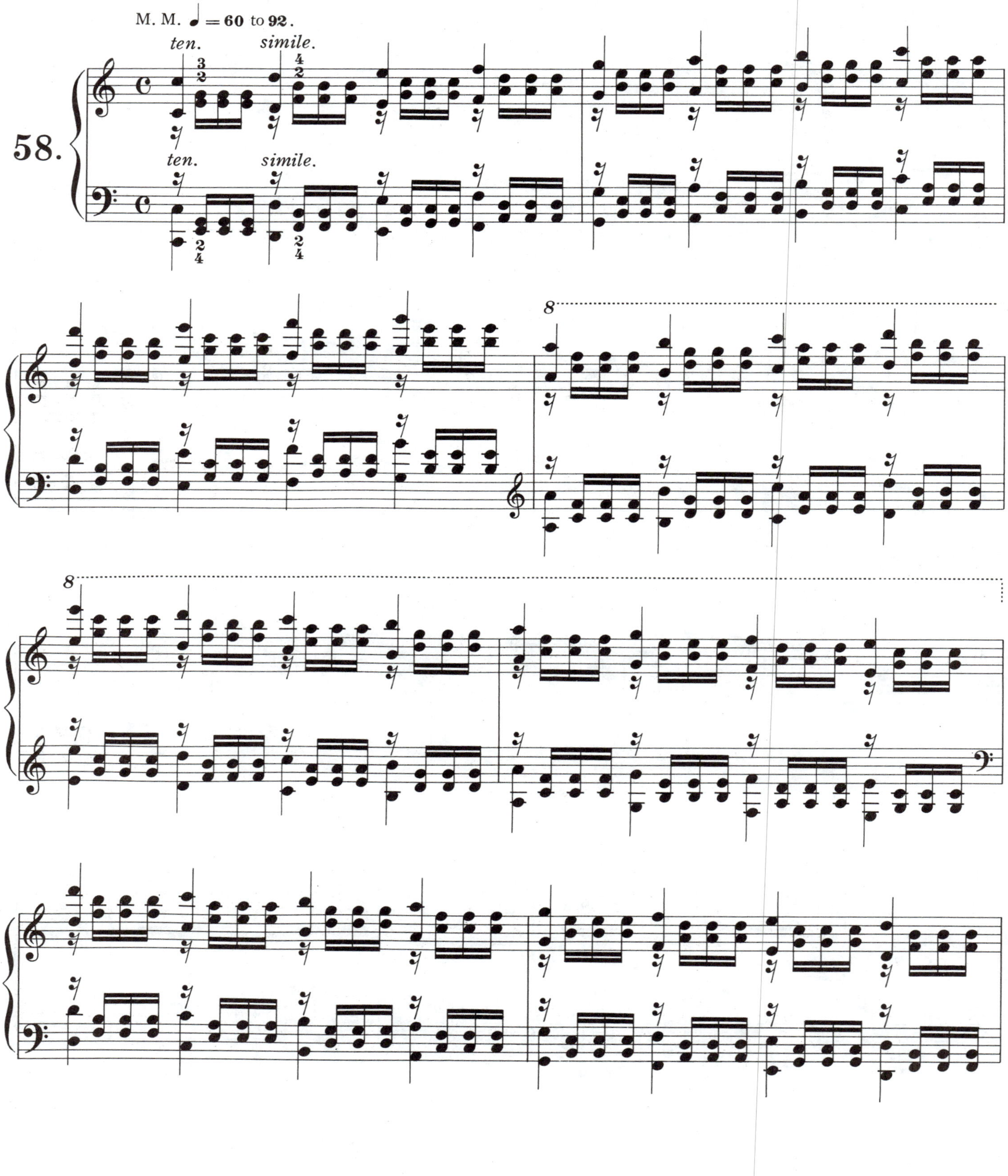

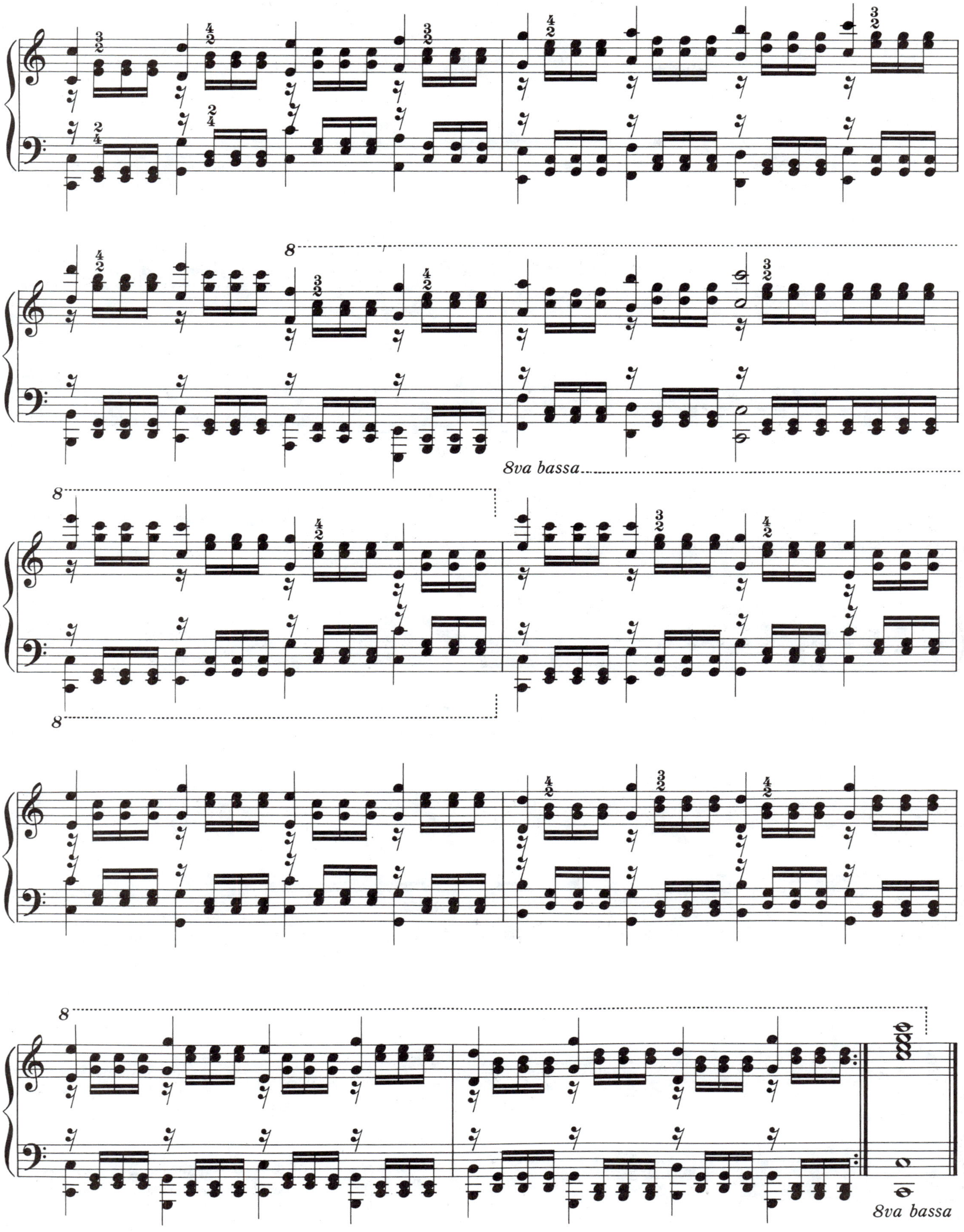
8va bassa
8va bassa

Four-Note Trill in Sixths

Combine the 1st and 4th, 2nd and 5th fingers of each hand. Do not move the hand or wrist while playing this exercise.

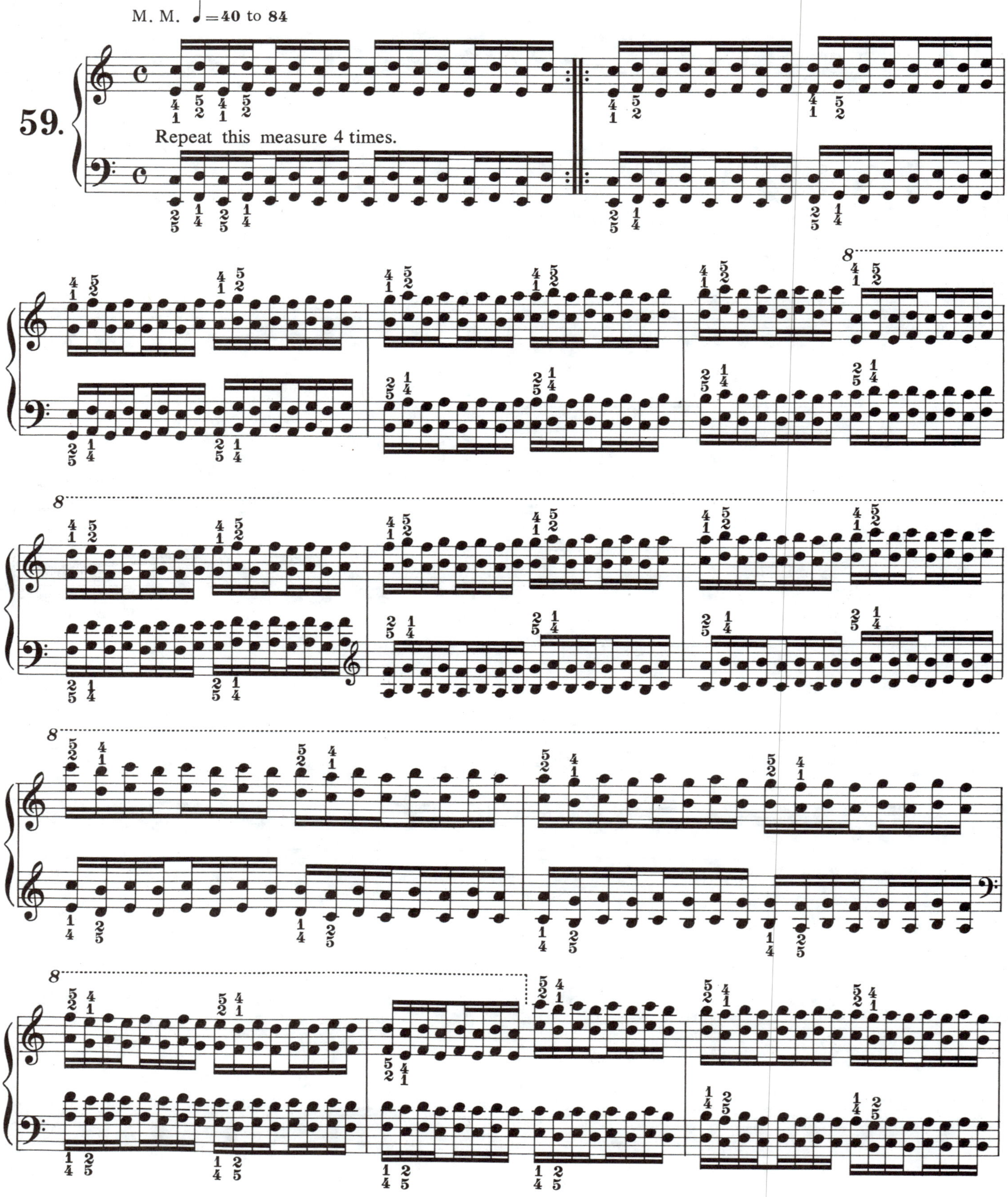

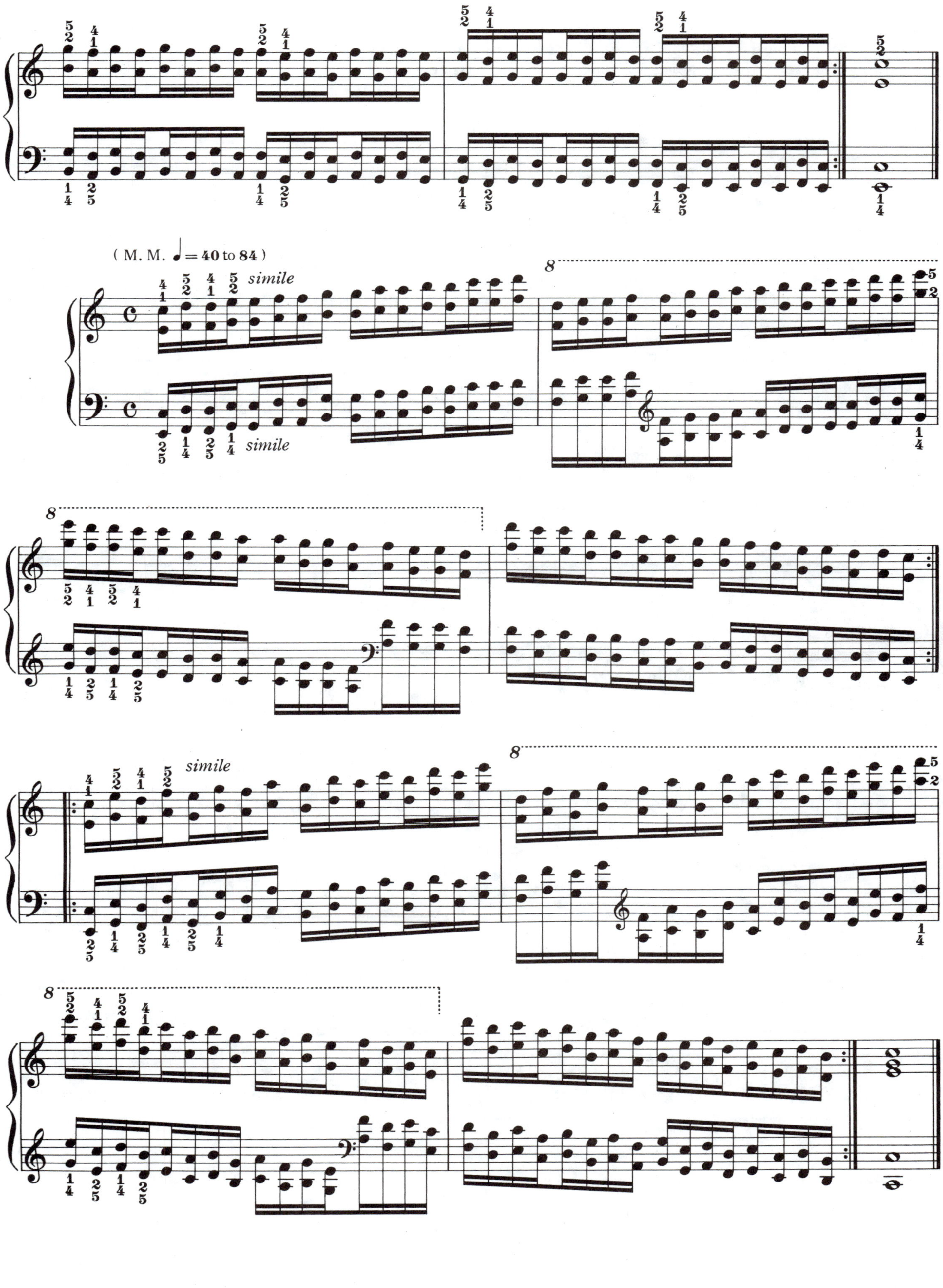
(M. M. ♩ = 40 to 84)
simile
simile
simile

The Tremolo

The tremolo should be played as rapidly as a roll on the drum. Practice slowly at first, gradually increasing the tempo until M.M. 72. To increase the speed even more, allow the wrists to turn rapidly from side to side. This exercise is long and difficult but the excellent results will fully repay the pianist for his efforts. Steibelt* made his listeners shiver by his execution of the tremolo.

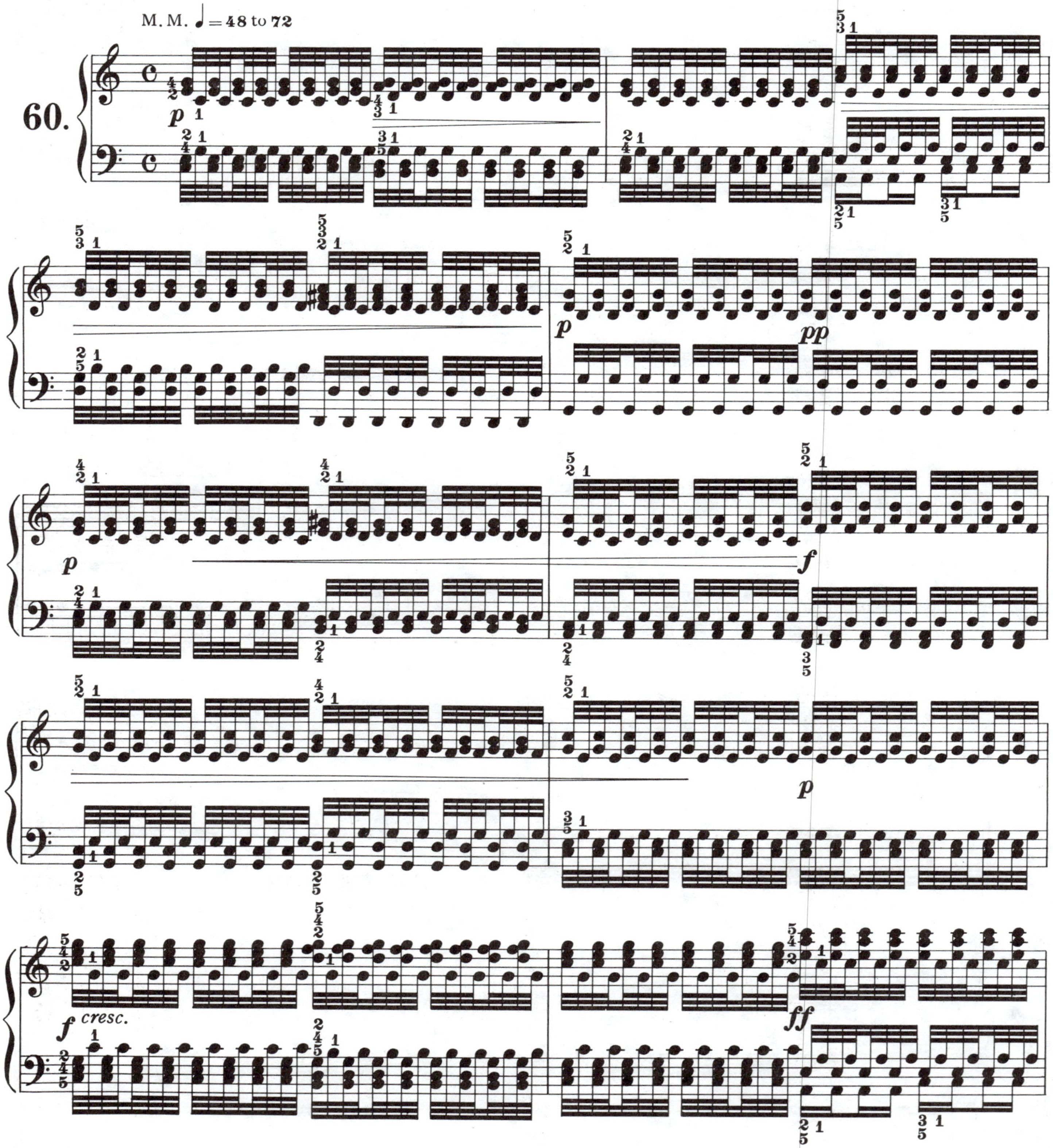

*Daniel Steibelt (1765-1823) was a German pianist and composer who was highly regarded in Europe during his life-time.

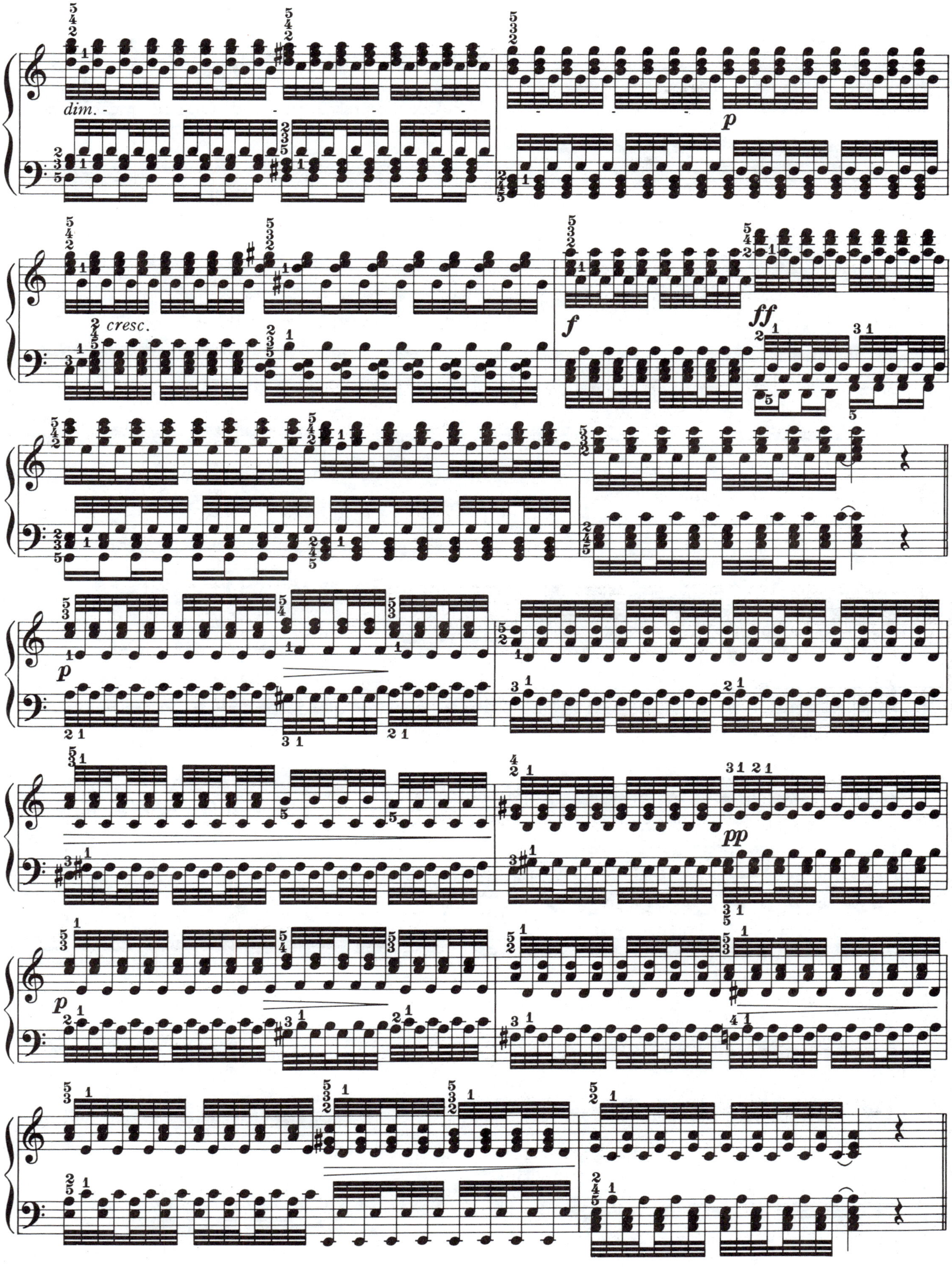
dim.
cresc.

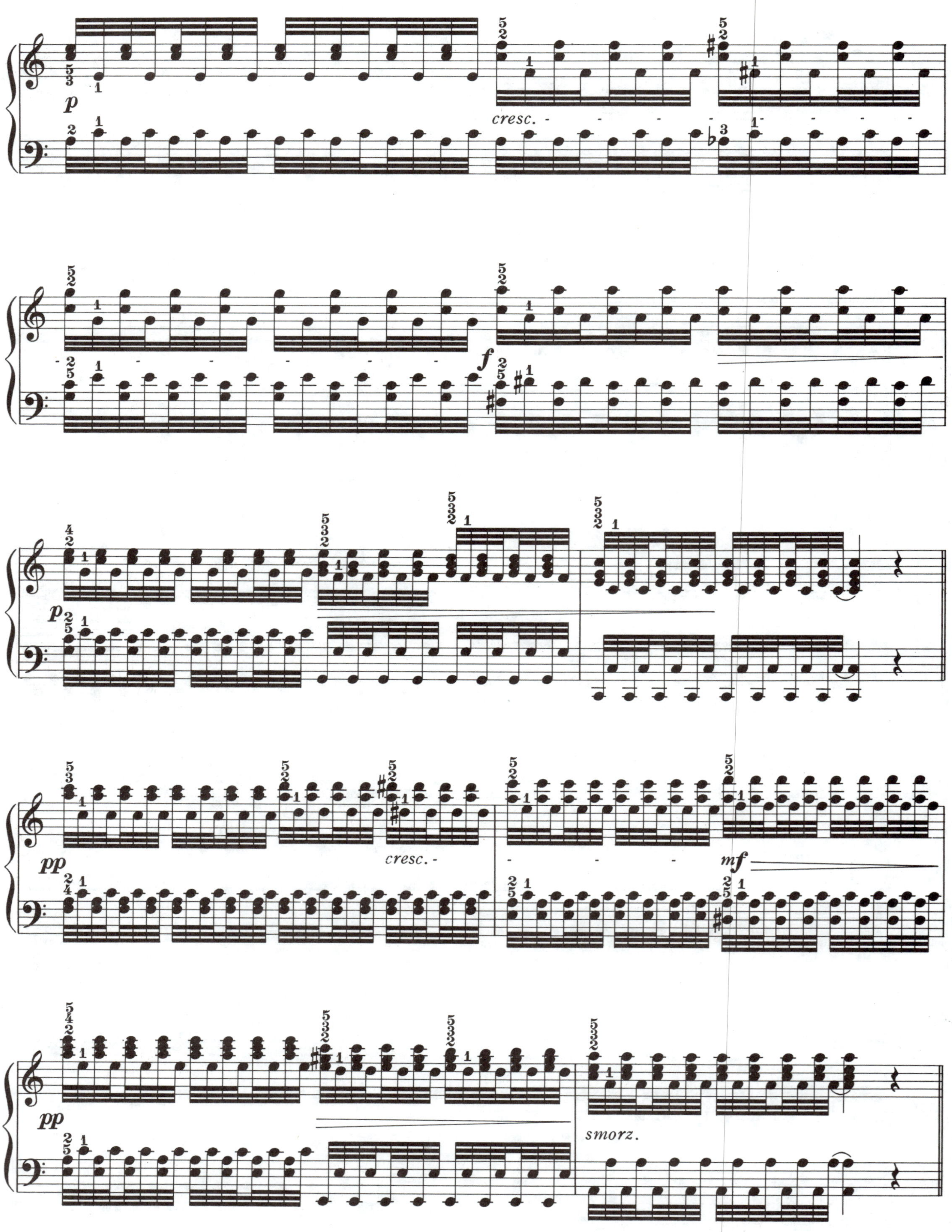
p
cresc.
f
p
pp
cresc.
mf
pp
smorz.

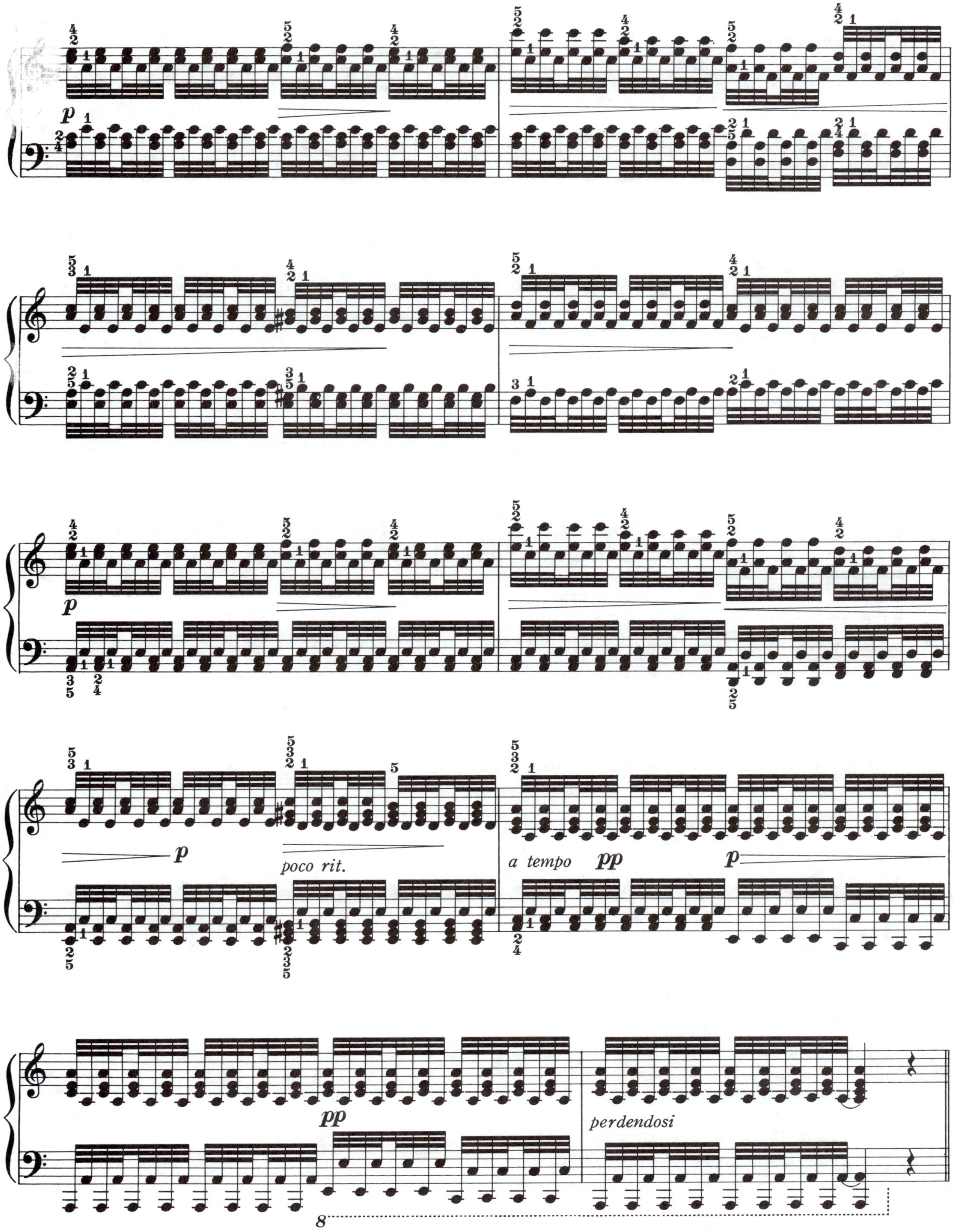
p
p
p
poco rit.
a tempo
pp
p
pp
perdendosi
8

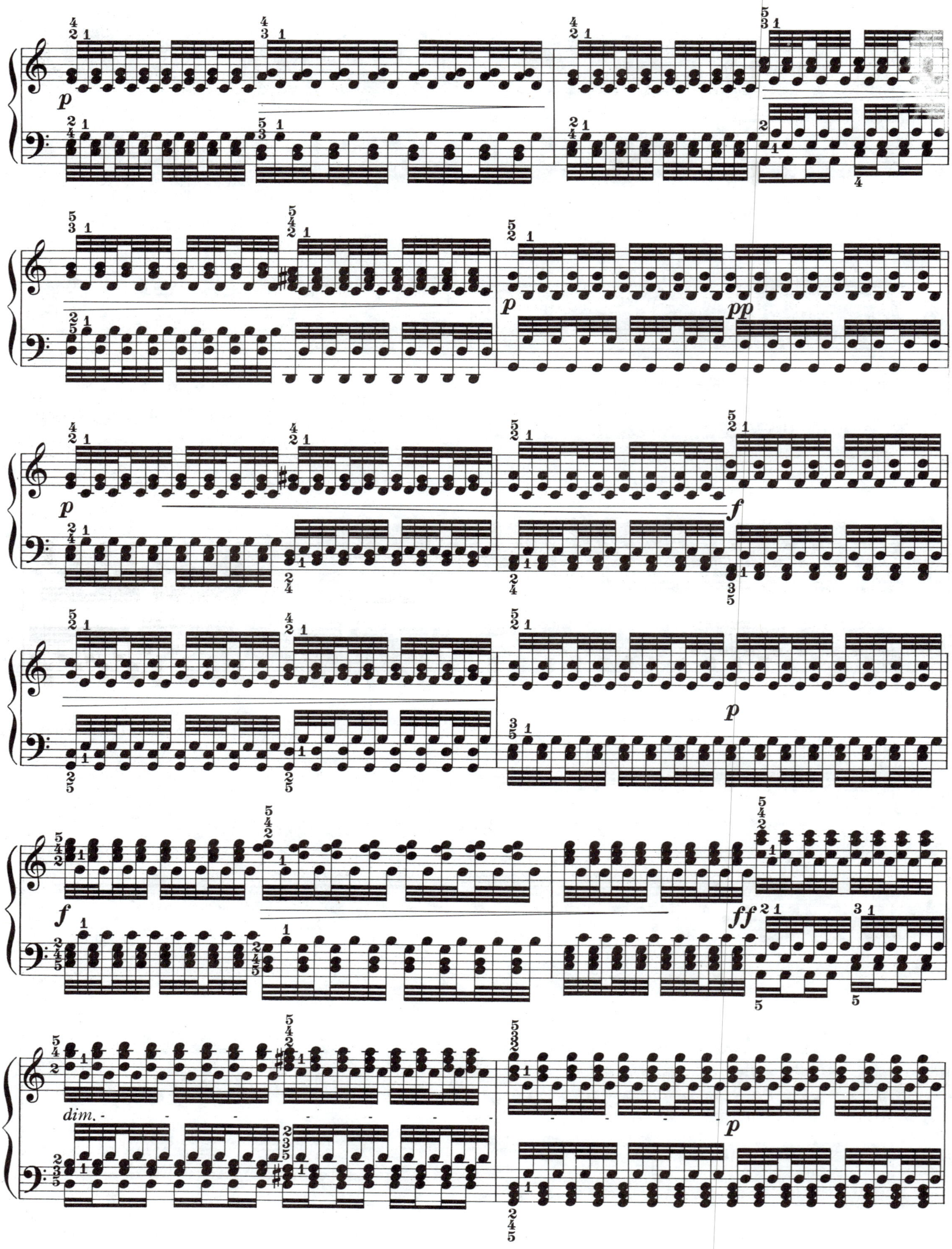
dim.

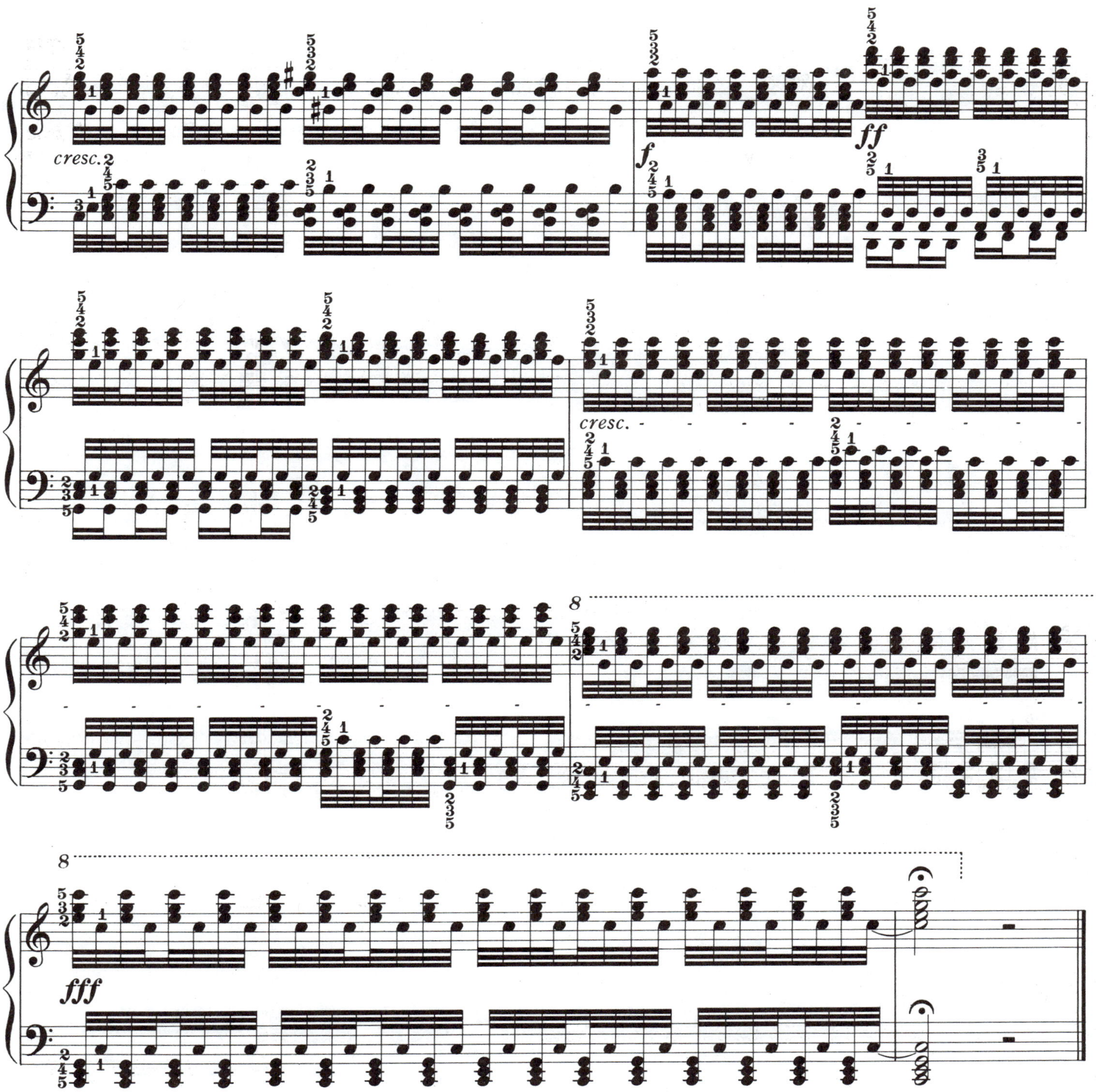

Concluding Remarks

Now that the student has completed this book, he should be familiar with the most important technical difficulties. But in order to retain the benefits of these exercises and become a real virtuoso, he should play through the entire book at least once a day. An hour is required to do this.

The greatest artists find it necessary to repeat exercises daily for several hours, merely to "keep their technique." It is no exaggeration, therefore, when it is suggested to the aspiring student that he play all the exercises every day.

$8.99 in USA

Charles-Louis Hanon's *The Virtuoso Pianist*, originally published in French, has been translated into many languages as pianists worldwide recognized its benefits. It has become, without a doubt, the most widely used piano technique book ever written.

Previous English translations, however, were not done particularly well. They were translated word-for-word by music editors, not experienced translators, which resulted in a stilted style and left Hanon's instructions somewhat obscured. This translation clarifies what Hanon intended and corrects errors that previously misdirected pianists to play the exercises in incorrect sequences. Also, because of old engravings, many other editions have an unpleasant, blurred appearance. This easy-to-read edition, from new engravings, clearly displays the music and fingerings. Alfred has tried to make this edition of *The Virtuoso Pianist* the most accurate and attractive one presently available.

Since Hanon (1820–1900) lived his entire life in France, a work of a popular French artist was deemed appropriate for the cover art of this edition. Presented here, as a suggestive representation of the patterns often found in the exercises in *The Virtuoso Pianist*, is a reproduction of the work *The Bees* by Henri Matisse, which displays repetitive elements and waveforms. Matisse created this work in the summer of 1948.

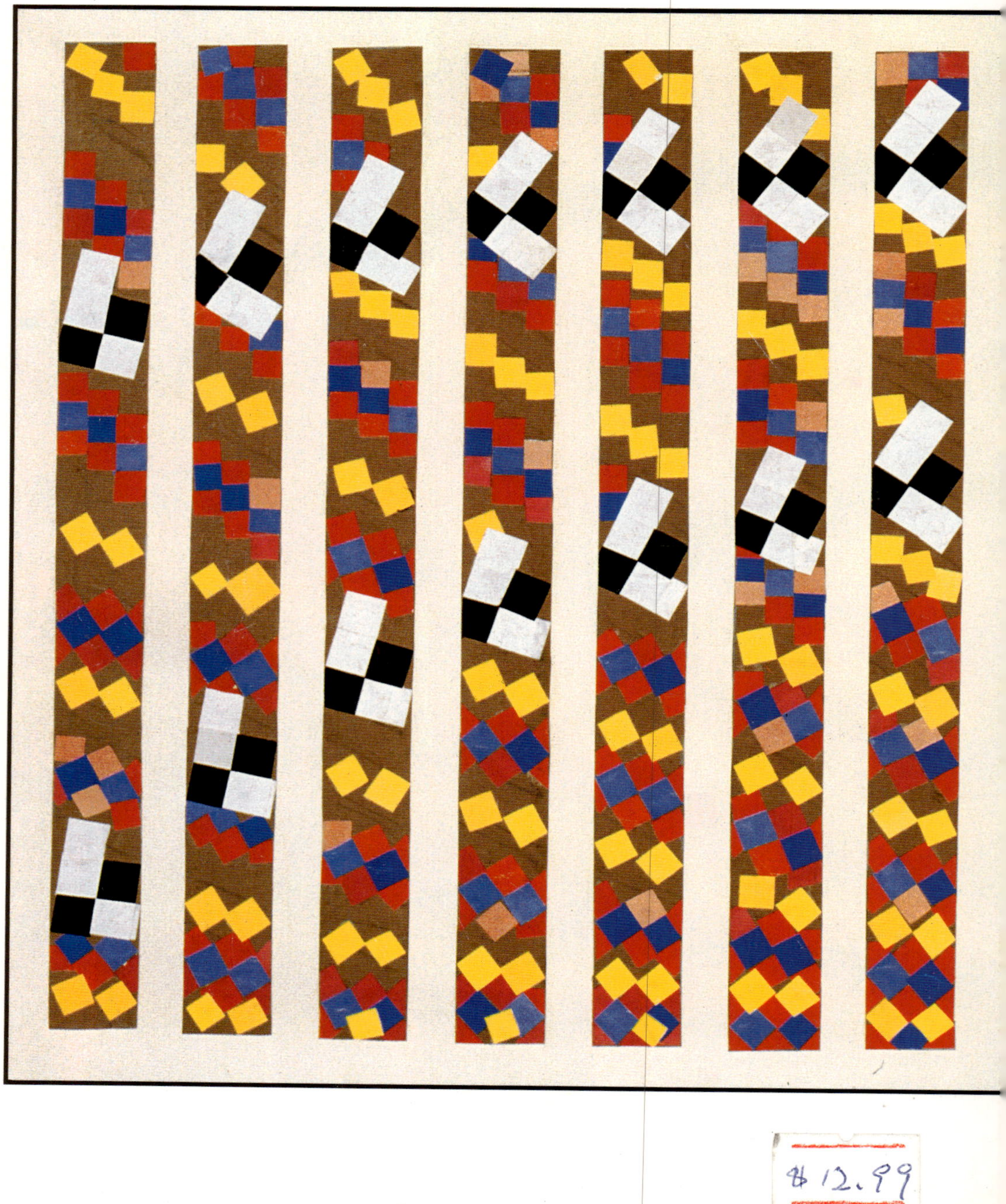

LAY-FLAT BINDING

Alfred has made every effort to make this book not only attractive but more useful and long-lasting as well. Usually, large books do not lie flat or stay open on the music rack. In addition, the pages (which are glued together) tend to break away from the spine after repeated use.

In this edition, pages are sewn together in multiples of 16. This special process prevents pages from falling out of the book while allowing it to stay open for ease in playing. We hope this unique binding will give you added pleasure and additional use.

$12.99

ALFRED PUBLISHING CO., INC.
16320 Roscoe Blvd., P.O. Box 10003
Van Nuys, CA 91410-0003
www.alfredpub.com

ISBN 0-7390-1733-0

0 38081 01237 7